FANDOM, THE NEXT GENERATION

FANDOM & CULTURE

Paul Booth and Katherine Larsen, series editors

FANDOM,
THE NEXT GENERATION

edited by Bridget Kies and Megan Connor

UNIVERSITY OF IOWA PRESS, IOWA CITY

University of Iowa Press, Iowa City 52242
Copyright © 2022 by the University of Iowa Press
uipress.uiowa.edu
Printed in the United States of America
ISBN 978-1-60938-833-1 (pbk)
ISBN 978-1-60938-834-8 (ebk)

Design and typesetting by Ashley Muehlbauer

No part of this book may be reproduced or used in
any form or by any means without permission in
writing from the publisher. All reasonable steps
have been taken to contact copyright holders of
material used in this book. The publisher would be
pleased to make suitable arrangements with any
whom it has not been possible to reach.

Printed on acid-free paper

Cataloging-in-Publication data is on file with the
Library of Congress.

For the fangirls who came before us and for the fangirls of the future

Contents

Introduction.. 1
Bridget Kies and Megan Connor

PART ONE: REBOOTS, REVIVALS, AND NOSTALGIA 7

"I Ain't Afraid of No Bros": The Generational
Politics of Reboot Culture 9
Bridget Kies

Reopening *The X-Files*: Generational Fandom,
Gender, and Bodily Autonomy 20
Bethan Jones

Missing Time: *Twin Peaks, The X-Files,*
and the Rise of Aging Fans 33
Siobhan Lyons

Truly, Truly, Truly Outraged: Anti-Fandom
and the Limits of Nostalgia 43
Andrew Scahill

PART TWO: GENERATIONS OF ENDURING FANDOMS 55

Like Father, Like Daughter: The Intergenerational Passing of
Doctor Who and Star Wars Fandom in the Familial Context 57
Neta Yodovich

Examining Pop Music Fandom through a Generational Lens 68
Simone Driessen

Looking Back, Looking Bi: Queering a Lifelong
Fandom of the Baby-Sitters Club 78
Megan Connor

The Man from U.N.C.L.E. Fandom: A Community of Cousins 90
Cynthia W. Walker

Fans of Female Film Stars in Turkey: The Case of Türkan Şoray 101
Yektanurşin Duyan

"I Named My Daughter Ripley": Fan Gifting and
Internal Hierarchies in the Alien Fandom 112
Janelle Vermaak-Griessel

"The Power of the Jane Austen Fandom": Bridging
Generational Gaps with *The Lizzie Bennet Diaries* 123
Meredith Dabek

PART THREE: GENERATIONAL TENSIONS 133

Star Wars Fans, Generations, and Identity 135
Dan Golding

Roads Go Ever On and On: Fan Fiction and Archival
Infrastructures as Markers of the Affirmational-
Transformational Continuum in Tolkien Fandom 149
Maria K. Alberto and Dawn Walls-Thumma

"Fannish Sensibilities": Fissures in the Sherlock Holmes Fandom . . . 161
L. N. Rosales

The Fandom Is a Welcoming Place Unless I Know More
Than You: Generations, Mentorship, and Super-Fans 172
Mélanie Bourdaa

Contributors 181
Notes 185
Bibliography 221
Index 237

Introduction

Bridget Kies and Megan Connor

The NBC sitcom *Friends* premiered in September 1994 to lukewarm reviews as one of many in "the horde of 20-something comedies crowding the schedule . . . [where] most young people do nothing but drink coffee."[1] By its finale ten years later, *Friends* had become a global phenomenon with over 50 million viewers tuning in. The series' success continued in syndicated reruns in the United States and other countries during and after its broadcast. When streaming rights for the series were bought by Netflix in 2015 for the steep price of $100 million, some twenty years after the pilot was first broadcast, it was breaking news, and many longtime fans celebrated the opportunity to revisit the series on demand.[2]

Revisiting *Friends*, however, calls attention to how television has changed dramatically since the mid-1990s. Apart from aesthetic developments, such as the decline in popularity of the laugh track, many social values have changed since the series' original broadcast. A crowd-sourced article on Buzzfeed, for instance, lists the many problematic aspects of the series, including the male characters' disrespectful attitudes toward women, the use of antigay and transphobic jokes (most often directed at Chandler and his father), and the lack of any long-running characters of color.[3] Another long-standing joke on the series was that the character Monica (Courteney Cox) was once overweight. In fact, rumors that Cox had anorexia were common during the series' original broadcast, and Cox herself admitted in 2007 that she was too thin on the show.[4] As Geraldine DeRuiter puts it in an insightful blog post, the series frames Monica's fatness as a problem she must surmount to find success in her career and love life, but the real problem isn't her size; it's that viewers "were told that her joy, and self-confidence, that her mere existence was something to be laughed at," that fatness is reduced to a punchline.[5] By today's standards, in which fat shaming is understood as a harmful form of unacceptable bullying, there is a worldwide obesity epidemic, and overweight celebrities like Lizzo are featured on the cover of British *Vogue*, jokes about "fat Monica" seem woefully out of touch.

New generations of viewers can become fans of *Friends* thanks to syndication and the convenience of streaming, both of which help longtime fans continue their love for the series. But in revisiting the series and recognizing how social discourses on gender and sexuality have changed, some may only be left with nostalgic appreciation for the role the series played in shaping television—and their lives—at the turn of the century. As an example, Bridget recalls watching the pilot episode as a young teenager, and soon after Thursday nights revolved around NBC's sitcom lineup with *Friends* as the high point. Now, however, she finds the series' humor excruciating and refuses to watch. For other fans, affection for the role a media text played in their personal history may allow continued consumption and appreciation. Outdated material can be fun to identify, a reminder of how society has changed. In contrast to Bridget, Megan's nostalgia for the series is strong enough that she finds it to be soothing bedtime viewing, has a tradition of watching the annual Thanksgiving episodes each year, and finds pleasure in pointing out the outdated plotlines and inappropriate jokes.

In May 2021, the *Friends* cast reunited publicly in an HBOMax special for the first time since the end of the series seventeen years earlier. However, the long-awaited reunion, speculated on for years, then confirmed in early 2020—but then delayed by the COVID-19 pandemic—and costing millions in appearance fees for the six primary cast members, couldn't help but fall flat in the face of so many nostalgic expectations. TV critic James Poniewozik found "the whole affair feels a touch less special . . . because of a glut in the nostalgia market," noting the many other past sitcoms that staged Zoom reunions in the previous year, including *The Office, Community, Parks and Recreation, Happy Endings, The Fresh Prince of Bel-Air*, and more.[6] More critically, NPR pop culture correspondent Linda Holmes suggests that the *Friends* reunion shies away from the true dynamic of nostalgia: "instead of being willing to accept that notes of melancholy are perfectly normal parts of reminiscing, it skitters away every time it's clear that time is stretching out for these actors in some unnerving way."[7] Certainly it is hard to discount the passage of time as the cast wanders a re-created version of the set, interspersed with clips of their fresh-faced debuts almost thirty years earlier.

Friends reminds us that media is transitory, created to be alluring to audiences of its time, both in the physical proof of actors aging and in the cultural aging of humor and social values. Comedies are especially fraught with the latter, since humor is often situational and context driven. However, rebooted or perpetually rebroadcast media texts like *Friends* persist, forming a body of what we call transgenerational media fandoms. A result of industry-standard reboot culture (remaking and expanding the canon of existing intellectual property) and new media technologies for distribution

2   *Introduction*

and exhibition, transgenerational media fandoms include growing cohorts that value their fan objects for different reasons and from different chronological and technology entry points.

FANS AND GENERATIONS

A quick glance online may make the idea of a "transgenerational" fandom seem unfathomable in the current social climate. Popular press articles and clickbait listing the things Millennials have killed abound; people born roughly between 1980 and 1995 are blamed for the cultural deaths of everything from marriage to doorbells, though more nuanced examination of these claims finds these "deaths" (really, just declines in popularity) are better attributed to economic scarcity and changing social values.[8] Many of these articles are written by older people who can be labeled Gen X or Baby Boomers. In turn, Millennials and the younger Gen Z invigorated the expression "OK, Boomer" as a meme, a "sophisticated, mass retaliation" against older generations who have shaped politics, the environment, and society in ways that younger people now see as misguided.[9] Yet Gen Z and Millennials also have their cultural and social battles against each other: whether to part one's hair on the side or in the middle, whether jeans should be skinny or baggy. Given this popularized intergenerational warfare, studying the ways media fandom can bridge divides between people raised with different economic and social norms seems fitting.

While the essays in this collection do reference the popular sociological understanding of generations—Baby Boomers, Gen X, Millennials, Gen Z—we argue that a nuanced perspective of transgenerational fandoms must move beyond these limited and occasionally arbitrary labels. In its own work on generational research, the Pew Research Center says that a "cohort spanning 15–20 years will necessarily include a diverse assortment of people—and often there are meaningful smaller cohorts within these generations."[10] In addition, within the fifteen to twenty years that make up a societal generation are often significant social and cultural changes that result in any two people having dramatically different relationships to media texts and fandoms. As Derek Johnson notes, "the difference between one designated generation and the next reflects perceived changes in tastes, technological use, participatory media practices, and more," and these perceptions in tastes influence and are influenced by industry practices and strategies.[11] This book proposes new ways to define and deploy the term *generation* as an organizing rubric for fan groups. Many contributors propose

Introduction 3

unique taxonomies for fan generations, from medium-based (Meredith Dabek's print-first versus screen-first) to kinship-based (Neta Yodovich's father–daughter familial sharing). Diversifying our understanding of generation allows us to more clearly see points of contention and connection in transgenerational fandoms.

Finally, we also understand *generation* as a synonym for the life course, what Harrington and Bielby describe as "fans' sustained engagement with media objects over time and the transformations of fandom in later life."[12] Göran Bolin argues the moment of discovery and youthful fandom is formative not only for individuals but for the self-construction of generation.[13] Specifically, as the individual fan moves through different stages of life, from childhood to adolescence to early adulthood and so on, their relationship to media evolves. Their relationship to a singular media text may make "new and varied meanings from the series as they have aged."[14] Although work on fandom and the life course has been scarce in the past, it is a growing area of interest for fan studies scholars, and we hope to demonstrate how the life course approach coincides with larger studies of inter- and transgenerational fandoms.

CONCLUSION

This book intends to further the conversation about how generational fandom is influenced by and, in turn, influences technologies, industry practices, and social and political changes. To accomplish this, a range of methods are used, from quantitative survey research and in-depth interviews to autoethnography, textual and industry analysis, and star studies. While gender is a persistent focus of this volume, the collected chapters represent a broad range of fandoms across geographical boundaries, genres, and age demographics.

Part One investigates the cultural reception of reboots, remakes, and revivals among fans. Bridget Kies finds a common bond of dissatisfaction with reboot culture between different generations of fans. Whereas fans of original media texts are sometimes turned off by the "politicizing" of reboots through more diversity in representation, many new fans are frustrated that these efforts at diversity are not good enough. The subsequent chapters by Bethan Jones and Siobhan Lyons explore how nostalgia has shaped the reception to rebooted properties. Jones examines how the revival of *The X-Files* undermined the "Scully effect," in which girls were encouraged to pursue studies in science as a result of the appeal of Gillian Anderson's character Dana Scully, as discourse during the revival shifted to talk about

4 *Introduction*

Anderson's aging body and Scully's sexuality. Lyons similarly investigates how revivals are affected by fan perceptions of aging but contrasts different reactions to male and female stars of *The X-Files* and *Twin Peaks*. Finally, Andrew Scahill investigates the disappointment that comes when a reboot fails to live up to fans' expectations. Using the film reboot of the children's program *Jem and the Holograms* as a case study, Scahill finds that it created a generational anti-fandom rooted in nostalgia. With focus on reboots and revivals in their numerous meanings and iterations, this section of the book demonstrates how transgenerational fandoms negotiate new additions to canons across political and cultural ruptures.

In Part Two, we turn our attention to the longevity of fandoms across generations and how reboot culture (and sometimes the lack thereof) sustains them. Neta Yodovich offers a provocative study of female fans who were introduced to science fiction media by their fathers. Her study challenges assumptions about how family interests and hobbies tend to be passed between same-gender parents and children while calling attention to women science fiction fans who are often overlooked or are considered exceptions. Simone Driessen presents research into female fans of 1990s pop bands that have reinvigorated their media appearances and concert tours in the twenty-first century. Her findings show how fan practices change, sometimes becoming more committed, as fans mature into financially independent adult women. Megan Connor uses an autoethnographic study of her fandom of the Baby-Sitters Club to demonstrate how girls' relationships to media texts evolve through adolescence, particularly regarding changes in sexuality. Connor is especially interested in the role that ancillary texts play in shaping retrospective understandings of beloved media. Cynthia Walker offers a closer look at the lesser explored "cousins" (fans) of *The Man from U.N.C.L.E.*, calling it a "fandom of waiting" that patiently sustained itself for nearly half a century before new textual iterations appeared. By contrast, Yektanurşin Duyan argues that the sustained stardom of Turkish actress Türkan Şoray can be attributed to her intergenerational appeal and the sense of immediacy fans feel. Janelle Vermaak-Griessel uses the framework of "fan-gifting" to demonstrate how Alien fandom is passed along in a familial context and the different modes its fans perform their fandom once initiated. For Vermaak-Griessel, no matter the style of fandom, those gifted fandom by their family are now part of a transgenerational legacy of fans. Finally, Meredith Dabek shows how transmedia adaptations of *Pride and Prejudice* like *The Lizzie Bennet Diaries* give different generations of Jane Austen fans a common experience through which to share their fandom. By focusing studies on inter- and transgenerational aspects, these chapters collectively offer more nuanced approaches to understanding long-established and polyvalent fandoms.

Part Three provides greater nuance to stereotypical depictions of generations at odds with one another, exploring fan divisions but also the bridges built between these divides. Dan Golding argues that each new iteration of Star Wars is "generationally thick"—carefully constructed to welcome back old fans while welcoming new ones and speaking to the politics and dominant mode of fandom of each iteration's time. Building on a survey circulated among fans of author J. R. R. Tolkien, Maria K. Alberto and Dawn Walls-Thumma demonstrate how different fan generations, concurrent with different additions to the Tolkien canon, pay more attention to aspects of sexuality and diversity. L. N. Rosales demonstrates how women were systematically excluded from Sherlock Holmes fan societies until the recent media age. Finally, Mélanie Bourdaa examines how mentoring in specific fandoms encourages a transgenerational kinship as older fans share their knowledge of the canon and common fan practices with newer fans. Despite tensions between different kinds of fan generations, each chapter ultimately suggests the potential for a culturally progressive broadening in choices for how fans experience their fan object, from greater canonical diversity to more sexually explicit fan fiction.

In his study of transgenerational media industries, Derek Johnson argues that the convergence era demands media industries "confront potential gulfs between their audiences—including perceived generational differences."[15] For Johnson, the growth of transmedia and media conglomeration have meant a collision of old and new media industries that also means "old and young audiences might collide too."[16] While Johnson's attention is on strategies the industries employ to manage this generational collision, greater attention toward strategies audiences and fans use is needed. As reboot culture continues, as franchises continue expanding over time, and as new technologies enable easier access to older media, much more investigation into transgenerational fandoms and intergenerational fan relationships must be done. This book begins that conversation.

PART ONE

REBOOTS, REVIVALS, AND NOSTALGIA

"I Ain't Afraid of No Bros"

THE GENERATIONAL POLITICS
OF REBOOT CULTURE

Bridget Kies

Where once fan studies sought to exalt the creativity and collaboration of fans, in recent years the discipline has become infatuated with the dark side of fandom. One of the go-to examples, mentioned several times in this volume, is fan response to the 2016 all-women remake of *Ghostbusters*. The infamy of the movie's trailer receiving the most dislikes by YouTube users is an often-told tale, as is the racist Twitter firestorm alt-right icon Milo Yiannopoulos launched at one of the movie's stars, Leslie Jones. In the wake of so much toxicity leveled at her Blackness, her acting, and the movie, Jones eventually responded that the best solution was to quit feeding the troll.[1]

With respect to Jones, this chapter ignores her advice and "feeds the troll" by examining fan responses to what I call "reboot culture"—an umbrella term for reboots, remakes, and revivals that have saturated the contemporary media landscape. With particular focus on representations of race, gender, and sexuality, I am interested in how evolving social norms and cultural values shape generational and intergenerational reception of reboot culture. On one hand, fans of the originals often argue that the remake, reboot, or revival is too different, granting a value judgment of badness as a result. At the same time, those who anticipate being fans of forthcoming remakes, reboots, and revivals—and who likewise call themselves fans—frequently get angry with new iterations because they expect more progressive portrayals of race, gender, and sexuality. *Ghostbusters* is one example, but TV revivals like *The L Word: Generation Q* (Showtime, 2020–) and remakes like *One Day at a Time* (Netflix, 2017–2019, Pop 2020–) similarly generate anxieties that their more diverse portrayals of race and queer identities are not qualitatively correct or quantitatively enough to meet a contemporary metric of acceptability.

Previous examinations of reboot culture often group fans into an older generation who prefers the original text and a younger generation who prefers the reboot or remake. This grouping limits opportunities to find points of convergence among different clusters of fans and anti-fans across age-based generations. As C. Lee Harrington and Denise Bielby explain, "media texts and technologies help unite cohorts, define generations and cross-generational differences, and give structure and meaning to our lives as they unfold."[2] The "so-called 'television,' 'computer,' and 'Facebook' generations" can all be understood as having different relationships with technology and socialization because of the burgeoning and dominant technologies when those generations were born and growing up.[3] But marking generations by time or age neglects other factors that shape reception to media texts. *Where* a fan is born—for instance, whether in a conservative neighborhood or diverse urban area—may be just as important at shaping their tastes and politics as when the fan was born. Furthermore, tastes and politics evolve over time and are influenced by a host of other factors. Rather than taking a sociological approach to generations (Baby Boomers, Gen X, Millennials, Gen Z) or an industry-focused approach (target or predicted audience compared with measured audience), I am more interested in how "generations" might be identified through their entry point to a canon, regardless of the fan's age and the release year for the media text.[4] (This strategy is also taken up in Dabek's and Alberto and Walls-Thumma's chapters in this volume.) I am specifically interested in how that entry may affect reception of future canonical developments, such as reboots, remakes, and revivals. What I call "original" fans are fans of the first incarnation of a particular media text, regardless of their ages or when they discovered the text. "New" fans are fans of that text as it is rebooted, remade, or revived. These fans may be younger and so may not have had access to the original media text when it first came out, but this does not have to be the case. It is inaccurate to think of "original" and "new" fan groups as mutually exclusive because in reboots "some elements of the original narrative are explained while others are left to the canon for explanation" to provide pleasure to the "attentive fan who will catch the reference."[5]

Different generations of fans and anti-fans of reboot culture do not often agree on whether representations of race, gender, and sexuality are too much or too little, but they often share a sentiment of dissatisfaction. Where previous studies of reboot culture have emphasized the schism between what I call original and new fans, this chapter highlights the ways their generational criticisms can overlap, despite their contradictory goals.

REBOOT CULTURE GOES TOO FAR: RUINED
CHILDHOODS AND NOSTALGIA

Popular and fan-led criticism of reboot culture often uses aesthetic and textual analyses to mask anxieties about the integrity of the franchise and the universe fans think it portrays. One common concern in critical reviews and fan metas is that new textual incarnations, especially those that foreground women and people of color, "ruin" the original text and, by extension, the childhoods of those who grew up with that original. After publicity for *Star Wars: The Force Awakens* (J. J. Abrams, 2015) began, the original generation of Star Wars fans expressed sentiments the film was "so bad, *it destroyed Star Wars*" (@Bvd788, Reddit, April 21, 2018). The complaints cite many factors, including the film's narrative, but the most noteworthy updates to the canon were its female protagonist (Rey, played by Daisy Ridley) and secondary BIPOC characters (played by Oscar Isaac and John Boyega) and the perceived romance or bromance between them. For some original generation fans, these choices were seen as political—moves made by producers purely for the sake of pandering to an audience that values diversity on screen without regard for narrative necessity or authenticity to the textual universe. In 2018, an open letter circulated declaring that Lucasfilm had "willfully and malignantly discarded the fans in the sole pursuit of a misguided political agenda" (@AzulaAr, Twitter, June 3, 2018). As Ross Garner notes, though, choices that appear to reflect "multiple contemporary sociopolitical discourses" are always measured against "branding requirements" and fan affect to protect and expand the brand franchise for its continued consumption.[6] Dan Golding's chapter in this volume takes up the Star Wars fandom in more depth, but this fandom example is useful for understanding how greater representational diversity in reboot culture is often perceived as political.

In a related example, Reddit user Crazylegsmurphy describes his personal relationship with the 1984 version of *Ghostbusters* and the pride with which he wore his original Ghostbusters T-shirt before the 2016 film's hype and release. He expresses his concerns about the announced reboot and fear that it might "destroy" the greatness of the original film. In his own words: "Wearing a Ghostbusters logo today sends a confusing message. Am I wearing it in support of feminism? Am I making a statement that there is only one Ghostbusters team?"[7] On the surface, his anxiety indicates concern about how he will be perceived by others. If the shirt is mistaken as merchandise for the 2016 film, he may be perceived as supportive of the film and its feminist reimagining. If the shirt is (correctly) perceived as merchandise for the 1984 film, he may be perceived as antifeminist, opposing the new film and asserting his support solely for the original, all-male version.

In the case of the Star Wars letter and the Ghostbusters shirt, the claim that reboot culture "ruined childhood" is less about rewriting favorite scenes and replacing favorite actors than about taking a media text the fan feels always had an "innocence about it" and turning it into something "political" through inclusive depictions of women, BIPOC, and queer people.

Accusations of childhood ruination are swiftly hurled at reboot culture, though they are just as swiftly met with numerous think pieces explaining how the "ruined childhood" argument is a mask for antifeminist sentiment.[8] *Ghostbusters* (2016) director Paul Feig plainly dismissed ruined childhood claims on the grounds of temporality: "The only way I could ruin your childhood is if I got into a time machine."[9] But flaws to the ruined childhood argument extend beyond the temporal. Crazylegsmurphy's perceived innocence of the 1984 film, for instance, neglects the film's rampant misogyny, in which a woman's body is sexually appropriated by an evil spirit, and its latent racism, in which the lone Black actor (Ernie Hudson) was excised from marketing materials.[10] As Reddit user OceanCyclone puts it, the original *Ghostbusters* film "had a shit ton of issues."[11]

The issue of whether material is "political" or "problematic" lies in the fan's identity and how that identity might be reflected in or shaped by the media canon. Richard Jenkins finds that personal choices and perceptions enable us to conceive of our own identities.[12] Building on this, Matt Hills argues that fans can shape their self-identities through their fandom, which means a threat to a canon can feel like a threat to their identities.[13] William Proctor similarly argues that memory and nostalgia are mapped onto texts like *Ghostbusters*, so that any threat "to the totemic object, then, can thus be felt as threats to self-identity, self-continuity, and self-narrative."[14] For Proctor, concerns like Crazylegsmurphy's are "not 'simply' or 'only' about gender" because any reboot—including a new all-male cast—would intend to erase the original, the totem, for contemporary audiences and would therefore be threatening to a fan's nostalgia and identity.[15]

While Proctor offers a detailed understanding of how nostalgia functions, his claim ignores the backlash to developments in media industries to increase representations of race, gender, and sexuality and any real-world consequence this backlash might have. He uses Crazylegsmurphy's commentary as an example of an average fan, yet this overlooks the occasions when this fan reveals his polarizing politics. In other posts and comments on Reddit, Crazylegsmurphy expresses the belief that sex is binary, denying the existence of intersex—or perhaps confusing sex with gender and denying the existence of trans and nonbinary people.[16] He applauds the concept of "straight pride parades," thus demonstrating homophobic ignorance of LGBTQ history, and, finally in a "men's rights" subreddit, admits: "I hate this movie because it stars four women."[17] Gender, it seems, is the driving force for an original fan who openly declares: "I am actually totally against the idea of any all-female cast because of everything that goes along with it."[18] What this example shows, and what Proctor conveniently neglects, is that the self-identity threatened by reboot culture is less about fannish identity than cisgender, heterosexual, white male privilege.

The online spaces where vitriol for reboot culture is expressed include sites like Reddit and Twitter, public forums that, according to Ryan Milner, presume white male centrality by design.[19] Adrienne Massanari adds that geek and nerd culture also presumes maleness, and so "to discuss geek and nerd culture is to discuss masculinity," which Massanari narrows to "white male masculinity."[20] As Crazylegsmurphy's Reddit post indicates, concerns that a gender-swapped *Ghostbusters* reboot might destroy one's childhood fantasies presuppose that the child in question was a (cis het) white male and that seeing other (cis het) white men in central roles in blockbuster movies was inspirational. Matt Zoller Seitz describes this presumed person as the "demographically specific fan (straight, white, male, and used to seeing himself as the hero in everything) whom the culture has until recently treated as The Fan."[21]

This ignores the childhoods of women, BIPOC, and queer people who want and deserve to see themselves reflected in the media texts they consume. In contrast to "The Fan," women and girls are less accustomed to seeing themselves in the role of the movie hero, a crisis that has spawned think pieces, academic study, and advocacy organizations like the Geena Davis Institute on Gender in Media. The "ruined childhood" argument is not simply, as Proctor argues, a shield for loss of memory and nostalgia. Gender and racial politics are at the very heart of it. It is an argument that demonstrates the divide between "The Fan" who self-identifies with the original text and those who do not or cannot.[22] This is not to say that girls/women, BIPOC, and queer people cannot identify with or idolize cis, heterosexual, white male heroes, for indeed they often do, perhaps sometimes in the absence of other main characters. The point is that the options for identification with characters of the same race, gender, or sexual identity are fewer.

In *Ghostbusters* (2016), Kristen Wiig's character, Erin Gilbert, loses her opportunity for tenure at Columbia University when a book about paranormal activity she co-wrote with Abby Yates (Melissa McCarthy) resurfaces. Erin confronts Abby, from whom she is estranged, only to find that Abby has continued her work on the paranormal with the help of Jillian Holtzmann (Kate McKinnon), an engineer who produces the gadgets and gizmos that assist with ghost hunting. After seeing a ghost in person, Erin is persuaded to join them. During their first case, they meet Patty Tolan (Leslie Jones), a conscientious subway worker who does not want ghosts affecting the flow of mass transit. Patty joins the team and brings an encyclopedic knowledge of New York history. The four Ghostbusters must stop a disenfranchised white male bellhop (the archetypal angry white male loner) from destroying Manhattan with the help of an army of ghosts, but their efforts are thwarted by Homeland Security, the white male mayor, and a popular myth debunker played by (white male) Bill Murray. They are subject to internet trolling after they post a video of a ghost encounter. In a parallel to the backlash the trailer received, Erin reads misogynist comments left on their video on YouTube. Ultimately, the Ghostbusters are successful at stopping the bellhop and his ghost army, and the film concludes with the mayor's office pledging support for their now legitimate business ridding New York of the paranormal. The male trolls, both living and ghostly, are defeated. While the original *Ghostbusters* theme song declared, "I ain't afraid of no ghosts," a more fitting description of the 2016 reboot might be: "I ain't afraid of no bros."

In celebration of the film's themes of women working together, Melissa McCarthy posted a photo on Instagram on August 25, 2015, that features the cast along with the many women who worked on the production. Each woman holds a sign with her job title on it, and the four principal actors hold a banner that says, "Girl Power." At the film's premiere, the standouts among the legions of fans waiting to see the four principal actors on the red carpet were girl fans dressed up as the Ghostbusters. A viral photo showed Kristen Wiig talking to the mini-Ghostbusters, captioned in several media outlets cheekily: "destroying someone's childhood."[23] Less publicized was that there were also adult men in Ghostbusters costumes along the red carpet, there to celebrate the premiere and greet the new cast.

According to a study by the Geena Davis Institute, men are shown in STEM professions (science, technology, engineering, and math) at a rate of five to one in family-oriented film and media.[24] Increasing rates at which young women study the sciences have been attributed to characters like Dana Scully (Gillian Anderson) from *The X-Files* (dubbed the "the Scully effect").[25] For some fans in the new generation, a gender-swapped film like *Ghostbusters* does the opposite of destroying a childhood; it sparks a childhood interest that may turn into a lifelong passion and career. For adult fans in this generation who already have career paths, the effect is to celebrate the opportunities shown as available to others. What distinguishes the new generation of fans is less about age than taste—and, as the male fans at the premiere emblematize, less about the fan's gender and more about their gender politics.

NOT GOING FAR ENOUGH: THE LIMITS OF PROGRESSIVE REPRESENTATION

While some fans feel frustrated by what they perceive as the politicization of reboot culture, others feel equally frustrated that reboots, remakes, and revivals are not politically progressive enough in their portrayals of women, BIPOC, and queer people. In a review of *The L Word: Generation Q* (2019–2020), a revival of the lesbian-oriented drama *The L Word* (2004–2009), Crispin Long describes the revival as trying to "absolve the original's sins," which included "its characters' carefree privilege, its tendency to tokenize people of color, and, most infamously, its crass, misinformation-laden depiction" of a trans man played by a cis woman.[26] It is perhaps not absolution but atonement that has driven the revival: the series' stars and executive producers (Jennifer Beals, Leisha Hailey, and Katherine Moennig) acknowledge that the original series had limitations and offer their hope that the revival will feature more diversity and "better" representation.[27] Even the series' new name, *Generation Q*, was intended to signify a shift to more inclusive portrayals of sexual identities, where the "L word" meant only "lesbian." The revival includes trans, disabled, and BIPOC actors and characters of lesser economic means. The "generation" in the title may refer to the more complex community depicted, which moves beyond racial, gender, and sexual binaries. It may also refer to a younger target audience. Gen Z (born between 1997 and 2002) is the least white American generation alive today.[28] Nearly 16 percent of them identify as LGBT, but 72 percent of those do not identify as specifically "gay" or "lesbian."[29] "Q" signifies a welcome marker of inclusion, since white, cis lesbians no longer push the envelope of representation.

At heart, *The L Word: Generation Q* remains a soapy drama with conflict and narrative tension dependent on troubled interpersonal relationships and plenty of sex scenes. This narrative setup mirrors the original series, which was continually evaluated on whether it seemed "good" or "authentic" in representation, as one of very few series (still) to feature an ensemble of

"I Ain't Afraid of No Bros" 15

queer women. TV critic Naomi Gordon-Loebl argues that *The L Word* was never "a series whose primary interest is in exploring the political and cultural issues that cut through LGBTQ communities" but instead was a prestige version of a queer soap opera.[30] As part of the same universe, the revival should be expected to similarly represent political issues but not necessarily explore them with any "correctness" agreed upon by divergent audiences. Instead, Gordon-Loebl argues the value of the original and the revival is that, as melodramas, they are "capable of pulling at our heartstrings."[31]

Following the first season, *The L Word: Generation Q* was criticized, along with other contemporary TV series with BIPOC characters, because "the 'wokeness' is performative" (@_kuki_sanban, Twitter, March 27, 2020). In addition to what some feel is superficial diversity, some fans expressed frustration at the amount of sex and drama: "It's a whole load of mess why is everyone sleeping with everyone and cheating on each other" (@jsl90, Twitter, March 24, 2020). A. Andrews similarly echoed: "i didn't know it was possible but the l word generation q is literally worse than the l word" (@anghost, Twitter, December 16, 2020). Among the hundreds of tweets I reviewed using a search for "l word generation q," this is the only one that expressed general dissatisfaction with the series. Most tweets were positive, even if they acknowledged some troubling aspects of the series. Criticisms were largely about the lack of storyline for a trans character and promiscuity and infidelity that—while attractive for a premium cable series—may not show the LGBTQ community in its best light.

Revivals like *The L Word: Generation Q* are intended to speak to fans of the original as much as they want to welcome new fans. The involvement of actors from the original series, now serving as executive producers, demonstrates how thinking of generations by age is limited. Instead, the generations of fans can be organized by how social changes shape reception. For instance, an original fan could have enjoyed the original series until it appeared socially unacceptable, as trans rights became more openly discussed and legislated and as popular discussions of sexuality shifted from a gay/straight binary to a spectrum. The trans rights movement and existence of a sexuality spectrum, of course, preceded *The L Word*'s original broadcast, though arguably without the same visibility in popular discourse as they have had since the end of the original series. Given this social change, some fans—and even stars—of the original series may see critical flaws that push them into being fans of the new generation.

Promotional material for *The L Word: Generation Q* hyped the evolution of politics and values among the show's producers as a way to reassure audiences that the revival would also be updated for today's politics. The sitcom reboot *One Day at a Time* similarly promised in social media, critical reviews, promos, and interviews that it would push the premise of the original (a single mother raising teenagers) to address social issues in a way consistent with a generation committed to diversity. On fan boards, viewers of the original *One Day at a Time* (CBS, 1975–84), even those who call themselves fans, agree the series was not very good (though explanations of "good" vary). O Don Piano says, "I'm 'meh' about it. If I do watch, it's for nostalgic reasons," while Jupiter8's assessment is more extreme, describing it as the "most irritating show ever."[32]

A defender of the original series, Billoneeg, doesn't contradict that the show's plots were unbelievable or the characters irritating but explains: "The reason I loved this show is because I suspended reality & watch them without expectation."[33] DLD adds that the lack of cable and streaming in the late 1970s meant that viewing options were severely limited compared with today, and many people became de facto "fans" in that they watched every episode without the real emotional connection typically understood as emblematic of fandom.[34] Among the discussion threads I reviewed, fandom of stars Valerie Bertinelli and Mackenzie Phillips, who played the teenage and later young adult children in the original series, were primary reasons viewers remembered watching.

The rebooted *One Day at a Time* changed the family's ethnicity from white to Cuban American, peppered the dialogue with Spanish, added a sassy grandmother (played by the inimitable Rita Moreno), and changed the setting from Indianapolis to the more urban and diverse Los Angeles. As with the original series and all of creator Norman Lear's works, the reboot features moral dilemmas that anchor each episode's plot as the family discusses race, gender and sexual politics, drug use, veteran post-traumatic stress disorder, and immigration laws. The reboot kept the conventions of earlier sitcoms, including a three-camera set-up with a primary living room set and a laugh track. One Reddit user asked if younger fans who might have missed the original's broadcast found the sitcom conventions annoying. Users ranging from age twenty to thirty reported that they enjoyed the reboot, frequently noting that it felt "fresh."[35] We might speculate that this assessment of freshness is based on the series' content, rather than its aesthetics, though its traditional domestic sitcom aesthetics might feel fresh to viewers accustomed to modern single-camera sitcoms without laugh tracks. None of these new generation fans were alive when the original was broadcast, though they may have encountered it in rerun syndication.

"I Ain't Afraid of No Bros" 17

The format of the reboot was less important to these fans than the social issues foregrounded in the show's narrative; because those issues seemed contemporary, so did other aspects of the show.

The reboot explores the sexuality of both teen children. Elena (Isabella Gomez) comes out as gay but soon falls in love with a nonbinary person, Syd (Sheridan Pierce). In a third season episode, Elena and Syd book a hotel room to have sex for the first time, but Elena decides she is not ready, and they agree to wait. A fan campaign attempted to get the couple nominated for the Teen Choice Awards Choice Ship, and *TV Guide* declared "Sydlena" the cutest couple of the 2018–19 season. Elena's younger brother, Alex (Marcel Ruiz), is given lectures normalizing masturbation. The frankness with which teen sexuality is portrayed is a departure from the original series but one that is more consistent with contemporary TV storylines.

When Netflix announced the cancellation of the rebooted *One Day at a Time*, fans immediately rallied on social media, and the series was picked up by Pop TV for a fourth season. Pop TV president Brad Schwartz described the decision as "investing in fandom": "we have to put on stuff that people are so emotionally connected to."[36] The fan campaign and its success garnered attention for the series and Pop TV, as well as awareness about the power of fan campaigns. In contrast to the original series, which my research indicates was watched incidentally or with willing suspension of disbelief and taste, the reboot has passionate fans who worked in conjunction with the actors and producers to save a series they felt was "respectful and even subtle at times" in its treatment of social issues.[37] This is a rare example in which reboot culture is appreciated for its perceived progress, rather than criticized for not going far enough.

THE FANTASY OF REBOOT CULTURE

For reboots like *One Day at a Time*, social politics seem to be the anchor through which fans connect with the text. For some reboot fans, that also means a sense of frustration that political and social issues are not depicted with enough detail or attention to the myriad complexities—or the "correct" viewpoint (however any individual fan might regard "correctness").

For new generation fans, vision toward the future often drives a deep desire to see more diversity in portrayals of race, gender, and sexuality. These fans can become frustrated if a reboot does not "do enough," although they may celebrate steps toward progress. This approach is as critical as the approach of original fans who are led by nostalgia to lament changes to the canonical universe. The new generation approach presumes a linear progress to social issues, which is as mythical and romantic as nostalgia. In the case of gender and sexuality, for instance, there have been new laws protecting same-sex couples (most notably, federal marriage recognition) since 2015, but there has also been an increase in wealth disparity that often affects trans people more severely than cis people.[38] Media portrayals of trans people have increased, though real-life economic conditions have not improved.[39] For Cael Keegan, the quest for "good" trans representation is misguided because an increase in "positive" representation does not necessarily correspond with increasingly positive conditions for trans people in real life.[40] Similarly, Sarah Banet-Weiser notes that although portrayals of popular feminism have increased, so have incidents of popular misogyny because feminism and misogyny in popular media are "deeply entwined."[41]

Just as some original generation fans experience frustration with how the present and future iterations of a rebooted media text interfere with their looking back at the original, new generation fans may experience frustration with how the present reboot culture doesn't yet strive toward a more utopian vision of media. We often conceptualize these generations as at odds, focusing on their different textual interests. By focusing on their similarities, we can form a more complete picture of fan responses to reboot culture. Both original and new fans are often frustrated with the politics of reboot culture, especially with regard to race, gender, and sexuality, and these frustrations stem from a romanticized notion of how media operates, what it can do, and what it symbolizes to us.

"I Ain't Afraid of No Bros" 19

Reopening *The X-Files*

GENERATIONAL FANDOM, GENDER, AND BODILY AUTONOMY

Bethan Jones

On September 10, 1993, the pilot episode of *The X-Files*, featuring FBI Special Agents Fox Mulder (David Duchovny) and Dana Scully (Gillian Anderson), aired on the Fox network. The series, including the 1998 feature film *The X-Files: Fight the Future* (Rob Bowman), ended in 2002, but after the release of the 2008 movie *The X-Files: I Want to Believe* (Chris Carter), fans mobilized on social media in the hopes of persuading Fox to greenlight a third cinematic installment. Although these campaigns were unsuccessful, Fox confirmed in March 2015 that *The X-Files* would return as a short-order mini-series with Duchovny and Anderson reprising their roles.[1] This reassured (some) fans, who had feared that the original cast would be replaced, but others wondered how well the series would age. These discussions demonstrated how revisiting cult franchises can be complicated as the text, fandom, and actors age.[2]

In this chapter I am interested in exploring how fans of *The X-Files*—both original and new—perceive and receive the show and its depiction of gender. Initially lauded for its representation of strong female characters—the "Scully effect," whereby the character influenced young women to enter STEM fields, has been well documented—the series' recent incarnations have been criticized for being transphobic and misogynistic. Anderson's revelation that Fox offered her half the salary they offered Duchovny for season ten demonstrates a continued lack of gender equality in Hollywood.[3] A product of its time in the early 1990s, fans' responses to the revival suggest that the shifting attitudes to gender in the twenty-first century haven't necessarily been reflected in the series.[4] In a period that saw the election of Donald Trump as US president and the #MeToo movement, the way that different generations of fans deal with the show's hits and misses, particularly with regard to gender, suggests that nostalgia for a beloved show competes with progressive attitudes toward gender representation and raises questions for how we deal with being fans of problematic things.

In discussing generations, I use these terms to refer to cohorts of *X-Files* fans: "original" fans who watched the original series as it aired or shortly after (self-identified as fans for sixteen years and more); "second-wave" fans who watched the show after it finished airing but prior to the widespread use of streaming sites (self-identified as fans for eleven to fifteen years); and "new fans" who have come to the show more recently, through family fandom or its inclusion in streaming platforms such as Netflix (self-identified as fans for up to ten years). Analyzing four surveys reveals that these phrases are broadly aligned with generational identifiers: original fans are more likely to be Gen X and Millennials (80 percent of those who said that they had been fans for over sixteen years were aged twenty-six to forty-five, compared with 18.7 percent who were over forty-five and 1.3 percent who were under twenty-five); second-wave fans were predominantly Millennials (72.7 percent said they had been a fan for eleven to fifteen years), followed by Gen Z (20.8 percent) and Generation X (7.3 percent). New fans were more likely to be Gen Z (65.3 percent of those who said that they had been fans for less than ten years were twenty-five or younger, compared with 29.1 percent aged twenty-six to forty-five and 5.6 percent over forty-five). Yet *X-Files* fans are known for being early adopters of technology,[5] and the analysis of a specific fandom presented here may trouble the articulation between new technologies, new viewing patterns, and Gen Z as much as others may enable us to feel confidence in it.[6] This chapter interrogates how *The X-Files* and its fans navigated issues surrounding gender in both iterations of the show, as well as in the fandom and general discourse.

METHODOLOGY

Drawing on research undertaken in May 2015, April 2016, December 2017, and April 2018, I examine fans' responses to the original series and the revival seasons ten and eleven. I circulated a total of four questionnaires on Twitter and Facebook and in forums, LiveJournal communities, and Facebook groups. Respondents were asked sixteen to twenty-three questions, which contained demographic information as well as reflections on how they felt about a particular season, if and how their fandom had been affected, what their feelings were toward creator Chris Carter, and how they felt about specific storylines. In total the surveys yielded 2,688 valid responses, and data were explored for recurring patterns, rather than approaching it with a set of preset codes.[7]

Reopening The X-Files   21

"THE 'BETTER FAN' VIBE IS RIFE IN THE XF FANDOM AND I PREFER TO MAKE MY OWN CONCLUSION": INTERGENERATIONAL ANTAGONISM AND INTER-FANDOM RELATIONSHIPS

The X-Files's position as lauded media text and cult fan object has enabled it to maintain a position in the media's (sub)conscious even while off the air, and fan campaigns have maintained its status in fandom.[8] The announcement of the new series drew much hype, even before details on what it would actually entail were available. Thomas Austin, drawing on Barbara Klinger, suggests that "promotional operations of disaggregation and dilation" shape the assembly of the text, and "multiple bids to capture audiences are made intratextually . . . as well as extratextually."[9] Fox's marketing campaign seemed designed to capture both fans of the original series, by using "official" fan platforms run by original fans, such as X-Files News, and social media platforms like Snapchat for a younger generation.

Fans of *The X-Files* are often considered among the first to use the internet to create their own fan spaces, and Brian Lowry suggests that "fan reaction to the series has become as much a part of *The X-Files* story as the show itself."[10] The emergence of social networking sites such as Facebook and Twitter provided fans with new ways of communicating with other fans and media producers and has led to a resurgence of fan activity. Web 2.0 also saw studios begin to make use of social networks and blogs to communicate with fans, and Fox used this changing online landscape, undertaking a long social media marketing campaign ahead of the season ten premiere. This campaign was a coup for Fox, relying on fans posting photos and reviews to their own social media accounts to facilitate interest in the new season through word of mouth, as chief marketing officer Angela Courtin noted in an interview with *The Wrap*.[11] The premiere of the first episode of season ten at New York Comic Con, along with Fox's other tools such as #201DaysOfXFiles, airing a trailer during the Super Bowl halftime show (a marker that the series had "officially" moved from its cult TV status to the mainstream discourse), and sharing fan-produced posters on its social media accounts, speaks to a new kind of marketing strategy to promote contemporary televisual content.

Of the 758 respondents to my April 2016 survey, 8 percent said that they participated in or followed the 201 days of *X-Files* campaign, with many also following the official Twitter, Facebook, and Instagram accounts. Nine respondents attended the New York Comic Con panel and screening, while others attended the "Science of *The X-Files*" event at the University of Maryland and the screening at the Grove in Los Angeles. Official events were limited to key cities in the United States, a fact noted by many fans who completed the survey, but the use of social media by Fox and fan sites enabled fans in rural areas and overseas to take part in activity prior to the new season.

Twitter and Facebook were the most common ways for fans to engage with season ten on social media, although Tumblr, Reddit, and Instagram were also mentioned frequently, predominantly by younger fans.[12] 21st Century Fox maintained a presence on Twitter, Facebook, and Instagram specifically for *The X-Files*, and the main cast, including David Duchovny, Gillian Anderson, and Mitch Pileggi, also used those platforms to discuss the show. Fans, particularly younger ones, used their own time and labor to talk about season ten outside of official channels. Respondent 2016156, a female fan aged eighteen to twenty-five who had been a fan of the show for up to five years, detailed the social media activity they undertook:

> I followed the official *X-Files* Twitter account, as well as Gillian Anderson's, David Duchovny's, and Mitch Pileggi's accounts. Occasionally I would retweet things from them. My biggest contribution to social media regarding the revival, however, involves Tumblr: I run a Tumblr account devoted to *The X-Files*, which currently has around 3,600 followers. While Fox's "201 Days of *The X-Files*" campaign was going on, I devoted my time to creating one "gifset" per episode, posted on the days of the countdown that corresponded with each episode.

Both original and new fans thus used social media to discuss the revival in the lead up to and during season ten. Many of the older fans responding to my survey noted their enjoyment of the fandom around *The X-Files* during this period and the ways they were able to experience it differently from the original airing in the 1990s. There were more ways and means to engage in fandom, with real-time engagement as the episodes aired and easy access to more content—official and otherwise—even if these fans' enjoyment of the episodes themselves was more conflicted.

As Teresa Bridgeman observes, "the experience of narrative is always linked to temporal relations," and temporal patterns that structure the narrative are set against viewers' temporal experience with the text, "founded on memory and anticipation."[13] Thus, time and space are part of the fabric of narrative and "profoundly influence the way in which we build mental images" of the stories we encounter.[14] Heather Urbanski concurs, suggesting

Reopening The X-Files   23

that fan memories of the earlier text, as well as paratextual canon, "provide the material for a third layer of continuity [in the reboot], which is rewarded by references (major or minor) to the original versions [and] fandom and canon complicate this neat sense of authority because fans, armed with (in some cases) decades of canonical knowledge, often decide for themselves which sequence in a narrative they will follow."[15]

Yet in a revival, which attracts new fans as well as old ones, how do these memories and paratextual canon play into relationships between different generations of fans? I asked my respondents to reflect on their fandom following each season, and key among original fans was how new forms of engagement enhanced their experience of the show while also creating an element of nostalgia for the ways they had engaged with fans previously. Community, friendship, and connections with others were key themes coming out of original fans' responses, as respondent 2016128 suggests: "*The X-Files* brought me one of my oldest and best friendships, going on fifteen years now. The revival, from start to finish, was a way to reconnect in a way we hadn't been able to since the show ended. We still talked about old episodes over the years, but to have something new to talk about every week was exciting. We felt like giddy kids again!" (female, twenty-six to thirty-five, fan for eleven to fifteen years). This reference to "giddy kids" offers us a new way of thinking about fan generations and fan ages. Engaging with the fandom through the new series allowed this fan, who would have been between eleven and twenty at the time she began watching, to throw off the expectations of age and return to the "squee" of childhood and the unabashed enthusiasm of engaging with a beloved fan object. As Harrington, Bielby, and Bardo note, "older fans are held accountable to age norms in ways that younger fans are not (e.g. they are expected to 'grow out of' their fandom)."[16] However, by reverting back into their younger modes of fannish behavior, these fans occupied two generational spaces: their actual age and their fannish age. I consider the fannish age to align with the age the fan was when they had their most affective attachment to the show, whether that was during high school, college, or later. For respondent 2016128, this meant being able to talk about the show on a weekly basis with her best friend, replicating the activities they previously engaged in and allowing them to reconnect by reliving those early experiences. Similarly, respondent 2016003 wrote:

> I was a huge *X-Files* fan when I was in high school, but after the original
> series ended, I moved on with my life—and while I never forgot about

The X-Files and have always had the complete series on DVD, I didn't think much about the series anymore, and had moved on to my other, more current fandoms. The revival just rekindled my love of the series & brought my teenage fangirl self back to the forefront. It reminded me how much I loved the show and why I loved the show, and made me feel so nostalgic for what was, really, my "first fandom." (female, twenty-six to thirty-five, fan for sixteen to twenty years)

She also talked about how tweeting at commercial breaks reminded her of calling her friends during commercial breaks during the original series, which reflected what many other respondents said. They referenced their "original" or "earlier" fandom and talked about how watching the revival series allowed them to reenter that time and relive those experiences. Respondent 2018645 (female, thirty-six to forty-five, fan for over twenty years) wrote, "Both seasons 10 and 11 'awoke' my earlier dormant fandom. And it was different—more fun—in a way because when I was watching back in the 1990s, there was no social media to join in on." Thus, despite being older, these fans embodied their fannish age as a result of the revivals.

Engaging with others was an important element of this, and the idea of community was also mentioned by some new fans in a marked contrast to the behavior of fans of other rebooted and revived franchises: "The fandom is very welcoming, particularly to new members. I was not quite a year old when the pilot aired and no one has ever acted like I'm not a real fan because I'm younger/wasn't into it back then" (respondent 201669, female, eighteen to twenty-five, fan for zero to five years).

Other relationships between new and original fans seemed to generate more conflict. Respondent 2016301, a longtime fan of the show, suggested that new viewers may have engaged in mocking practices that affected their fandom:

I found myself much less willing to engage with other fans. I think the emotional resonance it had with me as a person made it difficult to be around those fans younger than I who took it much more as a joke and a novelty to admire the outdated fashion or the bad production values. Then again maybe I take all things I like too seriously. But to me it remains sacred, for lack of a better term, and I found being around the mocking atmosphere upsetting. (female, twenty-six to thirty-five, fan for eleven to fifteen years)

It is possible to frame this by drawing on Matt Hills's notion of inter-fandom antagonism.[17] These fans' responses may come from a kind of fan protectionism and boundary maintenance, which relates to their own individual fandom rather than a collective "old" fandom versus a collective "new" fandom. Leora Hadas writes about the tensions caused in Doctor Who fandom between fans of classic *Who* (1963–1989) and new *Who* (2005–) and notes that the show's revival in 2005 caught long-term fans by surprise. The science fiction classic, "long loved and cherished by a dedicated fannish minority, suddenly opened to a huge new flux of eager, often young, outsiders with little initial awareness and investment in the original text and no experience in the ways of its longtime fandom."[18] Although there were plenty of "old" *X-Files* fans who affectionately mocked the new series, much of this was accepted because of the subcultural capital those fans had accrued. In-jokes that were built and developed in the fandom over time were recognized as such and served to mock the show while retaining that nod to the community. As Kristina Busse notes, "length of fannish involvement is often used as an indicator of fannishness. . . . Years in fandom generates fannish cred by indicating time commitment and investment."[19] Original fans had thus invested more in the show than new fans had, and this time served meant they were more entitled to mock it. There is, then, an inherent conflict in new generations of fans bringing lifeblood to the fandom while also being othered and embraced ambivalently by established fans. This tension can cause divisions within the fandom, as respondent 2016570 points out: "It divided a lot of people, and many people left the fandom because of how different age brackets interacted with each other (e.g. the fresh very young teenage fans interacting with the old fans that watched during the original run). I saw a lot of bullying during the course of the revival between individuals, often over points of the show" (female, eighteen to twenty-five, fan for zero to five years).

Despite the differences between these old and new fans, there was one area in which there was almost universal accord: the treatment of Dana Scully.

"TALK ABOUT TAKING A MASSIVE SHIT ON YOUR LEADING LADY": BODILY AUTONOMY, GENDER, AND DANA SCULLY

The X-Files has been lauded for its depiction of a strong female character, and series creator Chris Carter has often discussed his decision to reverse the gender roles of the key protagonists, saying in his introduction to the 1996

26 REBOOTS, REVIVALS, AND NOSTALGIA

Pilot/Deep Throat VHS, "I wanted to flip the gender types, the stereotypes that we have. I wanted Mulder, the male, to be the believer, the intuitor, and I wanted Scully to be the skeptic. The one which is usually the traditional male role."[20] Fans and scholars have responded to the image of Scully as a powerful, strong woman, capable of holding power and taking on leadership, with Lisa Parks arguing that her "feminized body becomes the site through which scientific rational, technological and legal discourses are articulated and negotiated."[21] There are, of course, arguments to be made for the ways *The X-Files* undermines this favorable depiction of Scully, but respondents to my questionnaires repeatedly used words like *strong, independent*, and *feminist* to describe the character and her influence on their lives:

> Scully is my role model in life. The Scully effect affected my life in a very good way: I'm an independent, strong woman who is also a feminist and who wants to achieve her dreams and never gives up. (respondent 2015106, female, twenty-six to thirty-five, fan for sixteen to twenty years)

> *The X-Files* was a huge part of my preteen years. I am a direct result of the Scully effect. I majored in criminal justice and work in law enforcement. (respondent 2018267, male, twenty-six to thirty-five, fan for over twenty years)

However, reactions to seasons seven, eight, and nine had been mixed, particularly with regard to Scully's pregnancy storyline. In the season seven finale, "Requiem," viewers discovered that Scully was pregnant. (She had been pronounced infertile during season five.) The child was born at the end of season eight, and Scully named him William. Both she and Mulder referred to him as "our son," but he was given up for adoption during the end of the ninth season after it was revealed he was a "miracle child" important to alien conspirators. Many fans during the series' original run had been frustrated by this storyline, and were unsurprisingly divided on whether they wanted to return to William in season ten:

> [I want them to] Deal with the William thing. And do it in a way that does justice to the characters. So much has been taken from Scully, and when not one but two children [the second child referred to here is Emily, who was created during Scully's season two abduction and given to foster parents but died shortly after Scully found her at the

end of the season five episode "Emily"] were given to her only to be taken away again, I felt that crossed some kind of line. (respondent 2015100, female, twenty-six to thirty-five, fan for sixteen to twenty years)

Equally unsurprisingly, once season ten aired, responses remained mixed. William was a key feature of the season, with the second episode, "Founder's Mutation," showing Mulder discussing his fears that William was infected with alien DNA and episodes four ("Home Again") and six ("My Struggle II") focusing heavily on Scully's guilt in giving him up for adoption. For many fans, the execution of this storyline was underwhelming, particularly when it came to Scully and the way they felt she would act:

> I thought [the episodes] suffered a bit from Chris Carter's heavy hand-edness and the usual "women are just incubators" kind of schtick that always irritated me. (respondent 2016105, female, thirty-six to forty-five, fan for over twenty years)

> Scully's daydreams about William came down to basic '50s housewife kind of expectation/representation of having a child, without giving her dreams any personal side. Scully is a f*cking scientist, a pathologist, and a former fbi agent, she has a lot of interests/hobbies/experience, yet she dreams of reminding William about dinner when he runs past her? It felt flat, boring and a little ignorant. (respondent 2016602, female, twenty-six to thirty-five, fan for eleven to fifteen years)

Of course we inevitably deal with fans subjectivities when comparing season ten to *The X-Files*'s earlier seasons, and comparing the reactions of original or second-wave fans to those of new fans demonstrates the importance of recognizing these subjectivities and the weight they bear for different generations of fans when we talk about revivals. As respondent 2016635 (female, twenty-six to thirty-five, fan for zero to five years) pointed out:

> Perhaps it was binging it all at once, but I was more willing to be-lieve characterization & storyline as it was presented to me; I had no preconceived notions about what Mulder & Scully had been up to in time since season 9 or IWTB, as I had no "downtime" to consider it. I thought season 10 tied in well with the whole series and was excit-ed to see how the characters had aged & matured but stayed true to themselves.

28 REBOOTS, REVIVALS, AND NOSTALGIA

Unlike more long-term fans, who were adamant that Scully was acting out of character, the way newer fans engaged with the show and its fandom led them to view the characters differently.

In her discussion of reboots, Urbanski suggests that reimagined narratives "carry with them a more explicit, identifiable, and familiar background and history, and all the familiar elements of audience reception, such as genre, media hype, and viewer expectations, are magnified and complicated by the weight of history and what is known within fandom research as 'canon.'"[22] Faithfulness to the original series thus matters to the audience, and one of the key issues fans had with the revival was its lack of faithfulness to Scully.[23]

Season eleven opened with the revelation that Mulder is not William's father. Shown as a flashback to the seventh season episode "En Ami," the viewer sees Cigarette Smoking Man (CSM) arrive at a house with a sleeping Scully in the car. In the original episode Scully accuses CSM of drugging her; in this episode, we find out that he did. Discussing the events with Mulder and Scully's boss, CSM admits that he impregnated Scully with alien science and that he is William's father. Reactions were highly charged, with respondent 2018 (male, forty-six to fifty-five, fan for over twenty years) writing "Mulder not the father even though CC and Frank Spotnitz having admitted he IS the father? CC MUST NEVER WRITE AGAIN. He has ruined his own show," a sentiment echoed by respondent 2018234 (female, eighteen to twenty-five, fan for zero to five years) who said, "UGGGGHHHHH If I see one more reminder that the Cigarette Smoking Man is William's actual father, I'm going to scream." Few fans approved of this revision. Respondent 2018278 (male, eighteen to twenty-five, fan for zero to five years) was one exception: "I loved the twist that CSM was responsible for Scully's 're-fertility.'" Respondent 2018414 (female, thirty-six to forty-five, fan for over twenty years) was another: "I liked the twist of the story about [William]. It was tough, maybe cruel for many fans but I can live with that story." Responses were even more damning when Chris Carter stated in an interview that CSM "didn't rape Scully. He impregnated her with science."[24]

Emily Regan-Wills notes, "There are at least three different narratives in which Scully is feminized and rendered powerless: Scully as abductee, as sexually desirable, and as a (potential) mother," and indeed Scully has had much violence visited upon her body: abducted by humans and aliens, experimented on, medically raped, and the list goes on.[25] Both old and new fans referred to this in their responses to my questionnaires:

Reopening The X-Files   29

Chris Carter ret-conned a significant storyline (the William arc) in ways that I found unbelievable, disturbing and needlessly cruel. "My Struggle III" included the repeated physical brutalization of the Scully character, which is a well that Chris Carter dips into way too often for my liking. . . . "IV" was worse. Scully was completely sidelined, which is silly considering that the last time she was pregnant she was running around the desert trying to find Mulder. . . . Also to tell a story in which Scully has been raped; to not call it that; and to not provide a scene in which she is told this information and given the opportunity to speak about it, was reprehensible . . . especially in this day and age of "Me Too," it is completely tone deaf. The last scene was maybe the worst part about all of the "Struggles," and that's really saying something. For Scully to say she wasn't a mother to William was absolutely absurd and not in keeping with who we know Scully to be. (respondent 2018105, female, thirty-six to forty-five, fan for over twenty years)

After season 11, I hope Gillian Anderson tweets every single day about what an ass Carter is. For him to not tell her that stupid "I'm pregnant again! Whoooo!" twist until just before shooting the final scene . . . there's simply having bad ideas (OMG The Cigarette Smoking Man is William's actual daddy 'cause experiments and stuff!!!!) and there's being a total pig who showed no respect for his lead. (respondent 2018246, male, thirty-six to forty-five, fan for zero to five years)

It was a classic Chris Carter story-telling, however, "My Struggle III" made it obvious how little Chris Carter knows about/understands women, and how flippant and cruel he is to Dana Scully. To me, Chris Carter comes across as incredibly sexist. Dishing out all that he has to Scully and watching how she grits her teeth and bears it is a messed up way to show a strong woman. (respondent 2018258, female, twenty-six to thirty-five, fan for eleven to fifteen years)

Although there were nuances in what fans wanted to see and how they felt it had been handled in seasons ten and eleven, reactions to the treatment of Scully and Carter himself clearly demonstrate that *The X-Files*'s reintroduction in the twenty-first century wasn't entirely successful. Individual episodes, particularly the standalone monsters of the week, were on the whole considered the most successful, largely because they steered clear of

FIGURE 1. Gillian Anderson posted a GIF of Scully covering her face in disbelief two days after the season eleven finale aired. @GillianA, "Oh boy oh boy do I ever hear you," Twitter, March 23, 2018.

the mythology and Scully's pregnancy—elements of the show that proved most problematic. Fans of all ages, from different fannish generations, were cognizant of the #MeToo movement and recognized that much has changed about the ways we discuss gender and sexuality since the original seasons.[26] These shifting attitudes have clearly affected how *The X-Files* and other revived series are perceived.

CONCLUSION

The X-Files revival performed well in the United States and overseas, with over 21 million viewers watching the season ten premiere in the United States and nearly 7.5 million watching the season eleven premiere (figures include live and catch-up viewers). Despite the ratings, many fans and critics were unimpressed by the content of the revival. Chief among the criticisms was that Carter tried to do too much in too few episodes and that Scully as depicted in the revival was not true to that of the original show. I have focused on Scully's pregnancy and bodily autonomy, but these must be understood in the broader context of the #MeToo movement and gender inequality. Fans were aware of work Anderson had done to call for more female staff members on the show, and a tweet she posted following the season eleven finale suggesting that she shared fans' thoughts was widely circulated in both press and fan spaces (see Figure 1).[27]

Paratextual discourse, available because of improvements in technology since the early seasons, also played a role in determining how fans viewed the gender issues in the revival and how they responded to them. My discussion here has examined the complexities at work in reviving a beloved cult TV series for the contemporary televisual landscape, particularly when issues of gender are concerned. The fans who responded to my surveys came from a range of backgrounds and ages and had been identifying as fans from months to over twenty years. Although this brought inevitable differences in their reactions to the revival and the fandom, it was also clear to see commonalities, particularly in relation to gender. Issues of gender and sexuality have risen in other rebooted media texts, such as *Star Wars* and *Ghostbusters* (as discussed elsewhere in this collection), and *The X-Files* is not alone in disappointing fans in how it deals with these subjects. It is, however, one of the few long-running TV series that have been revived. Moreover, it is a series that features a female character who was universally regarded as a feminist icon. Unlike Rey, a new character introduced to the Star Wars universe, or the female ghostbusters in the 2016 reboot, *The X-Files* brings its original characters into the present along with all the expectations fans have for them. While society and fandom have progressed, the depiction of Scully has not. Recognizing how the world has changed when it comes to rebooting or reviving beloved, long-running texts is thus of paramount importance to both media producers and fans.

Missing Time

TWIN PEAKS, THE X-FILES, AND
THE RISE OF AGING FANS

Siobhan Lyons

After a twenty-six-year hiatus, the cult series *Twin Peaks* (ABC, 1990–1991) returned to premium cable TV network Showtime in 2017. *The X-Files* (Fox, 1993–2002) returned to Fox after fourteen years in 2016. The rerelease of these shows in the age of streaming platforms and the internet saw the emergence of cross-generational fandom. While original fans flocked to see the new installments in the height of the 1990s nostalgia boom, both shows also courted new fans, many of whom were not old enough (or even alive) to have watched the original series when it first aired.

The revivals have since fueled a dialogue around the aged appearance of the actors and how aging affects, positively or negatively, the enduring fandom of those who watched the original run. For *Twin Peaks* in particular, the extended hiatus meant that there was a significant gap between seeing the actors in what is considered the prime of their youth and the height of their sex appeal and seeing them in their forties, fifties, and older. This gap is important because it disrupts the ordinary conventions of fans aging in parallel with the actors in these shows. The jump from the 1990s to the revivals in the twenty-first century forces fans to evaluate how they, too, have aged and how their fandom corresponds to the inevitable process of aging, both for themselves and for the actors. In addition to critics, fans of all ages have taken to online mediums to scrutinize the aged appearance of the actors, demonstrating an important link between aging celebrities and fans of different generations who anchor their fandom in the appearance of these actors. While Millennials (1980–1994) are also fans of the original run of *Twin Peaks* and *X-Files*, having benefited from watching these shows via VHS and DVDs, Generation X (1965–1979) and the Baby Boomers (1946–1964) experience a specific temporal engagement with these shows, sharing the same generational bracket as most of the cast members (Baby Boomer cast members include Kyle MacLachlan, Peggy Lipton, and Ray

Wise, while Generation X include Sheryl Lee, Sherilyn Fenn, Mädchen Amick, and Lara Flynn Boyle). In this way, their fandom is irretrievably linked to their age and generation.

This chapter examines how the extended time span between the original run and the revival of both *The X-Files* and *Twin Peaks* gave rise to various fan responses surrounding aging and how online technology facilitated these discussions. Blogs and online forums became spaces of cross-generational fandom, with many Baby Boomers and Gen Xers using these spaces to reflect on how the actors (and characters) aged and what impact this had on their fan experience of the revivals.

AGE AGAINST THE MACHINE

Fan studies is a thriving field of scholarly enquiry, but its relationship to aging is underexplored. "Fandom in late(r) life remains under-examined," write Harrington and Bielby. "What does it mean to be a 40-year-old *Once Upon a Time* (ABC) fan who live-tweets each episode? Or a 60-year-old *Lord of the Rings* enthusiast who curates an online catalog of fan art?"[1] For Jerslev and Peterson, fandom is customarily viewed as synonymous with youth, while older fans are ridiculed for appearing inappropriate. Yet Jerslev and Petersen maintain that "studying cases of enduring fandom makes it possible to not only conceptualise how expressions of fandom change over the life course but also how the meaning of being a fan changes."[2] Indeed, as Hanif Abdurraqib observes, "fandom as an adult looks different, feels different, and is generally *performed differently*."[3] Today, the performance of fandom has shifted. For older viewers of *Twin Peaks* and *The X-Files*, fandom was defined by the constraints of time and space, synonymous with the arduous efforts of waiting patiently for the next installment, collecting memorabilia and videos, and participating in fan clubs. As fandom has migrated online, older fans are expected to pursue an online fan presence by engaging in online communities, posting opinions, and partaking in discussions to ensure their enduring fandom does not go unnoticed. The internet has become a platform not only for illustrating and maintaining one's fandom but for allowing cross-generational fans to converge.

On the Twin Peaks Gazette website, for example, a thread titled "Passing *Twin Peaks* to the next generation" features commentary by original fans about how they have "introduced" the show to a younger generation.[4] One user writes of her daughter watching the original *Twin Peaks*: "It makes me feel old, yet proud that teenagers are STILL interested and getting interested in *Twin Peaks* even now after all this time. It has a timeless quality to it, one you feel you can identify with" (comment by @Maddy, March 16, 2011). The sentiment of "feeling old" has appeared frequently online when fans discuss their favorite TV shows: "In high school we all had the *Secret Diary of Laura Palmer*. I also owned a 'boxed set' on VHS, so all of this makes me feel old."[5]

The transition from a fandom based on merchandise and collecting to the immateriality of online networks has given rise to a cross-generational network of fans that congregate in online forums like Reddit. For Baby Boomers in particular, online platforms have given them the opportunity to comment and reflect on the inevitable issue of seeing their beloved actors age in the revivals. Since the time span between *Twin Peaks* and *The Return* is particularly substantial, a more significant generational gap was witnessed—one that threatened to alienate older fans. Hills explains that "*Twin Peaks: The Return* is frequently marked by the aging or loss of its older generation. Part of its generational seriality involves a self-reflexive awareness," one that considers the deaths of some of the original cast members.[6]

Most of the original cast members returned for the third season, and most, as various commentators have noted, have aged, in some cases considerably: "A lot has changed in 25 years. The original cast members, who are mostly back on board, have all aged heavily and visibly."[7] E. C. Flamming concurred, writing, "The past 25 years are etched clearly upon their wizened faces, and yes, it is a bit unsettling to see these characters we love looking so, well, elderly."[8] Noel Murray writes: "Seeing a middle-aged Laura Palmer and a Cooper in his late 50s isn't really a fun nostalgia trip. Given the time we've spent with these characters, the wrinkles and graying hair are a sad symbol of time lost."[9]

Peter Ormerod wrote of fan anticipation for the return: "For some, the appeal will lie in nostalgia. For others, it will be in seeing how the cast have aged and how their characters have developed."[10] The interest in the aging characters is evidenced in the plethora of "*Twin Peaks* Cast Then and Now" articles and images showing the sometimes stark contrast of the actors' appearances between 1991 and 2017. A large number of news outlets and social media threads emerged in the wake of the revivals, all dedicated to scrutinizing the actors' aged appearances.

While the progression of a TV series ordinarily shows the cast aging with the show, the significant gap between seasons two and three for *Twin Peaks* alters the temporal process by which the characters (and the actors) naturally and gradually age. The effect is shocking for an audience accustomed to seeing the stars—many of whom, perhaps due to the show's cult

Missing Time 35

status, did not have too many roles following *Twin Peaks*—in the prime of their youth. The effect is also necessary for showing the realistic effects of time on figures who are often not allowed to age in an industry defined by youth and appearance. As Sabrina Qiong Yu argues, "The aging star body is probably not the favorite of the industry, but it does not necessarily mark the end of one's stardom."[11] In fact, she writes, the natural process of aging can be used to the advantage of the star's career, if incorporated well. Jerslev and Petersen similarly note:

> A range of television and film series have returned with revival of older shows, for example *Doctor Who* (1963–89, 2005–), *Twin Peaks* (1991–1992, 2017), *X-Files* (1993–2002, 2016–), *Gilmore Girls* (2000–2007, 2016). These returns have created an opportunity for fans of the original series to immerse themselves in the narratives once again and engage in playful exchanges on social media platforms at the same time as they can follow celebrities' aging processes, both enjoying and scrutinizing their aging appearances.[12]

The way the actors aged became an important factor for fans of both *The X-Files* and *Twin Peaks*, but particularly for older fans, who measured their own aging process against the actors'. Fan comments on community websites like Reddit show that the better aged the actors appeared to be, the more positively fans reacted to the revivals. For example, David Duchovny, who, in addition to his role in *The X-Files*, starred in *Twin Peaks* and *The Return* as Denise Bryson, was commended for his appearance by many fans of *The Return*. On Reddit, one user writes of Duchovny: "Congratulations to the most well-aged actor of *Twin Peaks*" (@Arcatus, May 25, 2017). Another user commented: "David Duchovny is doing good, probably in the aged best" (@curious_Jo, May 28, 2017). On another Reddit thread, titled "Who didn't age at all of the returning cast?," fans comment favorably on the appearances of many of the male actors: "Ray Wise, goddamn. Looks literally the exact same as he did when he was in the cell" (@mwcope, June 4, 2017); "Bobby went grey but seems to have held up pretty well otherwise" (@MaryVanNostrand, June 4, 2017); "Dana Ashbrook is damn good looking as a silver fox" (@LordHoot, June 4, 2017); "He may even look better now, and that's saying something" (@back2missoula, June 4, 2017). On Whirlpool, an Australian forum website, one user posted: "Agent Cooper does not look a day older! He's aged better than Laura Palmer that's for sure" (The Jimmy, May 26, 2017).

Mädchen Amick, the youngest of the original cast members, was also positively received in several comments on the Reddit thread: "She looks even better in my opinion" (@Nihilokrat, June 4, 2017); "she's the real goddess now" (@NABAKLAB, June 4, 2017); "She's unreal" (@NostalgiaZombie, June 5, 2017); "I would have to agree about Mädchen looking even better" (@PeakTrap, June 4, 2017). The ability to maintain one's youthful looks appears to be a significant factor in reinforcing fandom. It seems that the more aged an actor becomes, the more fans return to earlier episodes, when actors are at their most youthful. On an *X-Files* Reddit page, for instance, two users explain how they seek refuge in the earlier seasons of the show, when both Duchovny and Gillian Anderson were younger:

pwrof3: "Every time I watch the series in its entirety, I start to feel sad at the end and then end up watching the first season all over again."

xxgreenhornet: Same!! Especially the later seasons seeing Mulder and Scully as older.[13]

Similarly, when a "first look" at Mulder and Scully was tweeted in 2015 prior to the revival, one Twitter user responded: "omg they look old noooo" (@boygaga1996, June 10, 2015). On a review of the eleventh season, one person commented: "I had a hard time watching the revival simply because the actors look old."[14] Blogger Nick Person also criticized the aged appearance of Anderson and Duchovny:

The one thing that struck me about this new series is how old Duchovny and Anderson look. Seeing them as spry FBI agents (and Duchovny doing his all stunts no less) back in the 90s make them look even more haggard and useless now. They've aged, they look old and tired, worn out even. I'm not going to buy the fact that they can pull off half the things they managed in earlier seasons.[15]

Although many fans embraced the aged appearance of these actors, commending what they considered to be their youthful appearances, these other comments attest to the unflattering link between how well an actor ages and how a person's fandom is tested. For older and younger fans alike, agelessness is a significant contributing factor to fandom, since fandom rests partly on how well a show and its actors look and age.

Missing Time 37

WRAPPED IN PLASTIC (SURGERY)

Both *Twin Peaks* and *The X-Files* fans focused more on the aged appearance of the female cast members. Sabrina Qiong Yu argues that "there is a common perception that aging is less an issue for male stars than female stars, since appearance weighs much more on a female star's career."[16] She maintains that "males have to confront the challenges of aging and old age as much as female stars," citing the careers and aged appearances of Harrison Ford, Bruce Willis, Clint Eastwood, and Sylvester Stallone.[17] Kirsty Fairclough-Isaacs disagrees, saying that while men "are closely scrutinized for attempting to hide signs of aging, particularly hair loss," women, in contrast, "are routinely maligned if they fail to hide the signs of aging."[18] Indeed, she argues, "Older men by contrast can often maintain long and successful careers, aging without the negative treatment of the media."[19] While American media is preoccupied with aging in general, this preoccupation is "concentrated on women," and she notes that the mass media is "profoundly ageist in its attitudes to women."[20]

For *Twin Peaks* and *The X-Files*, fandom hinged more on how well the women aged, from Sherilyn Fenn's Audrey Horne to Gillian Anderson's Dana Scully. For example, a *Daily Mail* article in 2016 discussed the possibility of Anderson turning to Botox, complete with a graph scrutinizing her facial features according to plastic surgery "experts."[21]

In another *Daily Mail* article titled "The Botox Is Out There: *X-Files* Fans Claim the Biggest Mystery of the New Series Is How Mulder and Scully Haven't Aged a Day," Anderson is the primary target of Botox accusations, featuring a sample of fan tweets, including: "Scully hasn't aged much—probbaly [*sic*] all the Botox inflicted by aliens" and "The aliens clearly implanted a LOT of Botox in Scully's face."[22] A number of similar, alien-themed tweets followed: "All that Botox has made Scully the most alien looking thing in *The X-Files*," "What has Gillian Anderson done to her face? That face-lift and Botox make her look like the aliens she's after," and "Scully's overuse of Botox is making her look somewhat alien."[23]

Because women are more often discussed in regard to standards of "beauty" than men, they are expected to maintain this beauty but in ways that appear seamless, rather than obvious. Women who have successfully navigated plastic surgery are applauded while those who have had bad or obvious enhancements, or who have ignored surgery altogether, are maligned:

Although contemporary media increasingly advocates the ability to age naturally, with actresses like Helen Mirren and Meryl Streep frequently cited as natural older beauties, natural aging is only accepted to the extent that this look of naturalness is appeasing. Unflattering, unaltered naturalness, on the other hand, is demonized, with such women encouraged to turn to the knife after all in order to achieve a more acceptable look of natural aging, one that will inevitably and ironically provoke further criticism. For women considering plastic surgery, they are damned if they do and damned if they don't.[24]

This double standard is evident when considering the fact that the men in *Twin Peaks* and *The X-Files* fared better in discussions of their aged appearances. Matt Prigge writes that "it's one thing to go from seeing, say, early 30s MacLachlan, his face still babyish, to witnessing late 50s MacLachlan, who frankly still looks super handsome. Ditto Michael Horse, the rugged and laconic and soulful badass of the first two seasons, whose hair is now sparkly white. (And he still looks handsome, too.)"[25]

While Duchovny was frequently praised for his rugged appearance in the new seasons of *The X-Files*, he stated in an interview with *The Guardian*: "I can't play it the way I played it when I was 33 or 32, because that would be obscene and weird. It's like seeing a 95-year-old guy in a toupee. . . . We don't have to change Mulder, but he's going to keep getting older."[26] Clearly, for Duchovny, the issue of aging is more in line with his physical abilities and craft as an actor than with his actual appearance, illustrating a clear and unfair distinction between the how men and women are "allowed" to age.

While MacLachlan was praised for his appearance in *The Return*, he was also suspected of having plastic surgery, but without the same level of judgment leveled against Anderson. As Hills writes: "The older Kyle MacLachlan has been described by TV critics as remaining 'preternaturally youthful.'"[27] A Fashionista article titled "The Real Reason Agent Cooper Doesn't Look Much Older Than He Did in the Original *Twin Peaks*" featured an interview with a dermatologist who purportedly gave MacLachlan a "tie tuck" treatment.[28] More favorably, a forum on *Welcome to Twin Peaks* was titled: "Kyle MacLachlan Is in Excellent Shape for a Man of His Age."[29]

X APPEAL

The focus on the aged appearance of the actors in the revivals was important to Baby Boomers who, willingly or otherwise, compared how well they were aging with the actors in the shows. As one person commented on Facebook: "You sure aged better than me lol! Gillian fan forever!"[30] A person on Pinterest posted in response to a photo of Anderson and Duchovny: "Love this picture, they've aged better than i have."[31] Inevitably, questions about the sex appeal of people in their fifties, sixties, and older were raised by fans and in the media, spurred by revivals. Sezin Koehler wrote of the female actors of *Twin Peaks*: "From the RR Diner's Shelly Johnson (Mädchen Amick, 46) and Norma Jennings (Peggy Lipton, 71) to Audrey Horne (Sherilyn Fenn, 52) and Nadine Hurley (Wendy Robie, 63), *The Return*'s older women are complicated, still beautiful, and many are sexually active, in roles that are far more than just set dressing for younger and newer cast members."[32]

Like the women of *Twin Peaks*, Anderson's appearance and role as a sex symbol in *The X-Files* revival was also under much scrutiny among fans and the media. The state of her sex appeal as a woman in her mid-forties was highlighted in the tenth-season episode "Mulder and Scully Meet the Were-Monster." In this episode, Scully appears in a sex scene revealed to be a fantasy of the episode's suspect, Guy Mann (Rhys Darby). Scully is first shown unbuttoning her shirt before the camera pans to her up against a wall with her legs entangled around Mann. Of this scene, Liz Shannon Miller of *IndieWire* writes: "It only took 22 years, but Scully finally got to have sex on camera on *The X-Files*," further observing that "certainly many Gillian Anderson fans got a kick out of her turning porn star, and scenes like this prove to be very valuable in reminding us that Anderson has some incredible comedic chops."[33] In *Slant Magazine*, Chuck Bowen writes that Scully is "redefined" in the episode, which, he says, "discard[s] the iconic earnestness that the season has already been gradually backgrounding, while foregrounding the character's sexual confidence."[34] He notes that "Scully is a beautiful, intelligent woman, who's used to being underestimated by jack-offs in a men's profession and wearing her tragedy and turmoil as scars of survivor's honor."[35]

The scene is purposefully out of character for Scully, an ordinarily reserved, no-nonsense agent, which accounts for some of the comedic tone. The scene works to showcase Anderson's continued sex appeal for an audience that first watched her disrobe in the pilot episode in 1993. There are several scenes in the original series in which audiences catch glimpses of Scully partially clothed, obligatory hints of her attractiveness and sex appeal to assure early viewers that Scully—customarily dressed in suits and long coats—was a flesh-and-blood desirable woman. Yet the over-the-top sex scene in the were-monster episode demonstrates the apparent necessity to self-consciously assure these early fans that both Scully and Anderson are still desirable, all these years later, rewarding their continued fandom and patronage of the show with a hyperreal sex scene that, in all likelihood, would never have appeared in the original run of the series. But the scene's use of comedy unwittingly suggests that however attractive Anderson may still be, she and her character are comparatively less desirable than they were in the original run of the series, when a Scully sex scene wouldn't have necessitated any comedic element whatsoever.

Despite the positive reception that Scully received for her sex scene, *The X-Files* nevertheless felt the need to include younger counterparts alongside its famous older actors, as if to communicate the message that Millennial viewers might not wholly embrace characters over a certain age without younger cast members to balance them out. The tenth season introduced two young characters that fans immediately recognized were thinly veiled replacements for Scully and Mulder: Liz Einstein (Lauren Ambrose), the scientific skeptic complete with Scully's trademark red hair, and Kyd Miller (Robbie Amell), the supernatural believer. *The Return* is also gratuitously peppered with young, stereotypically thin and attractive actors, many of whom are primarily depicted in sexual roles, including Madeline Zima, Amanda Seyfried, and Nicole LaLiberté, the last of whom is brutally murdered while wearing lingerie.

These "updated" counterparts in *The X-Files* and *Twin Peaks* illustrate the problematic approach to time and aging that befalls many revived franchises, such as Star Wars, Indiana Jones, and *Blade Runner*, in which younger actors are used to aid aged actors and potentially take the story in another direction for a new generation. "By introducing new, younger characters alongside aging favorites," Hills writes, franchises attempt to strategically position themselves between various generations, thereby securing a wider fan base.[36] The strategic mix of younger and older actors suggests that although these shows are interested in broadening their fanbase across different generations, both *Twin Peaks* and *The X-Files* are ambivalent about their relationship with aging and the overall message about what older actors and older characters are capable of. The shows portray actors in the same kinds of action sequences from the shows' heydays while also suggesting that these actors are past their prime, necessitating the inclusion of "young blood" to truly revive the series.

Yet while both shows remain ambivalent about aging, there is a clear disparity between how the women and men are treated in regard to aging. While MacLachlan and Duchovny were scrutinized for their changed ap-

Missing Time 41

pearances, the women were under greater scrutiny by critics and fans to maintain their sex appeal and conceal the aging process in a way that is seamless and not obvious. Arguably, for older fans, the aged appearance and continued sex appeal of these actors was important in not only reinforcing their fandom and reminding them of the original run of the series but in reassuring themselves that they have also aged well in the years that have elapsed since the shows went off air.

CONCLUSION

The return of *Twin Peaks* and *The X-Files* to television after a significant hiatus created a frenzy of interest from fans and critics, many of whom were fascinated by what their beloved actors would look like after so many years. In this way, the revivals were unwittingly framed by various conflicting discourses on aging and what it means to be a fan of a long-standing show in a different time. It was overwhelmingly important for older fans in particular that the actors in *Twin Peaks* and *The X-Files* did not appear too old or too different from how they looked in the original run of the series. Not only would their changed appearance violate the nostalgic image fans had sustained since the shows went off the air, compromising their fandom, but this also reflected on the fans themselves and how they saw themselves in comparison in a society obsessed with youth and sex appeal. Although the opinions of fans and critics widely differed on how the actors looked, the comments in online communities nevertheless showed how important it is for fans that a show and its actors age satisfactorily, and how much one's fandom hinges on the continued attractiveness of its aging cast.

Truly, Truly, Truly Outraged

ANTI-FANDOM AND THE
LIMITS OF NOSTALGIA

Andrew Scahill

Jem and the Holograms (Jon M. Chu, 2015) is a film of notable distinction. Not critical distinction—the film, a live-action reboot of a children's cartoon from the 1980s, was universally panned by critics and holds a 22 percent approval rating on Rotten Tomatoes. Nor was it distinguished by its cult following; in fact, fans of the original cartoon actively worked against its promotion. Rather, *Jem and the Holograms* is a notable film for the spectacular nature of its failure.

With an almost two-year promotional campaign targeting the nostalgia of Gen X fans and a YouTube discovery narrative designed to appeal to Millennial and Gen Z fans, the film was projected to return $5 million in wide release (2,413 screens) on its opening weekend. But on release, the film returned only $1.4 million, resulting in only $569 per theater.[1]

Jem and the Holograms's numbers plummeted 72 percent the following week, making only $387,925 or $160 per screen.[2] Two weeks after its release, Universal Studios pulled the film from theaters, a retreat that industry insiders described as "an unheard of move for a movie that was in theaters nationwide."[3]

These factors combine to make this fairly unremarkable film a remarkable case of fan antipathy and rejection. Not only was *Jem and the Holograms* the worst opening for a studio film in 2015, it has the added distinction of being the fourth worst opening ever for a film on over 2,000 screens and the worst opening weekend ever for a film released by a Big Five major studio.

How did Universal Studios so overestimate the transgenerational appeal of this property? What might the spectacular failure of this film reveal about the limited elasticity of nostalgia and the affective economies of fan betrayal and antipathy? Where fandom studies traditionally examines the productive and participatory nature of fan love, recent scholarship in the field has proposed fan hatred, or anti-fandom, as a neglected area of study.

Yet examining failure illustrates how negative emotions often comingle with the positive emotions of fandom—how love of one text is intensified by hatred for another or how first-generation fandom can be enabled by hatred toward a second-generation renewal. In examining a broad range of fan responses to the promotional campaign of the *Jem and the Holograms* reboot, this essay analyzes how fans of the original cartoon became anti-fans of the Hollywood reboot. But rather than an act of mere negation, the #NotMyJem anti-fandom allowed adult fans to reassess the subversive pleasures of their childhood spectatorship and even produce content that celebrated, rather than commodified, their shared nostalgia.

JEM 1985: DISCO SCI-FI SUPERHERO

The original TV series *Jem and the Holograms* (1985–1988) was a Sunday morning cartoon that ran three seasons in first-run syndication and then three more years (1989–1992) in off-network syndication on the USA network. The show began as a joint venture between Hasbro, Sunbow Productions, and Marvel Entertainment group. This collaboration had already generated several successful transmedia franchises, such as *My Little Pony* (1986–1987), *The Transformers* (1984–1987), and *G.I. Joe* (1983–1986). As with Hasbro's previous cartoon properties, *Jem and the Holograms* was designed to be "toyetic," or created with the purpose of marketing tie-in merchandise like dolls, play sets, and costumes.[4] The show's original air date was chosen to create buzz for the release of the Jem and the Hologram dolls at the New York Toy Fair in February 1986.[5]

Christy Marx, then one of the only female staff writers for *G.I. Joe*, was hired to write the show based on a basic concept and merchandising designs. Marx capitalized on the dominant presence of MTV by modeling the show after the rapid editing and stylized spectacle of the cable network. Quite novel for its time, each episode featured three fully produced musical numbers presented as largely nonintegrated music videos equally spaced throughout the twenty-three-minute run time. Each episode has a self-contained adventure while maintaining larger serialized narrative tensions (success and setbacks, a love triangle).

The show begins with Jerrica Benton discovering her father's AI technology (Synergy), which allows Jerrica to transform herself into pop star Jem with "starlight earrings" that project holographic illusions. Along with her sister Kimber and her adopted siblings Aja and Shana, Jerrica launches a successful music career.

The show functions primarily as a melodrama in that it centers around personal relationships (friends, romance, family), it elicits strong sympathy for its central protagonist through suffering or entrapment, and it tells its story in a heightened style (marked by spectacular effects, implausible coincidences, and a clear dichotomy between good and evil). As a romantic melodrama, it offers its protagonist the choice between romantic love and societal obligation, both of which require sacrifice.

This narrative is augmented by three other genres: the musical, science fiction, and the superhero genre. The influence of the musical is most readily apparent in the show's structure. Each episode is organized as a series of interstitial story beats providing narrative context for the central musical numbers. But the musical genre also informs the show's thematic preoccupations. It chronicles the trials and tribulations of show business and follows one naïve ingenue's rise to fame, much like *A Star Is Born* (George Cukor, 1954) or *Singin' in the Rain* (Stanley Donen and Gene Kelly, 1952).[6] It also shares the genre's preoccupation with the "authentic" versus the "inauthentic" performer and evidences that through the pairing of opposites. In this show, rival rock group Misfits represent Jem and the Holograms' contrasting opposite. Where Jem and the Holograms' pop disco sound recalls the safe girl power of Bananarama and the Go-Go's, the Misfits' punk rock stylings reference the rebellious and anarchic energy of the Runaways or Siouxsie Sioux. Their harsh war paint and acid tones also contrasted with Jem's feminine softness, and the program decidedly marks the Misfits as lower class, crude, and uneducated. This is a weathered trope in the show musical. Consider Lina Lamont (Jean Hagen), the brassy, low-class villainess of *Singin' in the Rain*, as contrasted with the innocent and feminine voice of Kathy Selden (Debbie Reynolds). Paradoxically opposed to our conventional understandings of modern music history, *Jem and the Holograms* presents the studio-crafted sound of pop music as more authentic and "real" than the raw, edgy sounds of punk rock. This is in keeping with the genre conventions of the musical, which consistently valorizes the ability of Hollywood to create an escapist fantasy far superior to the lived reality of its spectators.

The final two genres of the show, science fiction and superhero, are intimately linked in *Jem and the Holograms*.[7] Through the AI system Synergy, Jem pursues her dreams but must hide her true identity, Jerrica, from the rest of the world. Such duality and conflict is endemic to the "masked crusader" mode of the superhero genre, and Jem's inherited wealth and technology-augmented superpowers recall the benevolent millionaire origins of Iron Man and Batman. Like Batman, Jem's villains emerge from gutters and threaten

Truly, Truly, Truly Outraged 45

to destabilize her privilege. The title sequence literalizes this contrast, as Jem's anthem is interrupted by the Misfits lifting a manhole cover and singing from the sewer: "We are the Misfits / Our songs are better / We are the Misfits (the Misfits) / And we're gonna get her." As such, the Misfits serve as a constant interruption of Jem's true and authentic illusion: her bourgeois consumerist fantasy, marked by "Glamor and glitter / Fashion and fame."

JEM 2015: YOUTUBE INGENUE POP IDOL

The film reboot *Jem and the Holograms* takes place in the present day, as Jerrica Benton (Aubrey Peeples) and her sisters face eviction when their Aunt Bailey (Molly Ringwald) cannot pay the bills. Jerrica, disguised as Jem, becomes a hit on YouTube, and she and her sisters are offered a recording contract by Starlight Records producer Erica Raymond (Juliette Lewis), who schemes to break up the band and sign Jerrica as a solo artist. Jerrica's late father leaves her a small robot called 51N3RG.Y (pronounced "synergy"), which takes the girls on a scavenger hunt to find its missing computer parts. When fully assembled, 51N3RG.Y projects a hologram of Jerrica's late father, who offers a tearful goodbye. Jem and the Holograms perform their first concert and become featured on the cover of *Rolling Stone*, and it is revealed that the true owner of Starlight Records is Rio (Ryan Guzman), Jerrica's new boyfriend. In the end credits, Erica meets a group of punk rock girls she plans to mold into the rival band, the Misfits.

For first-generation fans, this updated story bore few of the nostalgic markers of the Sunday morning cartoon. Gone was the underground lair, the AI technology, the musical rivalries, and the pop stars as savvy businesswomen. When the trailer was released in May 2015, many openly questioned what became of the marketing that had directly asked fans to submit personal testimonials of their nostalgia for the cartoon series. Nearly a year earlier on March 20, 2014, Universal Studios announced the *Jem and the Holograms* reboot with a video by director Jon M. Chu and producers Scooter Braun and Jason Blum asking fans to participate in the planning and production of *Jem and the Holograms*.[8] "We want to invite you into our process and help us make our movie," Chu said. "From writing music to designing costumes, even to casting."[9] Producer Scooter Braun, the man who "discovered" Justin Bieber on YouTube, chimed in with this plea: "Help us find our star."[10] This open casting call seemed to represent a kind of synergy between the original cartoon and the Hollywood reproduction: the promise of instant stardom in a story about instant stardom.

46   REBOOTS, REVIVALS, AND NOSTALGIA

Within a month, some of that excitement waned as the film was cast through the usual professional channels. These initial concerns were echoed on May 13, 2015, when the film's trailer was released, as Universal Studios met with almost universal derision and mockery. The overall fan reaction to *Jem and the Holograms* reboot is perhaps best summarized by the Jezebel headline "Here's the New *Jem and the Holograms* Trailer. I Think I Hate It."[11] The hashtags #JemFail and #NotMyJem trended on Twitter for the day. The reaction was so swift and so negative that several entertainment blogs took note, including Polygon, Uproxx, Buzzfeed, IFC, DListed, Mashable, and Jezebel. Among the cacophony was even an inflammatory tweet from William Shatner, boldly going on to state: "I watched the Jem trailer. No star earring? Where are the misfits? [crying emoji]" (@WilliamShatner, Twitter, May 13, 2015). On YouTube, fans used the popular reaction videos subgenre, in which they simulcast their first viewing of the trailer, to express their disgust—replete with eyerolls, sighs, and exasperated interjections.

ANTI-FANDOM

What do we make of this community of first-generation fans who joined together in shared revulsion? How do the bonds formed through shared disdain compare to those formed by mutual love toward a media object? And finally, is anti-fandom only a process of negation, or does the rejection of an insufficient copy alter or even augment a fan's positive relationship to the original?

Anti-fandom is a fairly recent preoccupation in fan studies. While critics such as Camille Bacon-Smith and Henry Jenkins have identified viewer frustration as an impetus for reading selectively or creating fan fiction, neither explored hatred as a mode of user engagement. In 2003, Jonathan Gray published an "atomic" model of fandom, in which regular viewers of a show are neutrons, orbited by the positively charged fans and the negatively charged anti-fans.[12] Such a model allows us to think productively about inter-fan behavior on a continuum of affect-based interactions with media texts. Says Gray, "Although pleasure and displeasure, or fandom and antifandom, could be positioned on opposite ends of spectrum, they perhaps more accurately exist on a Mobius strip, with many fan and antifan behaviors and performances resembling, if not replicating each other."[13]

Other critics contend that the fan and anti-fan are not discrete identities as Gray's atomic model might suggest. In her analysis of male-oriented sports fandoms, for instance, Vivi Theodoropoulou argues that anti-fandom is a necessary result of the binarism of city- or college-based rivalries. The fan, she argues, "resorts to anti-fandom so as to protect her/his fan object from the threat its 'counterforce' poses."[14] Anti-fandom is also sometimes directed at a celebrity or actor. Emma A. Jane discusses the production and circulation of "e-bile," or online hate speech, facilitated through online mediums.[15] Similarly, Suzanne Scott notes how anti-fandom can be mobilized as a form of "containment," in which "true fans" police the boundaries of who is and is not allowed to be deemed a fan. In her study of the backlash against so-called fake geek girls by male fanboys, Scott argues that such "spreadable misogyny" is enabled by convergence culture's mainstreaming of (male) geek culture.[16]

One of the most infamous cases of misogynist e-bile came with the 2016 female-cast reboot of *Ghostbusters*. The trailer quickly became the most "disliked" trailer of all time on YouTube, leading many journalists to suspect a coordinated attack seeking to "downvote the film into oblivion" before it even reached an audience.[17] Anti-fan behavior escalated when one of its stars, Leslie Jones, became the victim of racist tweets as well as the hacking of her personal webpage and "doxing" of her private photos. (Bridget Kies's chapter explores anti-fan reactions to *Ghostbusters* in more detail.)

In 2019, Gray revisited his atomic model of fandom to include multiple modes of anti-fandom, including "hate watching," in which pleasure is derived from camp mockery or the communal act of shared revulsion, and "disappointed anti-fandom," in which a show's potential encourages fans to continue despite their disdain for the property's current state.[18]

#NOTMYJEM

The performance of disgust in YouTube reaction videos promises shared affect and community-building experienced through fan-love communities. In "Hatewatch with Me: Anti-Fandom as Social Performance," Anne Gilbert examines the sundering effect of performing disgust for other like-minded anti-fans. As she notes, "hatewatching as an anti-fan practice is inherently communal, whereas fandom is not necessarily so."[19] Anti-fandom performance videos allowed viewers to not only see someone else's anti-fandom but to experience it with them simultaneously. In the comments section, shared hatewatching became the impetus for a disappointed anti-fandom, which (re)generated first-generation nostalgia for the 1985 cartoon.

Some fans very well may have enjoyed the film or simply parts of the film (the music, the makeup), though this pro-fandom did not translate to box office returns. The scope of this study is limited to anti-fans who took to social media using the hashtags #JemFail and #NotMyJem to collectively express their disappointment. If left unexamined, one might assume that generational anti-fandom is driven by a fundamentalist fervor toward any adaptation that deviates from the original. On closer examination, however, narrative fidelity takes a backseat to more nuanced concerns over authorship, tone, ideology, and genre, revealing fans to be savvy deconstructionists of their own nostalgia.

Authorship

Fans were among the first to note show creator Christy Marx's absence from the rebooted property, using the hashtag #WeWantChristy to signal their support of the writer. On March 21, 2014, Marx released a statement on Facebook expressing her disappointment in not being consulted, adding, "I see two male producers, a male director, and a male writer. Where is the female voice? Where is the female perspective? Where are the women?" (@Christy Marx Clubhouse, March 21, 2014). Fans were attuned to the ideological shift of the text from female empowerment and friendship to passivity and compulsory romance. Darryn King noted the regressive gender politics of the reboot in his article "Here's What Happens When Men Try to Make 'Jem and the Holograms.'"[20] Consistently, fans found the character of Jerrica evacuated of agency and shuttled around by various male figures: first her father and then her boyfriend, who rescues her by inheriting the record label.[21] In contrast, fans retroactively praised the feminist and queer politics of the original show, which favored female bonds over heterosexual courtship.[22] Sara Gwenllian Jones has noted the queer pleasures of episodic television in its constant resistance to the narrative completion represented by heterosexuality.[23] Rather than simply decrying a lack of fidelity, however, fans were able to articulate these changes as a problem of authorship and gendered labor.

Fans also critiqued the film's manipulation of its intended fan base through its promise of participatory fandom and coauthorship of the film's narrative. As Kate Erbland notes, director Chu used the fan-submitted love letters to 1985's *Jem* and repackaged them in the film's narrative as heartfelt testimonials of support for the 2015 film. Says Erbland: "It boils down to this: Tell us why you love Jem. Tell us how she's inspired you and given you courage and made you want to be yourself. Then we'll use it to sell a reinvented version of her, a watered-down character borne from YouTube and social media, a reimagining that didn't even have enough creativity to inspire fans on its own merits."[24] Rather than using the testimonials as part of the authorship process, Universal Studios made them part of the internal marketing of the film, with fans offering tacit approval and tearful adulation to a cinematic representation they have never seen.

Tone

Fans also critiqued the film for betraying the tone of the original. One responder on Twitter suggested the alternate title, "Avril Lavigne and the Kohl's Discount" (@LouisVirtel, May 13, 2015). The objections to tone were twofold. First, fans objected to the softening of the show's edgy, kinetic style and the introduction of bland aphorisms like "be you" and "find yourself." They derided the style as made-for-TV or Disney Channel. Such complaints by anti-fans concerning the "kiddie" quality of the reboot underscore the tension in transgenerational media production that seeks to capitalize on the nostalgia of adult fans and attract new fans with generic codes that speak to their field of experience. The result is what Derek Johnson refers to as a "collision" between old and new media industries, the result being that "old and young audiences might collide too."[25]

Many of the anti-fans using the hashtags #NotMyJem and #JemFail also objected to the updating of the text to the present day—though not for fidelity reasons, as one might expect. Rather, they felt it was a "wasted opportunity" for a campy commentary on the social, political, and technological climate of the 1980s.[26] Instead, the film seems at pains to eliminate the over-the-top quality of the original text. One reviewer noted that "[the film] exists only because of nostalgia for the animated source material. And yet the film seems inexplicably embarrassed by its roots."[27] Often, the "decamped" reboot is a way of "rescuing" texts from being read as ironic or camp with an infusion of realism and violence, as is the case with *Dark Knight* (2008), *Man of Steel* (2013), even *Miami Vice* (2006). Often the word *gritty* is trotted out to describe these reboots, which seems at times a code for de-gaying a franchise that has become too soft or too camp. For fans, *Jem and the Holograms* was a text that offered a variety of feminist and queer pleasures both in its exploration of female agency and homosocial bonds and in its excessively camp rendering of the backstage musical plot.

Genre

The original cartoon offered a novel mixture of the musical genre with the superhero genre—Jerrica's secret identity, costume changes, and hidden tech lair recall a more playful version of the caped crusader. The live-action

Jem largely replaces the superhero elements of the original with coming-of-age tropes such as the exodus from the parental home, loss of innocence, and the discovery of self. More than one fan compared the reboot to the TV show *Hannah Montana* (2006–2011), and the weird feedback loop of intertextuality here is compelling. *Hannah Montana* is a sanitized copy of *Jem and the Holograms* minus the fantastic genre elements. Paradoxically, for anti-fans this reboot fails largely because it is a copy of *Hannah Montana* masquerading as the original. From a show that joyfully celebrates the triumph of the artificial over the authentic, fans ironically detest its apotheosis: a hologram of a hologram of a hologram.

Much of the *Jem* reboot outrage comes not simply from disappointment but from the promise of participation and coauthorship. The disappointed anti-fandom directed toward the movie allows lovers of the original program to deem themselves "true" fans and demonstrate their authenticity through their derision toward its imitator. Rebecca Williams has noted how first-generation fans of the band Muse policed the boundaries of "true" fandom by denigrating recent fans who discovered their music through the movie *Twilight* (Catherine Hardwicke, 2008).[28] Dubbed "interloping fans," second-generation fans of the band were treated as unwelcome tourists by longtime fans. Similarly, the invocation of *Hannah Montana* is used to denigrate potential fans of the reboot as "interlopers" in the more long-standing fandom of the cartoon.

Ideology

In its evacuation of the queer camp aesthetics of *Jem and the Holograms*, the reboot also significantly transformed its ideology. The original series used the semiotic codes of the musical to validate the artificial and the escapist over the natural and the mundane. It also used the fantasy-making of the superhero genre to present "Jem" as an ego ideal formation for Jerrica and the spectator as well. The series provided the Misfits as a counterbalance, dangerous in their nihilism but appealing in their freedom and mobility. In replacing these genre formations with the coming-of-age film and the backstage musical/ingenue plot, the film instead validates the natural and authentic over the escapist. Instead of an ego ideal, "Jem" is a mask that hides Jerrica's true talent. It is only when Jerrica is stripped of the makeup and hair and reduced to an acoustic guitar on a bare stage that her true talent emerges. The original series encouraged spectators to queerly "try on" new identities like costumes, to embrace the escapism of fantasy and play. The reboot believes such explorations of youth to be a series of holograms,

Truly, Truly, Truly Outraged   51

and that like Dorothy Gale in *The Wizard of Oz*, maturity comes when the dreaming ends and the child returns home. For fans of the original, one of the queer pleasures it offered is that Jem could be just as "real" as Jerrica, and she never had to rescind her fantasy to return home.

NOSTALGIA AND PLAY

Most of the fan objections were short interjections or questions—an invitation to other fans to join and share their pain. Often what followed were lengthy discussions and analyses of the trailer and the original TV show, as well as of the viewers' affective relationship to the program and its meaning in a formative period of their lives. Indeed, even the simplest of fidelity objections seemed more like a call to explore the complexity of their collective nostalgia and betrayal.

Our nostalgia for the media of our youth could be understood as a longing for a time in our lives as much as for the media object itself. In the case of toyetic properties of the 1980s like *He-Man and the Masters of the Universe* (1983–1984), *G.I. Joe*, and *Jem and the Holograms*, nostalgia likely extends far beyond the cartoon itself and into paratextual domains like music and toys. To understand the scope and fervor of anti-fan statements like "the *Jem and the Holograms* reboot ruined my childhood," one must understand how a media property can become synonymous with a childhood space of fantasy and imaginative play.

Fan studies has long sought to transform the image of the passive spectator to one of a dynamic, engaged, and transformational fan. I close with such an instance, a humorous example of how one group of fans mobilized their disappointed anti-fandom into a more productive avenue. In June 2015, Charley Feldman, an LA-based writer and actor (and longtime *Jem and the Holograms* fan) created a short YouTube video called "Jem Reacts—to the New *Jem and the Holograms* Trailer," in which the Holograms and the Misfits, friends and enemies alike, bonded in a mutual experience of hating the trailer.[29] Shot in a mockumentary format, the characters ruminate on all the ways the trailer disappoints, reiterating many of the claims about tone, character, genre, authorship, and gender that the #NotMyJem anti-fans articulated on social media. The short ends with a music video titled "Totally Missed the Point."

Using the video as a launching pad for their Kickstarter, Feldman and her friends raised $13,286 from 286 backers to produce the thirty-minute film "Truly Outrageous: A Jem Fan Film!"[30] Described as a lost episode in the show's final season, the short film is a work of fan love that reproduces the campy excesses of the original cartoon while lampooning the live-action reboot. The short film also intervenes in the world of *Jem and the Holograms*, showcasing the subtextual queer romance between Jem's sister Kimber and Misfits member Stormer. This is a manifest example of recuperative fandom, where the creative activity of fans is mobilized by both fandom and anti-fandom—a communal sense of frustration funneled into the production of new narratives.

Studying anti-fandom and the processes by which fans can become alienated from loved objects provides new insights into our relationship to media production. At first glance, we might often dismiss anti-fans of reboots as overly sentimental first-generation fans, too blinded by nostalgia to appreciate the reimagined. But by studying anti-fan critiques and the rejection of commodified nostalgia, we can begin to analyze the productive nature of negativity in fandom.

PART TWO

GENERATIONS OF
ENDURING FANDOMS

Like Father, Like Daughter

THE INTERGENERATIONAL PASSING OF DOCTOR WHO AND STAR WARS FANDOM IN THE FAMILIAL CONTEXT

Neta Yodovich

When Rose (thirty-eight, UK), one of my research participants, was a young girl, she waited for what she used to call "*Doctor Who* day." Only five years old at the time, Rose knew that there was a particular day of the week when she went to her father's home and got to watch her favorite TV show, *Doctor Who*. Only later, she learned that *Doctor Who* day has a more mundane name: Wednesday. Throughout the years, and as Rose grew up, she continued following the series. After becoming a mother, Rose shared the object of her fandom with her daughter. Such experiences of intergenerational passing of fandom and long-term fandom are the focus of this chapter.

The family nucleus and parent-child relationships are a rarely explored terrain in fan studies.[1] Most research conducted on the subject so far has focused on fandom socialization, a process in which parents instill values in their children that are embedded in the object of their fandom.[2] For instance, Hills referred to the contribution of fandom in the socialization of gender roles and identities, depicting it as an inheritance that passes "from father to son, from mother to daughter."[3] Assuming that family members of the same gender pass fandom, Hills and other scholars neglect intergenerational passing that is asymmetrical in terms of gender.

Intergenerational passing of fandom is explored here as part of a broader exploration of fans' life course in which many change roles: from children to adults to becoming parents themselves.[4] Throughout this process, the object of fandom not only accompanies fans in their lives but also serves as an anchor or a point of reference fans return to for evaluating how they have grown and changed over the years.[5]

The junction between fandom and the life course could reveal discrepancies where content appears appropriate only for a particular age group or for a limited amount of time, forcing some fans to "grow out of it."[6] Because fandom is often framed as an experience that occurs in childhood, adolescence, and young adulthood, studies on older fans have captured their experiences of stigmatization and exclusion.[7] In other cases, research on long-running franchises such as Doctor Who or Star Wars revealed ownership clashes between older and younger fans, where veteran fans and newcomers battle for the right to define the franchise, its canon, and the fan community.[8] For instance, the works by Golding and Bourdaa (which are featured in this volume) examine the ways older and younger fans negotiate their engagement with the fandom. Golding's accounts focus on potential tensions between fans, and Bourdaa explores mentorship practices that bridge veterans and newcomers in fandom.

This chapter inspects intergenerational passing of fandom among three generations: from fathers to daughters and daughters to their own children. "Generation" or "intergenerational passing" are mainly understood here as kinship descent. Based on thirty interviews with female fans of Doctor Who and Star Wars between the ages of nineteen and fifty-five, this study examines the values and ideas inherited through fandom, especially when parents and children are not of the same gender, from fathers to daughters. The second intergenerational passing of fandom, as well as changes in roles in interviewees' lives, allow the opportunity to explore how interviewees fine-tune their children's fandom socialization based on their own experiences.

Findings reveal that even though female fans were encouraged by their fathers to consume science fiction, they internalized the notion that science fiction fandom was a masculine identity that prioritized boys and men over girls and women. In an attempt to break the cycle of educating children according to conservative gender scripts, participants used their favorite science fiction content to challenge gender inequality with the new generation of fans they were raising.

The primary contribution of this research is its exploration of the intersection between intergenerational fandom, life course, age, and gender and their impact on one's perception of and interaction with fandom. Examining such intersections is paramount as it allows us to reveal a deep and nuanced understanding of how fandom develops, shifts, and changes over time in the family and in different life stages. This chapter further engages with broader sociological issues in fandom studies, such as sexism, aging, and ageism. As many studies continue to focus on fandom among adolescents and young adults, scholarly scrutiny of the life course and long-term fandom has yet to be exhausted.[9]

METHODOLOGY

The following study, which was conducted in late 2017, includes thirty in-depth semi-structured interviews with self-identified female fans of Doctor Who or Star Wars between the ages of nineteen and fifty-five. The average age of interviewees was thirty-seven. Based on this, participants whose age was above average were defined as "older fans" for the purpose of the analysis, and those below average age were called "younger fans."

Star Wars and Doctor Who were chosen because of their longevity in popular culture. Choosing long-running franchises meant a potential broad age range of interviewees, a vital consideration in this research. The fact that Star Wars and Doctor Who debuted more than fifty years ago means that their fandoms include those who have followed these franchises since their inception and younger followers who joined later. Aside from their Star Wars/Doctor Who fandoms, participants were part of other fandoms, which they referred to during interviews. The analysis and findings will focus on Doctor Who and Star Wars but address other franchises where relevant.

Semi-structured interviews were chosen to provide participants with the opportunity to share their experiences as fans through an open conversation. The majority of interviewees were British (albeit some were not born in the United Kingdom). Seven participants were from other European countries, such as Spain, France, and Italy. Interviews lasted approximately ninety minutes and were conducted either face to face, via Skype, or over the phone.

The following sections unpack interviewees' recollections of becoming fans during childhood, being fans during adulthood, and passing fandom to their children. These accounts are reviewed chronologically, focusing on participants' struggles against sexism and ageism in science fiction fandoms.

FINDINGS

Childhood

All interviews began by asking participants to reflect on the first time they became fans. When constructing their autobiographical narrative, interviewees reminisced about their childhoods and their relationships with their parents. In contrast to early descriptions of solitary science fiction fandom, parents were involved in the development of their daughters' fan identities through activities that were framed as familial quality time.[10]

Most interviewees notably attributed becoming fans to their fathers. For instance, several younger interviewees recalled watching the rebooted *Doctor Who* for the first time after being prompted by their fathers:

> I think I was ten, eleven when it came back, my dad built a lot of the hype around it, he was always into sci fi and he said, "you need to watch *Doctor Who*." (Sarah, twenty-two, UK)

> I was pushed into sci-fi by my family. My dad, for example, I remember watching the first *Doctor Who* episode with him. (Nina, twenty-five, UK)

Since their first exposure to *Doctor Who*, female fans like Sarah and Nina continued watching the series with their fathers as a weekly, ritualistic habit. Since previous research did not emphasize questions of gender in intergenerational passing of fandom, this finding raises an important question: what do female fans learn about their identities after being socialized into them by their fathers? I argue that the inheritance of fandom from father to daughter led interviewees to perceive science fiction fandom as a territory that favors boys and men.

Many participants, of all ages, reminisced about growing up as "one of the boys," since they were the only girls who enjoyed what they perceived as traditionally masculine practices:

> I self-identify as a geek, the girl who was into science fiction, and that's part of how I viewed myself . . . I identified myself as being into these boys' things. (laughs) (Jane, forty-six, UK)

> Girls were into *Dawson's Creek* [popular teen drama, 1998–2003] and drawing flowers everywhere, and it was just not me. (Courtney, twenty-nine, Germany)

Like Jane and Courtney, Lucia (thirty-nine, Spain) also recounted being a "tomboy" during her childhood, an identity that was encouraged by her father:

> Fortunately for me, my dad was a nerd as well . . . he supported that kind of thing, even though he was really sexist in many things. When one year, I wanted to dress up as a Ghostbuster, all the other girls dressed up as princesses, and my father built the gear for my Ghostbuster costume.

Lucia, Jane, and other participants recognized that their geekiness distinguished them from other girls their age and made them feel unique and special. They favored what they identified as traditional masculine interests over feminine ones and appraised them as symbols of their individualism and nonconforming behavior. While these female fans felt special, in contrast to other "girly" girls, they internalized misogynistic conceptions that deemed "girly" content inferior. Simultaneously, they understood that the content they enjoyed was first and foremost for boys, not for them.

I argue that the acknowledgment of science fiction fandom as a traditionally male-oriented interest was partly a side effect of how interviewees' fathers introduced them to science fiction. Samantha (forty-six, UK), for example, recollected the double standards she experienced in her and her brother's upbringing:

> My brother came with us [her and her dad] to watch Star Wars. He enjoyed them, but he didn't become obsessed by them. He was vaguely interested, but I was the one who knew every tiny detail about it. He was the one who got all the toys. He was the one who got a Dalek, which I stole . . . I got Barbies, my brother got the sci-fi toys. He couldn't care less. It was me who loved it, I was the actual fan. . . . I understood that it was boys who got these toys and the girls steal the toys.

Samantha explained that she implicitly learned not to ask for Doctor Who toys from her father. Assuming that his son would be a more "natural" fit to science fiction, he taught his daughter, perhaps unintentionally, that Doctor Who fandom is not intended for girls. While exposing both of his children to science fiction, Samantha's father raised his children according to traditional gender scripts in which girls should be ultimately interested in Barbies and princesses and boys in action figures and science fiction. Regardless of whether their fathers helped them construct their Halloween costumes or ignored their wishes for fannish merchandise, female fans internalized that science fiction was primarily for boys. They may have grown up feeling special in comparison to other girls but were simultaneously second-class citizens in their fan communities of choice.

When comparing younger and older participants, it appears that younger women's transitions into the fandom world were smoother than their older counterparts, as could be understood by Nina (twenty-five, UK): "my dad got me into Star Wars. My dad is a massive feminist, and that's really good." Nevertheless, interviewees in this age cohort also reported feeling that their

Like Father, Like Daughter 61

fathers raised them differently from their peers' parents. Sarah (twenty-two, UK), for example, depicted how being a fan of the Terminator franchise at the tender age of seven was found odd: "other kids' parents seemed strict with the types of images they were viewing and films they were watching, while my dad was pretty chill about it." Similar to older participants, younger fans grew up with the understanding that the franchises they were exposed to by their fathers were not necessarily the type of content young girls were expected or socialized to enjoy.

Adulthood

Feelings of exclusion from what was ingrained in their perception as a male-dominated fan community followed participants into adulthood. Lucy (forty-one, UK), who worked in a comic book shop in her younger years, shared feelings of alienation when walking into one now: "When you're young, and you're female, especially if you're slim and pretty, people, I mean, men, they will make some amount of space for you . . . even if you're not going to sleep with them, they think you might one day . . . as women, we reach, probably even mid- to late twenties, when you either become invisible or you're treated like a hostile . . . like you don't belong there." Lucy's experiences as a young woman working in a comic book shop echo the "male fan's girlfriend" trope, wherein female fans are perceived as faking interest in the content to appease their boyfriends or find a romantic partner.[11] She believed that the reason she was hired was not because of her enthusiasm for and connoisseurship of comic books but because of the prospect she would date one of her colleagues.

Older interviewees' accounts revealed the ageist and sexist undertone of the "girlfriend" trope and depicted the process of transforming from "someone's girlfriend" to "someone's mother": "I know that men my age can go [to a movie premiere] on their own and can go as a group, and it's fine, but women my age, you're only there if you're someone's mom. When we get to conventions, I'm really aware of it as well. There's the moms. You're so irrelevant or invisible, you're just not part of it" (Lucy, forty-one, UK). Interviewees like Lucy were discriminated against twice: first for their gender and second for their age. What was once a somewhat valid lifestyle in their younger years became a complicated challenge as they got older. Despite being fans for years and decades, older participants felt they could no longer attend movie premieres or conventions without their children because they seemed idiosyncratic in these venues.[12] Their presence at conventions, comic book shops, or movie premieres was not only conspicuous in the eyes of younger fans, it was also an invitation for backlash or ridicule, according to Lucy.

Interestingly, some of the participants in the younger cohort also experienced ageism in fan communities. For instance, Emily (thirty-four, UK), whose age is lower than interviewees' average age, situated herself "on the older end of fandom." In contrast, another interviewee of the younger cohort, Lily (thirty-one, UK), indicated that male fans call her "a girl" when they want to dismiss her opinions: "they never call me a woman, even though I'm in my thirties." These statements demonstrate the subjective construction of age, especially when it comes to female fans. Depending on their opposers' intentions, female fans could be deemed too young or too old to be taken seriously in science fiction fandoms.

Older interviewees addressed merchandise as a primary site that embodies their exclusion from fan communities. Fans are conventionally perceived as "ideal consumers," who eagerly buy merchandise related to their fandom.[13] Based on this understanding, manufacturers produce a plethora of fannish commodities, such as posters, clothing, action figures, mugs, books, box sets, video games, and more. Even a cursory look at the science fiction fandoms' merchandise supply in stores or online reveals that most products are designed with boys and young men in mind, not older women, especially when it comes to fannish fashion.[14] Ally (thirty-nine, UK), a Star Wars fan, addressed the implied ageism in its merchandise: "I do like clothes, and I do like fashion, and I like expressing fandom in a way that is not just the stereotypical nerd, a nice item you'd like to own anyway. I can go to the supermarket and buy men's T-shirts, I can even go to the Disney store, they have a great Rey jacket, but it's for girls. If they did it in my size, I would buy it." Petersen used the concept of subjective age in her examination of Sherlock Holmes fans over the age of fifty.[15] She explained that her participants felt younger than their biological age, thanks to their fannish engagements. In contrast, the participants of this study did not necessarily express feeling an incongruence with their biological age. Instead, they were eager for people their age to be embraced and accepted by fans, producers, and manufacturers alike. One of the prominent symbols they used to assess the level of their inclusion or exclusion was through Star Wars and Doctor Who merchandise. Based on the lack of clothing and accessories made for them, older female fans learned that as they aged, they were pushed further away from their fandom.

The efforts to include girls and women in the merchandise and fashion manufactured for Star Wars fans were reported in Johnson's study on

Like Father, Like Daughter 63

HerUniverse, a clothing brand for science fiction fans and "geeky" women.[16] Johnson's main argument was that such brands reflect postfeminist and neoliberal mindsets, which frame consumption as an act of empowerment.[17] The pleas of interviewees in this study could be read through a similar prism; the focus on clothes as a sign of inclusion or progress overlooked a deeper and more nuanced understanding of institutionalized ageism and gender inequality that permeates fan communities and society as a whole. In the next section, which follows interviewees' transitions into motherhood, I suggest that consumption could be used as a significant educative conduit.

Motherhood

Nine of the thirty interviewees in this research (two from the younger cohort and seven from the older one) had entered a life stage that is also important when examining the development of long-term fandom: motherhood. Like their fathers before them, these interviewees reported passing their fan identities and fannish practices to their children. Rose, for example, shared she could not wait to share *Star Wars: The Force Awakens* (J. J. Abrams, 2015) with her young daughter because it featured a female protagonist, Rey: "I thought that as soon as it comes on DVD, my daughter has to watch it, she would love her."

Perhaps because of their negative experiences, fan mothers were keen to use fannish merchandise as a practice to imbue their children with feminist, inclusive values. Their eagerness that their children, sons and daughters alike, would play with female Star Wars action figures was met with a limited supply of Rey-centered merchandise:

> You can't find Rey merchandise. I have a son, and it's something we've bonded over, and I have this big thing that he has the female figures as well as the male ones. . . . It's quite a big deal for me to find female characters, to model things to my son, to not grow up to be a jerk (*laughs*). It's not Disney, it's the guy who ran the company that makes the figures, he said, "boys buy action figures, and boys wouldn't buy figures of girls," which is crazy. At the moment, my son's favorite action figure is a female character. (Ally, thirty-nine, UK)

Participants like Ally addressed the #WheresRey controversy, where despite being the leading character of the new trilogy, Rey was almost entirely missing from the merchandise that accompanied the release of *The Force Awakens*.[18] The scarcity of Rey merchandise was perceived as yet another demonstration of the explicit exclusion of female fans from science fiction fandoms. Lucy also criticized the paucity of Rey action figures: "The decisions that were made around Rey were huge errors, massive errors. How much money are they losing by doing this? It's not making sense. I guess they made these decisions because 'boys won't play with them,' but they're forgetting that women are fans, and moms. We're the ones buying things. They also overlooked that boys want a Rey character to play with, as much as anything else." Interviewees contested the thought process that concluded with the absence of Rey merchandise in which boys, the target audience of Star Wars, are not interested in playing with a Rey figurine. This line of thought not only neglects the female fans of the franchise but fails to acknowledge that boys could also be fans of female characters.

In the previous section, I reviewed claims that frame fans' emphasis on merchandise as a part of a neoliberal, postfeminist culture that equates consumption with agency and activism.[19] In contrast, other scholars, such as Brown, claim that "*Star Wars* merchandising is not a mere fannish obsession ... it is a recognition that political elements worth fighting over permeate every facet of our modern culture."[20] For the female fans in this study, fannish consumption holds political meaning that goes beyond fandom: women tire of being ignored and demand to be acknowledged and included in the public sphere. Interviewees' motivation to purchase merchandise featuring female characters was part of a grander effort to stake their claim in what continues to be accepted as male-oriented fandoms. Female fans' focus on consumption could also be read as their challenge to conservative gender scripts. Fan mothers shared the object of their fandom with both boys and girls and exposed them to a more versatile array of fannish merchandise. For instance, they consumed female action figures for their boys, not just for their girls.

Fan mothers' feminist education of their children through fandom did not stop at consumption. Watching Star Wars and Doctor Who alongside their children allowed them to share their fandom and reflect on gender inequality together: "She already talks to me about gendered elements in *Doctor Who*, like, 'why do the girls always fall in love with him? Why is it always a girl companion?' It is almost becoming a vehicle for exploring gender in her developing worldview" (Rose). Interviewees did not make a conscious link between their upbringing and that of their children. Nevertheless, it appears that they attempted to preserve the familial quality time they experienced with their fathers and remove traditional or old-fashioned gender-related perceptions their children might internalize from these in-

Like Father, Like Daughter 65

teractions. As their own fathers did, participants instilled their children with their love for science fiction and developed familial viewing rituals with them. Unlike their fathers, interviewees used science fiction fandom as a conduit to encourage their children's critical thinking and inspire them to question stereotypical representations in the media. Interviewees like Rose used their fandom as a starting point for open conversations with their children about gender. Acknowledging their experiences of exclusion from their fandom throughout the years, interviewees were adamant about mediating the content and fan community to their children and flagging any problematic aspects they might include.

CONCLUSIONS

This chapter examined a phenomenon that has not been often explored in fan studies: the passing of fandom from parent to child. The research captured the intergenerational passing of fandom among three familial generations: from father to daughter, and from those daughters to their children. Through interviews with female fans between the ages of nineteen and fifty-five, this study tapped into themes such as long-term fandom and ageism and sexism in fan communities. In particular, this research observed the values and norms that are passed through fandom socialization and the ways fandom is used by parents to shape and educate their children.

Findings revealed the challenges of navigating science fiction fandom in gender-asymmetrical intergenerational passing, as science fiction fandoms were accepted as male-oriented territories by both fathers and daughters. Encountering gender- and age-based exclusion throughout their lives motivated female fans to raise their children as more socially conscious fans. Participants' emphasis on consumption raised a debate about the significance of their actions: is buying Rey action figures a demonstration of agency and female empowerment? I contend that even though these acts of consumerism echo neoliberal traditions, they matter a great deal to fans, especially to parents who strive to raise their children to become not only good fans but good people. Although consumption might not contribute directly to dismantling institutionalized sexism and gender discrimination, these are small steps that are better than no action at all. This is especially true when consumption is taken as part of a more extensive set of educational practices.

The accounts captured in this chapter provide only a partial depiction of intergenerational passing of fandom. For instance, questions regarding fathers' incentive to expose their daughters to science fiction and their awareness of the implicit messages they were delivering remain unanswered. These autobiographical narratives depicted particular father-daughter interactions that do not necessarily reflect the diverse landscape of intergenerational passing of fandom and of gender identities (for instance, all interviewees were cis female and cis male fathers).

Despite certain limitations and the focus on a particular case study, the insights in this chapter provide the first step for opening a new or less examined avenue in fan studies. Future research could explore asymmetrical intergenerational passing in other fandoms beyond cinema and film and explore whether the same patterns emerge. Similarly, there is room to explore romantic relationships in which both partners are fans and the ways they engage with fandom among themselves, as well as with their children. I call on fellow fan studies scholars to continue developing the potential ties between fan studies and family studies.

Examining Pop Music Fandom through a Generational Lens

Simone Driessen

When we talk about female fans, frequently we refer to them as fangirls. This youthful association puts fans in a framework of youth, one's childhood, or teens. Being a youthful or teenage fan might carry a connotation of being naïve or even childish. Think about media descriptions of the hysterical fans of pop idols like the Beatles or One Direction. Such depictions have been particularly linked to female music fans.[1] But fans grow older, and many remain or return to their object of fandom at some point. More and more popular bands from a few decades ago have returned for reunion tours or picked up touring again and are releasing new music. What happens when boys and girls grow up and remain fans?

This chapter explores the transition of young music fans into adult music fans, a topic gaining more scholarly attention in studies of popular music, music sociology, (digital) fandom, and studies on media consumption across the life course.[2] To better understand current trends in the cultural industries, like reunion concerts, reruns and reboots of TV series, and film franchises, insights into why and how people maintain their affective feelings over time are needed.[3] By addressing how fans talk about, (have) experience(d), and reflect on being a fan in their youth and their fandom in their adult lives, this study offers such insights. This chapter draws on interviews, conducted in the Netherlands between 2014 and 2017, with (now) adult women from the Netherlands who have been long-term or recurring fans of the US boy band Backstreet Boys (1993–present, with a hiatus between 2002 and 2004). Pop music in general, particularly boy bands, forms a genre typically associated with youth that one is expected to outgrow as an adult, especially teen girls maturing into young women.[4] The interviews reveal how these women give meaning to fandom in their youth and now and consider these changes in the light of their generational identity—which I consider structured around the life cycle of the band, life milestones, and various life course developments fitting to and with growing older.[5] This study offers a unique perspective on aging music fans, a topic of academic interest gaining more attention in media, fan, and music studies.[6]

MUSIC FANDOM FROM YOUTH TO ADULTHOOD

Although fans often find it difficult to point out in their lives when their fandom precisely "happened," they do consider it a life-changing moment. Duffett argues that fans see this as an autobiographical turning point that changed their lives.[7] Harrington and Bielby consider this transformational moment a key event in one's autobiographical reasoning, a type of reasoning that helps situate fandom in one's life history.[8] Through this, fandom can become a structuring force in a fan's life: one might attach and connect various memories or even milestones of life to fandom.[9]

The social powers of fandom and a "becoming-a-fan story" are typically rooted and most powerful in one's youth. Despite fannish affection being of such importance and all-consuming, this phase of teenage fandom might later become a mere nostalgic period to revisit.[10] Hills described this as an abandonment of the object of fandom, which makes fandom more of a cyclical activity than a long-term, enduring investment.[11] However, in a later study Hills emphasizes how such reentries into fandom are a crucial part of what he calls "transformative self-narratives."[12] Like the autobiographical reasoning fans engage in, and considering entering a fandom as a pinnacle moment in one's life, this dipping in and out of fandom can be attributed a transformational power. For example, flexible (non)engagement allows fans to pick up their fandom when a band starts touring again and potentially picking up (old and new) friendships or now—as an adult—finally having the financial means to buy concert tickets.

The focus of this chapter on adult Dutch Backstreet Boys fans allows for an examination of an enduring or perpetual fandom, which implies that there is a long-term, ongoing commitment between fan and band.[13] This chapter provides an account of this particular cohort, more specifically a particular generation of fans, defined by and structured around the life cycle of the band, who were in their childhood or teens when Backstreet Boys started (1993). Now they have (along with the band—almost a reciprocal bond) matured into what Bennett and Hodkinson define as "post-youth," the phase of one's life in which one becomes financially and socially independent (e.g., earning their own salary, having their own duties and responsibilities related to family life as mothers or fathers).[14] These fans have grown into

Examining Pop Music Fandom . . . 69

adulthood, and Backstreet Boys have offered what Istvandy describes as the "lifetime soundtrack": a framework in which reflexive activities happen, considering music as a constant juxtaposition with our past selves and an instrument to create personal meaning in one's life.[15]

To better understand such meanings and experiences, particularly what it means to be an adult music fan, previous studies offer an indication of why people remain committed to their favorite band or artist. For some fans, like those discussed by Stevenson in his study on long-term male David Bowie fans, the singer appears to offer a resource for coping with issues and challenges in everyday life.[16] For Lavin, who gives an autoethnographic account of her fandom of singer Patti Smith, Smith appears to function like a big sister, whom she can confide in, consult, and rely on while growing older.[17] Like Bowie, Smith becomes an example to follow while making sense of her own life, its transformational events (like a divorce), and her process of aging.[18]

Besides these personal accounts, which offer strong examples of how fandom can be structuring or transformational for coping with what happens in life, there is also a social component to being an adult fan. Anderson's work on adult female Duran Duran fans is an illustration of this. In addition to still feeling affection for the music and the band, the escapism of going to a concert with friends as a grown woman is mentioned by one of the fans Anderson interviewed.[19] Moreover, the nostalgia of returning, through a concert, to a brief moment of one's youth is what matters for the women in their adult fanhood.[20] Attending a Duran Duran concert allows them to be carefree and young again, if only for a moment.

What these previous works into music fandom demonstrate is how there is a close link between growing older and fandom. For example, the aging punks in Bennett's study started to dress down or behave differently; instead of being at the front of a gig, they find themselves supervising the room from the back.[21] Being a fan might take a different shape across the various decades of being involved in a fandom, in addition to carrying different meaning(s) over time.

AUTOBIOGRAPHICAL REASONING ACROSS THE FANNISH LIFE COURSE

To explore how a boy band like Backstreet Boys features (or continues to feature) in fans' life across the years, this study turns to the autobiographical reasoning of the fans themselves. This allows for a unique insight into this particular generation's aging process and how fandom is experienced across one's life. Istvandy considers such reasoning about life narratives to recollect autobiographical memories of music as a means of switching between current and past identities.[22] In addition, this acumen highlights and helps a person revisit their memories. This reasoning helps one grasp these life narratives in and through their connection to transformational stages in life, like childhood, adulthood, and later life or the final phase.

To comprehend this process, this chapter scrutinizes the autobiographical reasoning of fans. I do so by analyzing the level of reasoning building on the narratives obtained through interviews conducted with twenty-two Dutch women, aged between twenty-five and thirty-three (at the time of the interviews, conducted between 2014 and 2017), who identified as (long-term or former) fans of US boy band Backstreet Boys. Interviews lasted forty to eighty minutes and were conducted in person or via Skype or email (the latter because some fans were hearing impaired). The fans had various educational backgrounds (from vocational schooling to university level) and jobs (from nurse to sports instructor). Some were in relationships or married, some were single, and some had children: all markers indicative of their post-youth status.[23] Some fans interviewed identified as people of color; however, they indicated in their interviews that besides being able to speak a second language due to their cultural background (for example), this did not change their fan experience. Nevertheless, it needs to be acknowledged that often fan studies, particularly music fandom, remains a space where whiteness forms our understanding of fans.[24]

Due to the Backstreet Boys' lengthy career, most women had been in the fandom for about two decades. Although in the United States the band has been performing since 1993, their international breakthrough (including in the Netherlands) happened around 1996–1997. Many fans declare that their fandom started sometime in these years. Although the band took a hiatus between 2003 and 2005, many fans remained invested, even when the intervals between albums became longer or when one of the members (temporarily) left the band.[25]

The interview questions aimed at getting to know the biographical story of the fans and focused on asking them about their fandom, whom they could share it with, how their fandom developed over time, and what kind of activities they (used to) do to express their fandom. The interviews were transcribed, and a thematic analysis was performed.[26] This led to identifying several core themes capturing and exposing how this generation of female fans experienced their route from young to adult fan.

Examining Pop Music Fandom . . .   71

GENERATIONAL MUSIC FANDOM

To discuss how the experience from young to adult female fan takes shape and is experienced, this section covers two core domains: the formative years (focusing and reflecting on childhood and teen autobiographical reasoning) and the adult years (highlighting and discussing current fan practices). The interviewed fans have not yet reached later life as a phase, which I would consider to be the period when one's children have become adults or when one has retired and taken their pension. They were asked to reflect on what they think their fandom will look like in the future. Most of them jokingly promised to still visit concerts when "old and gray," but since these events have not happened yet, they are not included in the chapter.

Taking this focus on the formative and adult years shows how this generation has experienced this transition from youth to after. Drawing on the autobiographical reasoning and memories of the interviewed women ensures such accounts are told through their eyes. The chapter unpacks how one experiences/d fandom as a young girl and how one does as an adult woman.

Formative Fannish Activities

There are a few typical elements that most fans mention when reflecting on their early ventures into Backstreet Boys fandom. Most interviewees were in their childhood or (early) teens, and some indicate they were entering puberty when they became fans. The interviewees indicate this life stage as the beginning of their "becoming a fan" story.[27] Some remember a precise moment, like seeing a video clip of the band on MTV or its Dutch equivalent, Music Factory. Esther, a twenty-nine-year-old office manager, reflects on this period as follows: "That was early puberty for me ... I remember when 'I Want It That Way' came on TV, and that was with some friends around, and then we could really be excited and glued to the TV, the three of us. Yeah, that was pretty frantic (*laughs*)."

Not only does Esther recall the practice of viewing these videos on TV (a popular pastime for teens in that decade), but particularly this aspect of watching together with her friends and being slightly frenzied about what they saw and heard. This element of togetherness or sharing returns in many of the interviewed fans' narratives. Twenty-seven-year-old student Sarah mentions how she was introduced to the band by an older babysitter who shared the albums with her. The babysitter and Sarah find themselves at the same age as most of the fans at the peak of the band's popularity in the Netherlands, making the early and mid-teens a specific generation defined by this media text. For Cynthia (thirty, real estate agent) being able to talk to her friends about being a fan mattered greatly: "Being a fan was just fun [at that age]. But also, because your friends like them. That meant you could gossip about who was the most good-looking or who they liked best and that kind of stuff." Being able to share her affection for the band seems important to Cynthia, as she points out. Listening to the music, watching the videos, and talking about the band members' looks: these can be considered typical activities teen fans would engage in.[28] Interestingly, in her work on adult Duran Duran fans, Anderson also uncovers this idea of having a continued communal experience as a vital element to maintaining one's fandom in later life.[29]

In addition to this communal experience that shapes or perhaps even helps create a generation of fans, some of the interviewees have very personal experiences of becoming a fan. Besides being able to watch videos with her friends, Esther emphasizes that she really liked the band's music. While being bullied in her teen years, she found comfort and consolation in the songs. Likewise, for Deshny (twenty-seven, student) the music offered comfort, warmth, and a sense of coziness, something she could escape in or to when she considered teen life challenging.

Another solo practice that mattered greatly to the interviewed fans in their younger years was collecting memorabilia—in the broadest understanding of the word. Cynthia illustrates this in the following memory she shared: "Cutting out pictures or photos from [Dutch magazines] *Hitkrant* and *Break-Out*, putting up posters in my room, duvet covers, pillows. . . yes, whatever you can think it, no matter how crazy, I probably had it at home." Equally, Sarah also is able to sum up her collection (pillowcases, posters, key chains, cassettes, CDs, newspaper clippings, interviews in English magazines, etc.), and so are other fans. Some have kept their collectibles in boxes or at their parents' house, and some have their collection still on display in their current homes (e.g., timeworn tickets from old concerts). Deshny indicates she would wake up in the middle of the night to record an interview with the band on TV.

That practical level of dedication seems to fade with aging, as I illustrate in the next section on adult fandom. However, as already clear from their references to TV, magazines, and CDs, this group of fans was perhaps one of the last fandoms to become fans without the internet being omnipresent. As covered elsewhere, internet access was on the rise in the Netherlands in the late 1990s and early 2000s.[30] Hence, the lack of digital access (and later the access to it) also shaped how this generation was able to perform

Examining Pop Music Fandom . . . 73

and experience their fandom in their childhood and teen years: much more analogue than fans growing up in today's world, where having immediate access (albeit unreciprocated) to an artist via social media seems to be normal.

Looking Back and Beyond Formative Fandom through Adult Eyes

Being able to follow a band for over twenty years or return to music from one's youth in adult life offers a rare perspective on long-term engagement with media. During this long-term affective investment, audiences might undergo different milestones and life events.[31] Building on previous research, one would expect that fans indeed consider this of great value. However, many fans point out how these transformative moments actually made them move away from the Backstreet Boys fandom. Esther reasons she had less time for the band and their tours when she grew older because she gained other interests that took up more time, like shopping with friends or dating boys. Some fans indicate that their jobs or their studies took up time, which made them less focused on the band and more on these new life events.[32] The transition from youth to the first steps of post-youth also led to discrepancies in the interviewees' fannish engagement.

Nevertheless, for some fans, adulthood also meant that there finally was a moment to engage (anew) with the band and its music. Miriam, a twenty-six-year-old social worker, considers 2005 (when the band returned to the Netherlands on tour after a few years of absence) a transformative moment in her fandom: "I see this [2005] as a turning point in my fandom because this is where it turned into a hobby that got out of hand. I met other fans online and together we travel the world for the band now. Concerts in New York, Dublin, London . . . promotional events in Copenhagen, Berlin . . . even a Backstreet Boys cruise in the Bahamas. I've done it all." Miriam's transition illustrates what adult fandom can entail, from forging new (online) friendships to traveling the world. This is possible because fans now have their own money to spend (as an adult with a full-time job in Miriam's case) instead of having their parents help out financially. But being an independent adult also means there is time to travel, or rather the perception of new-found freedom by being able to take off time from work and travel whenever you want, instead of being tied to a school schedule that does not allow for flexibility.

Elise, similar to Miriam, attended multiple concerts because she now was able to. After one of the concerts, she and a few friends tried to locate the hotel where the band was staying in the hope of getting an autograph or a selfie with a band member. This was something she could not have done in the past, for then she was either supervised by her parents at a concert or dependent on public transportation to get home. Without the internet it was much more difficult to trace the band and where they were staying. Now Elise could treat the concert attendance as a short road trip or holiday with friends with no parental supervision.

Many of the interviewees reflect on their adult fandom through the lens of how they experienced their childhood and teenage fan engagement. Accordingly, they compare these feelings and experiences of the past to their involvement today. For the interviewees, it is not so much about reclaiming this youthful phase in life, but it seems to be more about being able to position and discuss the level of affect they feel.[33] This shapes their discourse on what it means to be an adult fan. Interviewee Cynthia describes her experience: "Every time when you visit a concert and they appear on stage . . . Well . . . I get butterflies in my stomach, like 'oh here they are again,' and you're completely nervous about it."

Sarah shares the sentiment that Cynthia sketches—the nice feeling, the giddiness of the situation: "It's like being back in puberty or the likes. Not that I'm screaming all the time, but at times I do get a little overenthusiastic." These accounts illustrate how "feminine" feelings (having butterflies, feeling back in puberty) belonging to the frenzy of youth (hysterical teens' Beatlemania) still pop up in adult fandom. Yet the fans are now more reflective on these feelings and also a little critical. For example, interviewee Anya (twenty-six, PhD student) explains what she experienced when she and her friends visited an after-party (which they bought tickets for) where some of the Backstreet Boys members performed: "You get to see them really up-close and personal. And then I noticed that I really like felt like that twelve-year-old girl again, so . . . almost hysterical. I became really nervous and hot, and well . . . I was kind of surprised to feel that way. I didn't expect that, I thought that phase would be over." What her reflection shows is how Anya is surprised by and almost polices her behavior. That "almost hysterical" part was unexpected in this adult fannish moment. Although she did not expect to feel this way, the general stigma of being a "hysterical fangirl" does seem to transfer to adulthood.[34] Anya mentions how other people (colleagues or friends outside the fandom) consider it silly, almost disapproving of when she talks about attending the Backstreet Boys concerts: "I often still have to defend myself. People don't really understand. . . . I never had a moment where I considered the BSB silly. I always loved them and I will continue to do so."

The notion of having to defend why, as an adult, one still listens to the band's music or visits their concerts might sound like there is still somewhat

Examining Pop Music Fandom . . . 75

of a stigma on fandom at a later age. Elise (thirty-two, childcare worker) finds herself in a similar position to Anya at work: "When the concerts begin, and that wave of screams comes through the crowd from back to front . . . goosebumps! I always explain to my colleagues, who consider me a bit foolish for this, that once a year I just have to scream for an hour and a half, putting all my worries aside . . . the only worry I have is that it will end too soon." Elise almost attributes a mindful quality to the screaming: it allows her to not think of anything for a time. Whether screaming held a similar function for her in her youth does not become clear from Elise's autobiographical reasoning on this practice. However, being able to put that feeling into words fits with being an adult, when one can be more reflective on such feelings, having witnessed this across the life course.[35]

Having to explain oneself as a fan raises the question of whether it is typical for female fans to get remarks like this, if there is such a thing as an age-appropriate time to be a fan, or if the pop genre plays a role in how serious adult fans are taken. The (chiefly) male adult fans of (the more serious genre of) glam rock star David Bowie did not have to deal with such questions, for example.[36]

Besides this defense mechanism the interviewees seem to put up to the "outsiders," many of them chiefly consider the perks of being an adult, socially and financially independent fan when talking about what it means to be a grown-up fan. Cynthia recalls how she used to rely on her parents for taking her to the concert venues and saving money for a show. Now she can spend her money on whatever she pleases: a concert ticket, a photo opportunity with the band, or a meet and greet with them. However, her responsibility as a mother constrains her adult fandom slightly, she explains: "Well, I also have my responsibilities, bills to pay and that kind of stuff. So, it's not like I can attend eight or nine concerts or travel the world." Even so, she emphasizes that attending a concert also puts her in a carefree position, "just being me, not a mom, but just Cynthia," which makes spending the money worth it.

For the interviewees, a greater level of financial and social freedom seems to play an important role in their adult fandom and fannish engagement. On the one hand, having steady adult income allows them to—temporarily—be free of worries and responsibilities and spend their money on tickets in ways they couldn't as teens. On the other hand, that feeling might be reminiscent of the carefree period in their lives when they became Backstreet Boys fans and could spend all their money on the band.

CONCLUSION: A GENERATION'S REFLECTION ON MUSIC FANDOM

By exploring how a generation experiences the transition from childhood to adult fandom, this chapter looked at a particular group of female adult Backstreet Boys fans from the Netherlands. These fans' autobiographical memories and reasonings illustrate different experiences of fandom in the youthful, formative years of their fandom and the adult, long-term affective investment in the band.

What is characteristic for this childhood period is that the fandom experience seems to be about forging friendships and having a shared experience—listening to music together or going to a concert. In addition, being a fan is and was an individual experience, through starting and maintaining a fan collection or using the music as a means to cope with certain feelings. Reflecting on these experiences as adults reveals how this generation developed into post-youth women, who are now socially and financially independent. This transformation offers a lens for reflecting on these childhood practices of fandom and how they compare with current fan engagement. Moreover, being an adult fan in this generation of fans offers new opportunities and types of activities one could not commit to or conduct as a kid or teen (e.g., going on a Backstreet Boys cruise or attending multiple concerts on a road trip).

This generational lens, looking back as an adult via music memories on one's childhood or teenage fannish practices, is a unique way to explore long-term fan engagement. More and more reunion tours (e.g., the Spice Girls in 2019, a Take That quarantine reunion during 2020's pandemic) and continuing tours of bands (from the Rolling Stones to New Kids on the Block) are taking place. This study shed light on the phenomena of remaining or returning to being a boy band fan in later life. It would be interesting for future studies to scrutinize why some fans quit these fandoms after youth or decide not to return to them or to examine more closely how genre plays a role in adult music fandom. (Is rock fandom more accepted?) Although there were a few fans of color included in the group of interviewees, this has not been fleshed out further, but it would be interesting to do. Even so, the chapter offers an insight into how women are adult pop fans, but whether that is different for male pop fans is left unaddressed.

Examining Pop Music Fandom . . .   77

Looking Back, Looking Bi

QUEERING A LIFELONG FANDOM
OF THE BABY-SITTERS CLUB

Megan Connor

On February 28, 2019, Netflix announced a series order to adapt the iconic young adult book series by Ann M. Martin, the Baby-Sitters Club (BSC).[1] Two weeks later, the Society for Cinema and Media Studies held its annual conference in Seattle, Washington, and I, a graduate student attending alone for the first time and a lifelong fan of the BSC, repeatedly employed this entertainment news as an introductory anecdote to connect with new colleagues and old friends. This strategy proved remarkably effective, generating enthusiastic conversation with many academics—primarily white, US-based women—who shared my nostalgia for the series, even providing the first inkling of an idea for what would become this edited collection.

An adaptation of the BSC was not surprising to anyone I spoke with, indicating the extent to which reboot culture has saturated our media landscape. Granted, these conversations took place at an international conference for media scholars, but I was still struck by how easily conversant everyone I spoke to was in the language and conventions of reboots. Notably, each individual's remembrance and enthusiasm for the series seemed deeply tied to their personal identity. That is to say, many women who were BSC readers in their youth connected their fandom to their identity as girls, and especially to a particular BSC character. The five primary members of the Baby-Sitters Club, their names and titles neatly printed on the back of each volume, are a refrain I have been able to rattle off since I was six years old:

Kristy Thomas, President
Claudia Kishi, Vice-President
Mary Anne Spier, Secretary
Stacey McGill, Treasurer
Dawn Schaefer, Alternate Officer

Fan identification along a fandom's in-text classification system is not uncommon, whether it is which version of Doctor Who they prefer, which Hogwarts house they belong to (Harry Potter), or which Disney princess is their favorite.[2] In particular, there is a femininely gendered mode of fan identification, labeled as "extra-cinematic identificatory practices" by Jackie Stacey in her study of female fans of female Hollywood stars in Britain after World War II.[3] Stacey describes a process "where the star's identity is selectively reworked and incorporated into the spectator's new identity" in their daily lives.[4] Today, this mode of identification as fan play is still common for media texts that center on groups of women, like *Sex and City* (HBO, 1998–2004), *Pretty Little Liars* (ABC Family/Freeform, 2010–2017), or *The Golden Girls* (ABC, 1985–1992), where each character performs a different archetype of femininity.[5] Fans commonly discuss which character they identify with the most based on these archetypes: are they an Aria (the artsy one) or a Spencer (the preppy one)? In interviews regarding the 2020 Netflix adaption of the BSC, showrunner Rachel Shukert performs this fan identification with an added twist, proclaiming herself "a Claudia with a Kristy rising" in multiple interviews.[6] It is hard not to read this incorporation of astrological language as coded signaling to queer communities.

Given the renewed interest in this girl-centric fandom among my generational cohort, this chapter provides an autoethnography of my lifelong fandom of the BSC, thinking through its various iterations and its importance in defining my identity at various stages in my life, what Harrington and Bielby call a "life-course analysis" of my fandom.[7] I weave between the two main threads of reboot culture and identification, first looking at my childhood and considering how my fandom of the original series was bound up in my identity-making process. I also address the series' specific cultural importance through the Japanese American character Claudia Kishi, who provided a novel point of identification for Asian American girls and entry point for girls of all races (including myself) to be exposed to a nuanced representation of Asian identity. I then turn to my current and renewed fandom of the series, examining how different expressions of the BSC have or have not appealed to fans like me. In my case, this is based on my positionality and preoccupations as a bisexual woman and feminist media studies scholar.

Unlike the chapters in this collection that look at many different generations of fandom over time, this chapter uses autoethnography to move through time firmly connected to one generation. Autoethnography is a growing scholarly methodology defined by Adams and Herrmann as "us[ing]

Looking Back, Looking Bi 79

selfhood, subjectivity, and personal experience ('auto') to describe, interpret, and represent ('graphy') beliefs, practices, and identities of a group or culture ('ethno')."[8] Fan studies scholars often use varying degrees of autoethnography in their work by including their own subjectivity and fandom, as evidenced by the popularity of the term *aca-fan*. Evans and Stasi have suggested that self-reflexive autoethnography can be an innovative tool for fan studies to "develop narrative accounts of what it means to take up these subject positions and use them to create a sense of self as a lived experience."[9]

To return to my positionality: writing this as a thirty-year-old, I fit easily in the generational label of Millennial, defined as those born between the early 1980s and mid-1990s. The use of generational labels can merit the same concerns as autoethnography, implying that a personal, subjective experience can be taken as a universal or objective truth for a wider group. Generational scholars like Strauss and Howe argue that each generation has a unique "peer personality" built on their shared social and cultural history that all members of a generation engage with in some sense.[10] This belies the truth that Millennials are a disparate group of around eighty million individuals in the United States with different genders, ethnicities, socioeconomic classes, and life experiences. However, my identity in this group—a white, middle-class, female Millennial—positions me in the specific demographic that the BSC was originally intended for. My use of autoethnography can then grapple with both a generalized experience of BSC fandom for a generation of girls and the experience specific to my identity as a queer, feminist media scholar, moving through the moments of a life-course analysis.

"SAY HELLO TO YOUR FRIENDS"

My childhood fandom with the BSC is a well-worn family anecdote and shorthand used to explain my personality.[11] According to my mom, when I first began reading the series, I would repeatedly discuss the latest happenings in Stoneybrook, Connecticut (the fictional location of the series), and the members of the club as if they were real people at a level that toed the line into concerning. Years later, it is still a family joke to say, "You know they're not real, right?" with faux concern when someone animatedly recounts any sort of fictional narrative. This type of negative reception to fannish devotion is common to the fan experience, critiqued as the "fandom as pathology" model even in some of the earliest fan studies scholarship.[12] A pattern in my life began to develop where I would grow invested in a media text and then frustrated when my investment was dismissed culturally or specifically by people in my life, followed by a search for strategies to convey the legitimacy and importance of the media text to others. It took graduate school for me to have the particular language of fan studies to criticize the unmistakably gendered nature of this pattern, wherein texts for girls and women are the ones most routinely dismissed and criticized.[13]

Harrington and Bielby suggest that media fans' life narratives are composed of "complex interactions between our 'real' life (our biography), our autobiography (our storying of our life), and the media texts which help construct, give meaning to, and guide the relationship between the two—and that age along with us."[14] It is clear that that I have made my sincere and deep investment in stories of any medium—books, movies, TV—part of the "story" I tell about myself. The story I tell about my fandom of the BSC can be read as an origin story for my academic profile as a scholar of feminized popular culture, seeking to make space for and legitimize media texts for women. For other girl fans who grow into adults, the story of their gendered experiences with fandom might lead to building lifelong friendships or even parenting philosophies, as chapters by Driessen and Yodovich in this collection explore.

The story of my entrance into the world of the BSC begins in 1996, when I was in the first grade. I acquired the books in three ways. First, they were prominently featured in the Scholastic Book Fair catalog, a staple of 1980s and 1990s middle-class American childhoods. I would strategically mark up the thin, colorful paper, circling more books than I could possibly read as a negotiating tactic for the few I really wanted. The days the Scholastic Book Fair came to my elementary school were a true highlight of my childhood. I nervously carried my own money to school to find the magic of a mini-bookstore sprung up in the gymnasium. My fingers would trail across each book as I debated seriously before making a final decision. Second, growing up relatively lower middle-class with parents who love a good bargain, I spent many early Saturday mornings with my mom hunting through the newspaper classifieds for garage sales. The bulk of my BSC collection is well-loved copies of the original print run, acquired for a dollar or less as I learned how to haggle. Third, and as a last resort, I would get BSC books from the library. I loved the library, but I preferred the books in my permanent possession, where I could reread them whenever I wanted. I trace my current book purchasing rule—a book must be read and then reread with the same level of pleasure before being added to my bookshelf—to the high volume of books I read at that age, making the library a vital testing ground.

Looking Back, Looking Bi 81

There were plenty of books to read: the Baby-Sitters Club is a prolific universe of more than 350 books, including 131 volumes in the original series, along with special collections like extra-long Super Specials (in which the whole club would go on special adventures to camp, Hawaii, and a road trip), the spooky yet still age-appropriate BSC: Mysteries, and spin-off series like BSC: Little Sister about Kristy's precocious little sister Karen, and the California Diaries, a slightly more mature series that follows Dawn and her friends after she moves to California. The series published at least one new book every month from their start in 1986 until 2000. Alongside this steady stream of reading material, there was BSC merchandise (including multiple lines of dolls, a board game, and clothing), a fan club to join, and the TV series and film to watch. I watched the 1990 HBO TV series often as it reaired regularly on the Disney Channel from 1994 to 1997; the theme song, "Say Hello to Your Friends," is still a frequent earworm for me today. The BSC was an ideal fan object for a voracious young reader like myself, providing a seemingly endless amount of stories about my favorite characters.

"SHE IS CLAUDIA KISHI / WE ARE CLAUDIA KISHI"

Claudia Kishi is perhaps the most memorable member of the BSC, known for her bold and eclectic fashion and her treasure trove of a bedroom that served as the club's meeting place.[15] Both were lovingly described in the formulaic introductory chapters of each BSC book, which introduced each character—their personality, their appearance, their clothes. Numerous blogs are devoted to chronicling and re-creating Claudia's fashion exploits, such as the popular late 2000s blog *What Claudia Wore* (WCW), demonstrating the character's enduring style legacy across my generational cohort.[16]

Certainly, Claudia was my favorite BSC member. I remember wishing I could be like Claudia or be her best friend—in retrospect, a common sentiment for nascent queer women. I received my own eighteen-inch Claudia doll from Santa in 1996. She came dressed in an emulation of one of her well-known looks from the first book: a lacy white blouse, purple short overalls, hot pink tights, and purple cowboy boots. I remember being deeply resentful that she did not come with any of my favorite whimsical accessories (lobster earrings, sheep barrettes) and trying to create my own. I was later an avid reader of WCW, and I still consider Claudia a style icon, attempting to inject color and bold elements into my outfits just like her.

Beyond her stylish clothes, Claudia's room is a focal point of her appeal. It is filled with hidden caches of art supplies, Nancy Drew novels, and candy. More important narratively, Claudia's room is the meeting place for the BSC. The dedicated attention to her bedroom makes sense, as girls' media studies scholars have long noted the importance of "bedroom culture" to girls' cultural lives.[17] Although emphasis has often been placed on the active yet consumerist focus of girls' bedroom cultures (e.g., trying on make-up, reading magazines), the BSC is more in line with Mary Celeste Kearney's updated theorization of the bedroom as a productive space. In particular, Kearney notes the incorporation of "productive media technologies" like video cameras and personal computers that have altered how girls use their bedroom spaces from the 1980s and onward.[18] Indeed, it is Claudia's personal landline phone in her bedroom that makes it the ideal space for the club to meet so baby-sitting clients can call to schedule care for their children. The phone is what merits Claudia's designation as vice-president of the club. A private landline was both a necessity for the BSC in a pre–cell phone world and a glamorous luxury for a middle-school girl.

However, beyond Claudia's cool clothes and room, her legacy is cemented by the specific meaningfulness of her Japanese American identity. Her widespread cultural impact as one of the only fully realized Asian American characters in popular culture in the 1980s and 1990s is explored in the 2020 documentary short *The Claudia Kishi Club*. Director Sue Ding's film stresses the importance of representation, figuring Claudia as one of the few bright spots in a bleak cultural landscape of Asians only depicted as background characters and racist clichés. As an Asian girl who doesn't excel academically, Claudia is specifically praised for breaking the stereotype of the "model minority."[19] Throughout the series, Claudia is known as an awful speller—crossed-out words and misspellings litter her handwritten entries that begin each chapter of a BSC book—and her grades are so terrible she is forced to repeat seventh grade. At the same time, she is uniquely creative and aspires to be an artist; many plot lines involve her artistic endeavors. Relatedly, the documentary ties Claudia's iconic and eccentric fashion sense to her racial identity, described by Sarah Kuhn as "tween girl meets Asian auntie."[20] Kuhn and C. B. Lee further identify Claudia's essential coolness by noting that she was the one "everyone wants to be . . . rather than the de facto Asian character" and by describing childhood playground anecdotes of girls arguing over who would get to "be" Claudia in a game of BSC.

Looking Back, Looking Bi 83

For non-Asian readers of the BSC such as myself, Claudia's Japanese identity was notable, yet less poignant. While I can clearly recall details of books that emphasized Claudia's Japanese heritage, particularly her close relationship with her grandmother, Mimi, it was only one facet of many of my favorite character. In fact, when asked about the differences between myself and Claudia as a young reader, I was more likely to note that I was a better speller than anything to do with race. That is to say, Claudia's appeal was so multifaceted that many young white readers like myself adored her and identified with her without realizing the significance of such a nuanced and nonstereotypical portrayal of Asian American identity, opening the door for a normalization of, and even desire for, more diverse stories.

My subjective experience might seemingly argue that Claudia's appeal transcends race. However, the overwhelmingly white world of Stoneybrook places this nuanced characterization of Claudia in a vacuum that provides already limited representations of diversity removed from the actual challenges of prejudice and discrimination that Asian Americans face.[21] Phil Yu comments on this in *The Claudia Kishi Club* documentary and on his blog, *Angry Asian Man*. He notes that issues of racism are rarely addressed in the series, outside of one book, no. 56, *Keep Out, Claudia!*, in which a new family the club baby-sits for is revealed to be racist. Yu further highlights the dissonance between Claudia's relatively racism-free life and the lived experiences of Asian Americans by renaming Claudia-focused books in the series with titles like *Claudia Kishi, Only Asian at This Damn School* and *Claudia Just Realized This Boy Has Yellow Fever*.[22]

The documentary closes by making a case for Claudia's legacy. Ding draws a straight line from her subjects identifying with the character as young readers and thirsting for more Asian representation in media to becoming media professionals who create their own Asian representations. For example, Kuhn is the author of the Heroine Complex series, about a duo of Asian American superheroines, and Lee is the author of the Sidekick Squad, a young adult series with a bisexual Chinese Vietnamese protagonist.[23] Other documentary subjects have continued to engage with the BSC in their professional lives. There is Yu's *Angry Asian Man* blog and Yumi Sakugawa's comic "A Few Important Facts About Claudia Lynn Kishi, Age 13."[24] Gale Galligan writes and illustrates the ongoing graphic novel adaptation of the BSC (2008–present), and Naia Cucukov is an executive producer of Netflix's recent BSC adaptation. These works by Claudia Kishi fans demonstrate yet another "story" for lifelong fans of a feminized media text, as an origin story for their own creative and professional labors.

84 GENERATIONS OF ENDURING FANDOMS

"WE'RE GROWING UP TOGETHER, NEVER TO PART"

The next chapter in the story of my BSC fandom is a reinvigorated interest in the series as I returned to my hometown to begin my PhD studies in 2015.[25] In the moving process, I unearthed my collection of BSC books from my childhood closet and proudly arranged neat rows of pastel spines on the bookshelves in my new apartment. I had already begun doing research on young adult series literature for my master's thesis and was working toward defining myself as a feminist media studies scholar, focusing on popular culture and girls' media. Beyond bookshelf aesthetics, my first deeper reengagement with the fandom was ultimately unsuccessful.

Specifically, I discovered a distaste for the fan podcast *The Baby-Sitters Club Club* (TBSCC). As a fan podcast about the BSC books, TBSCC fits neatly into the genre Lauren Savit labels "episodic TV podcast[s]": podcasts that are dedicated to examining a particular series by engaging with it through episode-by-episode analysis, or in the case of the BSC, book-by-book analysis.[26] Savit suggests episodic TV podcasts like *Gilmore Guys* (2014–2017), for fans of *Gilmore Girls* (WB/The CW, 2000–2007), and *Out on the Lanai* (2014–2019), for fans of *The Golden Girls*, merit further research that considers the effects of the identity politics of the podcast hosts, particularly when they are mismatched to the expected demographics of fans of the original series, and how the hosts' identities might affect the experience of fans of the podcast and the series it discusses.[27] TBSCC is hosted by Tanner Greenring and Jack Shepherd, two adult men discussing a book series written for girls. Beyond this initial mismatch of expected audience/reader identity, the hosts play off each other: Greenring is new to the BSC while Shepherd read his female cousin's collection of BSC books as a boy, given a lack of "better" reading material.

I began listening to TBSCC in 2018; listening to the podcast seemed an ideal reason to begin rereading the series, an idle goal of mine. However, I found myself talking back to the podcast with irritation almost immediately. Shepherd and Greenring approach the BSC with faux pretension, drawing on literary theory to analyze each book. For example, in an early episode, they repeatedly insist that father figures—not any of the women or girls—are the most central theme of the series. This masculinist, albeit playful, perspective was totally foreign to my own reading experiences and those of many fans; there was little to no discussion of what I thought were the most memorable and pertinent aspects of the books that had fostered my deep affective connection. In the moment of listening, I felt a deep

Looking Back, Looking Bi 85

territorial nostalgia and unhappiness that two men had staked what Savit calls a "proto-fannish authority" over a text so entwined with girls' feminine and feminist identity.[28]

In contrast, Suzanne Scott, fellow BSC aca-fan, began listening to the podcast in the summer of 2020, catching up on one or two episodes a day while doing other tasks. She eloquently summed up my discomfort by noting how the dissonance between the BSC, a formulaic book series for young female readers, and the "overly academic and performatively analytical" discussion on the podcast echoes Derek Johnson's arguments surrounding prestige television.[29] Specifically, Johnson finds that prestige television rebrands femininized soap opera conventions through masculine discourses to give them cultural value and legitimacy. Ultimately, Scott views Greenring and Shepherd's deployment of these strategies in the podcast as performative and self-reflexive in a way that is pleasurable for her. Many others obviously feel similarly, as the private Facebook group devoted to fans of TBSCC (Baby Nation, as they call themselves) boasts more than 3,500 members.[30] However, I could not move past my perception of the masculinizing of a text so associated with my girlhood, so I stopped listening to the podcast.

Articulating dissatisfaction with this mode of BSC fandom solidifies and makes more legible my preferred reading: a queering of the text. Eleanor Patterson's work on *The Golden Girls* is a particularly apt framework for this analysis, as she notes the text's emphasis on female solidarity and homosociality. Specifically, Patterson examines *The Golden Girls Live*, an annual holiday drag show in San Francisco that reenacts the Christmas episodes of the TV series. She draws on the work of Charles Acland and Raymond Williams on residual media to explore how a once popular text is imbued with new and different meanings by an audience's continued engagement with it.[31] Reboot culture in some ways disrupts residual media by continually providing new, "canonical" meanings for a text with each iteration. However, residual media is a productive way to understand how the BSC, a girls' book series from the 1990s, can mean many things for different people today: the generative Asian representation of Claudia Kishi, the nerdy and complex theory-making of TBSCC and Baby Nation, or the potential for queer identification in a series focused on girls' homosocial bonds.

My initial exposure to a queer reading of the BSC came from women-centric culture blogs in the early 2010s like *The Hairpin* and *The Toast*. Patterson helpfully distinguishes between queerness and queer reading/queering in her work, defining queering "as a verb [that] refer[s] to the act of interpreting and imbuing media with queer meanings, whether or

FIGURE 2. Coauthor, Megan Connor, and her siblings in Halloween costumes, October 1998. Photo supplied by Connor.

not these meanings were intended by the producers."[32] The writing on the Hairpin and the Toast loosely fits into this definition, approaching the BSC from an adult, feminist lens I found subversive and intriguing. The article "The Baby-Sitters Club: Where Are They Now?" by Emily Weiss was a particular revelation to me, beginning, "Well obviously Kristy is a lesbian."[33] Kristy, consummate tomboy, lover of softball, disinterested in dating, neatly fit into lesbian stereotypes, but this was the first time I had seen it stated plainly in print. I had always identified as Kristy: her bossiness, organizational leadership, and knack for ideas. I even dressed as her for Halloween at age eight, hand-making my own BSC sweatshirt (Figure 2). What did this say about me then? If Kristy was a lesbian, was I queer too?

Although there was certainly not a one-to-one correlation between queering the BSC and my own coming out as bisexual, I found myself collecting evidence of potential queerness in the series and in other favorite media texts, both before and after coming out. To this end, when Ann M. Martin casually came out as a lesbian in the middle of a long profile in 2016 by mentioning her past female partner, it felt hugely significant.[34] Queer women across the internet celebrated the news, feeling a new sense of ownership over a series they already loved and identified with.[35] Martin's queerness gave sharper focus to the sense that there was something queer about the BSC although the text contains no canonically queer characters. Arguably, this queer sense is also informed by a Sedgwickian reading of the close, homosocial bonds of female friendship prioritized by the series.[36] While crushes and boyfriends come and go, the foundation of the BSC is the club and the girls' relationships with each other. To return to Harrington and Bielby, the search to connect the BSC—an essential part of my identity formation as a child—to my adult identity as a queer woman suggests the desire for a cohesive "storying" of my life. In doing this analysis, repeatedly asking myself why the series held such great appeal to me as a child, it was challenging to avoid depicting a smooth narrative trajectory toward my queerness. While queerness is an often studied aspect of fan studies, more scholarship is needed on this relationship between fans' coming-out stories and their fan objects.[37]

I recently rewatched the 1995 film adaptation for the first time as an adult. "All these girls are so gay," I declared with confidence to those watching with me. "Everybody only talks about how Kristy's such a lesbian, but they're all adorable varieties of queer. Claudia's an arty gay, Stacey's high femme fashion gay, Dawn's a granola hippy gay, Mallory's a book nerd gay." Browsing Wikipedia alongside the viewing, I discovered the film's director, Melanie Mayron, is also queer. This viewing felt significant as—rather than looking for evidence of queer potential—I actively performed my own queer reading of the BSC. In that moment, identificatory fan play, my nostalgia, and my queerness all coalesced, incorporated into my continuing story of my life and identity.

" 'CAUSE YOU KNOW THAT YOUR FRIENDS ARE ALWAYS THERE"

The excited conversations about the BSC at the 2019 SCMS finally paid off in July 2020 when Netflix released their adaptation of the series.[38] The adaptation updated the series to the present day (with some shockingly in-style-again 1990s fashion thrown in), cast age-appropriate actors, and retained the sweet, optimistic tone of the books. The series also notably increased the diversity of Stoneybrook: Dawn, who is blond-haired and blue-eyed in the original books, is portrayed by Latina actresses Xochitl Gomez in season one and Kyndra Sanchez in season two, and several adult characters are queer, including Dawn's father and the baby-sitting clients the Johanssens. In addition, one episode finds Mary Anne babysitting Bailey, a trans child, which the members of the BSC roll with matter-of-factly, even correcting adults who misgender Bailey.

In an interview with the Geena Davis Institute on Gender in Media, showrunner Rachel Shukert noted that diversity and inclusion were a priority going into the adaptation, with a goal to create Stoneybrook as an "idealized place [where] . . . things like gender identity don't have to be a story in and of itself."[39] Instead, added director Lucia Aniello, "gender identity [in the world of the show] is that simple: the outside reflects who you feel like on the inside."[40] While media scholars must continually caution against using mediated representations as a satisfactory measuring stick toward equity for POC and LGBTQ communities, watching the adaptation still felt monumental. How satisfying to see my beloved BSC characters rendered with more diversity after years of—consciously and not—hunting for traces of queerness and imagining my own! While reboot culture often demands conversations and close comparisons of changes made between one iteration and the other, Netflix's BSC series felt true in spirit to the original series, the fulfillment of the diverse potential that had drawn readers to the series so many years ago.

The contemporary prevalence of reboot culture has given fans more opportunities to weave their fandom into the continuing storying of their lives. Through an autoethnographic account, I have demonstrated the BSC's particular impact in shaping my life story as a feminist media studies scholar and a queer woman. But for others, like those featured in *The Claudia Kishi Club* documentary, fan stories include creating their own canonical contributions to their fan object. We must continue to look to fans of texts that are marginalized in one way or another (in the case of the BSC, by age and gender) as sites that plant seeds for the future. These fans age and grow into producers of their own stories, that include more and more of the diverse, progressive world they wish to see.

Looking Back, Looking Bi   89

The Man from U.N.C.L.E. Fandom
A COMMUNITY OF COUSINS

Cynthia W. Walker

To celebrate the fiftieth anniversary of the premiere of *The Man from U.N.C.L.E.* (NBC, 1964–1968), a team of fans including Robert Short, who now owns the U.N.C.L.E.'s gull-wing car, and Jon Heitland, who wrote the 1987 behind-the-scenes book, organized "The Golden Anniversary Affair," a weekend of events held in Los Angeles, September 26–27, 2014. Over one hundred fans and over a dozen professionals connected to the series attended a packed schedule of panels, parties, tours, and even a jazz concert of *U.N.C.L.E.*-related music. Awards were presented posthumously to Norman Felton, who conceived and executive produced the series, and Sam Rolfe, who developed it and served as producer during its crucial first season. Both men were represented by family members. Neither of the stars, Robert Vaughn and David McCallum, attended the event, but both sent well wishes. Judging from the comments left by the satisfied attendees on the event's website, a great time was had by all.[1] A month later, the Inner Circle, a Facebook group, was established, a fitting finale to the first half century of *U.N.C.L.E.* fandom.

But *U.N.C.L.E.* wasn't over—far from it. A new feature-length film starring Henry Cavill as American agent Napoleon Solo and Armie Hammer as Russian agent Illya Kuryakin with Hugh Grant as their boss, Alexander Waverly, was on the horizon. The film, directed by Guy Ritchie and written by Lionel Whigham, would be an origin story of Solo and Kuryakin's first mission together, set before the founding of the U.N.C.L.E. organization. After several shifts in release dates, the film was finally scheduled to debut in theaters in August 2015. How would the *U.N.C.L.E.* fandom, one of the oldest media fandoms, react? Would fans who had been focused for so long on the same characters played by the same actors in a single universe accept what was essentially a reboot? The question was of particular interest because appearances of *The Man from U.N.C.L.E.* have been few and far between.

In "A Brief History of Media Fandom," Francesca Coppa points out that although one might debate which is the oldest media fandom, there is no debate that media fandom emerged from the science fiction fan community.[2] It's not surprising, then, that the three media fandoms that vie for the honor of being first appealed to science fiction audiences. They are *Doctor Who*, which first aired in 1963; *Star Trek*, which first aired in 1966, and *The Man from U.N.C.L.E.*, which first aired in 1964. Although it was pitched and often described by the entertainment press as "James Bond for television," *U.N.C.L.E.* actually had as many connections to science fiction and fantasy, in creation and content, as it did to the spy genre.[3] For example, just as Starfleet protects the Federation of Planets in Star Trek and the Time Lords protect the universe in Doctor Who, the United Network Command for Law and Enforcement (U.N.C.L.E.), a multinational top-secret organization, protected the world, defending all nations, without regard to size, importance, or political system.

U.N.C.L.E. was also filled with technology that had a prescient, day-after-tomorrow feel to it.[4] U.N.C.L.E. HQ in New York was a multilevel maze of stainless steel corridors as sleek as a spaceship with banks of flashing computers and whispery sliding doors activated by the triangular badges worn by agents and visitors. When they traveled on their missions or "affairs," the agents "opened Channel D," using personal communicators disguised as pens that bounced transmissions off satellites circling the globe. They were armed with gadgets and advanced weaponry, including the U.N.C.L.E. Special, a modified Walther P38 automatic that could shoot both bullets and sleep darts. The antagonists, usually working for Thrush, had their own arsenal of fantastic weapons, everything from volcano activators to suspended animation devices. The organization was guided by a supercomputer programmed to predict human behavior using algorithms. It's no wonder that *The Man from U.N.C.L.E.* attracted the interest of the science fiction community, including professional writers like Harlan Ellison, who wrote two episodes and polished scripts for several others, and Terry Carr, who went on to edit a line of U.N.C.L.E. paperback novels for Ace Books. Carr, in turn, recruited young sci-fi fan writers like David McDaniel (a friend and housemate of Bjo Trimble, coordinator of the "Save *Star Trek*" campaign) and Robert "Buck" Coulson (husband of sci-fi writer Juanita Coulson), who wrote some of the best and most popular U.N.C.L.E. tie-in novels.[5]

As with Star Trek and Doctor Who, interest in *The Man from U.N.C.L.E.* attracted a loyal and dedicated international and multigenerational fandom. However, when *U.N.C.L.E.* is compared to the other two franchises, there is a notable difference: availability. During the same time period, Doctor Who had two separate runs—the so-called Classic Who (1963–1989) and the New

Who (2005–present)—as well as a 1996 TV movie. The Star Trek canon has been even more robust with eight regular series and thirteen feature films, including the 2009 reboot that featured an alternative timeline with a new, younger cast playing the original crew of the *Enterprise.*

By comparison with Doctor Who and Star Trek, not to mention more modern objects of fan appreciation like Star Wars and Harry Potter, *U.N.C.L.E.* sightings have been exceedingly rare. It is true that at the peak of its popularity, *The Man from U.N.C.L.E.* was telecast in sixty countries and consistently ranked in the top ten programs on US television. Eight feature-length films were made from two-part episodes and profitably released in the United States and Europe. *TV Guide* called it "the mystic cult of millions."[6] Even so, the series ran for only three and a half years. Its success spawned a sister series, *The Girl from U.N.C.L.E.* (NBC, 1966–1967), starring Stefanie Powers and Noel Harrison, but the spin-off only lasted a single season on NBC. After the original series ended abruptly mid-season, it was a decade and a half before a TV movie, *The Return of the Man from U.N.C.L.E: The 15 Years Later Affair,* ran on CBS in spring 1983. Written and produced by Michael Sloan and starring Vaughn and McCallum in their original roles, it was rumored to be a backdoor pilot, but nothing came of it.[7] The next three decades saw a number of attempts to revive *U.N.C.L.E.,* but for various reasons, none came to fruition. Even the long-awaited 2015 feature film has yet to see a sequel. No wonder frustrated fans talk about the "U.N.C.L.E. curse."[8]

How does a fandom survive and even expand over half a century without fresh, new material? Once a new film had finally arrived, could it satisfy older generations of fans while attracting new ones? As this chapter will show, there are a number of factors that have inspired, influenced, and fueled U.N.C.L.E. fandom. Prime among them was the way the original series invited its viewers-turned-enthusiastic-fans to not only watch but participate.[9] This continued with fans contributing to and collaborating with U.N.C.L.E.'s fictional universe and eventually each other.

THE IMMERSIVE EXPERIENCE OF
FIRST-GENERATION FANS

Unlike *Star Trek,* which posted mediocre ratings all through its original run but eventually found a second life in syndicated reruns, *The Man from U.N.C.L.E.* climbed more or less steadily in the ratings until by the second season it was a bona fide hit. An often repeated statistic maintains that Vaughn and McCallum were receiving ten thousand letters a week, more than MGM's historically most popular star, Clark Gable.[10] Even the special U.N.C.L.E. gun received fan mail.[11] One of the obvious appeals of U.N.C.L.E. at the time was that it was so ubiquitous. Not only did its success kick off what *Life* magazine called the "Great Spy Scramble," it was parodied everywhere, from situation comedies like *The Dick Van Dyke Show* to *Tom and Jerry* cartoons to advertising campaigns like "The Man from G.L.A.D."[12]

The U.N.C.L.E. universe bled beyond its own borders into other programming. The actors, masquerading as their characters, traveled the country on publicity tours and popped up in other TV shows and films. In 1965, Illya guest-hosted the popular teen music program *Hullabaloo* (NBC, 1965–1966) and spent the whole program being chased by Thrush, while Napoleon Solo made a blink-of-the-eye appearance in *The Glass Bottom Boat* (Frank Tashlin, 1966), a comedy-thriller starring Doris Day. When an episode of *Please Don't Eat the Daisies* (NBC, 1965–1967) showed the children becoming U.N.C.L.E. fans, Solo and Kuryakin appeared there, too. This led fans to pretend that, like Santa Claus, U.N.C.L.E. could possibly be real. The end credits of every episode included the words: "We wish to thank the United Network Command for Law and Enforcement without whose assistance this program would not be possible." This disclaimer was actually meant to avoid any confusion and possible legal problems with the United Nations, although UN visitors sometimes requested a peek at U.N.C.L.E. HQ anyway.[13]

For younger members of its global audience, the U.N.C.L.E. universe could be immersive. Notably, it was one of the first TV shows to be heavily merchandised.[14] There were hundreds of U.N.C.L.E.-themed items for sale, including games, trading cards, lunch boxes, action figures, Halloween costumes, and school book covers. Fans read paperbacks and comic books and listened to soundtrack albums released by RCA. They discussed U.N.C.L.E. incessantly, not only with friends but with executive producer Norman Felton, who often personally answered letters from fans.[15] Of course, they played U.N.C.L.E. because self-insertion was part of the mystique. Felton had conceptualized the structure of U.N.C.L.E. plots as including an "innocent," an average person (often but not always female) who would be recruited by the agents to provide valuable assistance with their missions. Anyone could be an innocent: teachers, secretaries, housewives, even school-aged children. Many fans preferred to imagine themselves as agents, and that was possible, too. For a $2 membership fee, fans could join U.N.C.L.E.'s Inner Circle, the official fan club, and receive a newsletter, autographed photos, and (most important) an U.N.C.L.E. identification card.

Despite its phenomenal success, for reasons that are still unclear, *U.N.C.L.E.*'s ratings in the fall of 1967 began to plummet. Some have blamed the series' inconsistency in tone from the third season's campy style to the fourth season's more serious approach. Others point to its unfortunate scheduling against two venerable CBS shows, *Gunsmoke* and *The Lucy Show*, that were favored by older audiences (i.e., parents) who often controlled the single household TV set. Or perhaps the craze had simply run its course. *U.N.C.L.E.* was canceled in January 1968, soon followed by other spy shows like *I Spy, Get Smart,* and *The Wild Wild West.* Within a few months, the toys, books, and merchandise had all but disappeared. However, thanks to its fans—which included Lowell Cunningham and Stan Lee, who were inspired to create *Men in Black* and *Agents of S.H.I.E.L.D.*, respectively—U.N.C.L.E. was gone but not forgotten.[16]

CHANNEL D REMAINS OPEN

In 1970, David McDaniel, along with three friends, established the Inner Circle II, followed by the Inner Circle III. Their newsletter, *Communique,* was soon joined by others, including *File Forty* and *For Your Eyes Only.* The first U.N.C.L.E.-themed fan fiction stories began to appear in Star Trek and multifandom zines, eventually leading to the first stand-alone U.N.C.L.E. zine, *The Blue Curtain Affair,* in 1975. A year later, a group of female college-age fans organized themselves as U.N.C.L.E. HQ with a monthly newsletter and annual yearbook. Nevertheless, the 1970s were lean years for the fandom.[17] Because of antiviolence campaigns by the PTA and other parental groups, TV series like *U.N.C.L.E.* that featured explosive action and gunplay were not widely syndicated.[18] Very rarely the three domestically released films might appear on local channels in late night or weekend afternoon programming. At one point, U.N.C.L.E. HQ had just sixteen members.[19]

The next decade saw the beginnings of a comeback. *The Return* TV movie was heavily promoted, with Vaughn and McCallum making appearances on talk shows like *Good Morning America.* U.N.C.L.E. reruns returned to the small screen the following year, airing on local PBS stations and, ironically, on the Christian Broadcasting Network's cable channel (CBN). Fans could record the episodes to watch and trade. They could follow along with *The U.N.C.L.E. Files,* a series of informational magazines written and edited by John Peel and Glenn Magee that were sold in science fiction and fantasy bookshops. In response, U.N.C.L.E. HQ, which had survived the 1970s, decided to hold a convention called Spy Con in the Chicago area. HQ membership increased past one hundred. In the United Kingdom, British fans started to publish their own newsletter, *The Network.*

The late 1980s and early 1990s saw more U.N.C.L.E. sightings, which in turn led to steady growth of the community. On Halloween night in 1986, *The A-Team* took advantage of the presence of Robert Vaughn, who had joined the regular cast, to present "The Say U.N.C.L.E. Affair." Filled with nostalgic callbacks, the episode featured Vaughn and guest star McCallum as ex-partners now turned enemies, a darker version of their relationship on *U.N.C.L.E.* A year later, Heitland's book was published with an introduction by Vaughn, who also hosted an *U.N.C.L.E.* marathon on Channel 61 in Connecticut.

Finally, in 1991, MGM/UA Home Video released twenty-two tapes with forty-four episodes of the show. It was less than half the original 105-episode run of the series, but after a decade of watching fuzzy bootlegs, fans could now own and watch clear, clean copies. Attendance swelled at HQ's Spy Cons, which now featured occasional guest appearances, including Rolfe and Felton. In the United Kingdom, U.N.C.L.E. fans began to meet annually; in the United States, they organized panels and parties at fan conventions. In 1995 at MediaWest Con, held annually in Lansing, Michigan, a group of fans decided to establish an electronic mailing list called Channel D. The list began with ten members and grew steadily over the years. By the time Yahoo! ceased hosting online forums in fall 2019, Channel D had grown to almost a thousand members from all over the world, with an archive of nearly 100,000 posts. As the fandom began to shift from print and face-to-face gatherings to online archives and communities, it expanded into more communities on Yahoo! Groups, LiveJournal, Facebook, and Tumblr, as well as dozens of individual websites devoted wholly or in part to U.N.C.L.E. On Archive of Our Own (AO3), there are over seven hundred stories for the TV series. On Fanfiction.net, *U.N.C.L.E.* is still in the top hundred television series, with over 3,500 entries.

The ebb and flow of U.N.C.L.E. appearances and popularity over five decades are reflected in the results of surveys taken within the fandom. The first formal survey, conducted in late winter 1995, found that U.N.C.L.E. fans could be divided into several cohorts or generations of "cousins."[20] Nearly three quarters of the respondents had watched *U.N.C.L.E.* for the first time during the series' initial run, a cohort the study labeled "First Cousins." In addition, after encounters with reruns, videos, or fan fiction, 13.5 percent became U.N.C.L.E. fans in the 1980s, while 12.5 percent came in during the 1990s. Only 2 percent had managed to come across the series for the first time during those lean years of 1969–1979. The average age of an U.N.C.L.E. fan was thirty-nine. Nineteen years later, a more extensive survey involving three and a half times the number of fans as the first sample found that the First Cousins had increased their numbers to nearly 80 percent of the community.[21] The average age was now fifty-six. Notably, these were not the same individuals who had taken the first survey. Fully half of the respondents in 2014 had joined the fandom after 2000, even though U.N.C.L.E.'s only appearance during that time had been as a boxed DVD set of the complete series plus extras released by Warner Home Video and distributed by Time/Life in 2007.[22]

What has motivated the fans—particularly the First Cousins—to be so fiercely loyal and devoted for so long? In interviews and replies to open-ended questions about what the series has meant to them, fans describe, often in detail, how the show offered them role models and shaped their values and worldview; how it influenced their careers, dreams, and aspirations; and how it brought back memories of youth and nostalgia for a certain idealistic vision of a better world.[23] "I am a better person for my exposure to the UNCLE universe," wrote one fan, "and it prepared me to withstand the latter part of the 1960s and tough times to come." Observed another: "Sometimes I wonder what a 64-year-old woman is doing being involved with this silliness, but I think it's kept me feeling younger than my parents did at my age." These kinds of comments are common, not only among the First Cousins but also among those fans who consider themselves second and even third generation. "My parents were fans and told me about the show before I ever had a chance to see it in syndication. I've written both fan fic and non-fiction work and I re-watch and discuss the series." No matter when they joined the fandom, the overwhelming majority say they are proud of their interest and their community and are happy, even eager, to self-identify as U.N.C.L.E. fans. "My first tattoo was the U.N.C.L.E. logo," one noted, and another revealed, "I still carry my gold U.N.C.L.E. I.D. card in my wallet." No doubt, he is not the only one.

THE ILLYA FACTOR

Despite the enthusiasm, loyalty, and memories that most U.N.C.L.E. fans share, there is one factor that influences what attracted them to U.N.C.L.E. in the first place and what activities might be pursued as part of the fan experience. That factor is gender. When asked in 1996 why they liked U.N.C.L.E., 66 percent of the female fans said that it was the characters and the actors who played them. This is in contrast to male fans, who offered a range of answers including nostalgia for 1960s television, a fondness for spy stories, and an appreciation of the style, gadgets, and overall concept of the show. This gender difference has remained consistent over the years. In 2014, 78 percent of the female fans chose the main characters and the actors who played them, and in 2020, it was 65 percent. In the surveys, the replies of male fans were distributed mostly among the other choices.

There is also a difference between male and female fans in their choice of favorite character. Most male fans favor Napoleon Solo over Illya Kuryakin or say they like both agents equally. With female fans, an overwhelming majority choose Illya Kuryakin. This has been tempered in more recent surveys by a growing group of female fans who favor the two equally. That so many female fans favor Illya is no surprise. During the original run of the series, Illya was the breakout character, much like Spock was on *Star Trek*.[24] Indeed, in 1997, Stephanie Schorow coined the phrase "the Illya Factor" for any time a co-star becomes more popular than the star.[25] Highly intelligent, emotionally distant, but physically adept, the Russian agent became a sex symbol—the so-called Blond Beatle. McCallum was consequently mobbed by teenage girls everywhere he went and constantly profiled in entertainment magazines.[26]

This preference for the characters over other aspects of the show has meant that female fans focus their efforts on different activities than male fans. The 1996 survey found that while male and female fans took the same initial steps in exploring the series, their paths diverged when it came to activities and involvement. All fans wanted to, in some way, "possess" their favorite show (see Henry Jenkins's concept of "poaching"), but male fans did so by researching facts and information connected to U.N.C.L.E. and collecting memorabilia, including props, guns, furniture, and even the car used in the series.[27] Female fans collected U.N.C.L.E. memorabilia, but their efforts were focused on re-creating the series through fan fiction and later videos. This has held true over the years, and with few exceptions nearly all U.N.C.L.E. fan fiction has been written by women. In 2014, fully half of the male fans said they had never read fan fiction, while 61 percent of female fans read it often or all the time. A number of female fans, particularly younger ones who were born after the series' initial run, say they were recruited into the fandom primarily through fan fiction and fan videos.

What has changed is how fans interact with each other. Of those responding to the community survey in 1996, 73 percent were women, and

27 percent were men. At that time, online connections were limited to the U.N.C.L.E. discussion lists housed on Yahoo! Groups, which were (with one exception) moderated by women. Women fans also reported having more face-to-face fan friends: 27 percent had twelve or more, while nearly half the male fans reported not having any. Almost two decades later, with the demise of print zines and newsletters and the fading of in-person fan conventions, face-to-face fan friends had dropped from an average of eight to three with only small differences between male and female fans. These days, regular meet-ups for U.N.C.L.E. fans are pretty much over. Spy Con ended in 1998 with the U.N.C.L.E. HQ newsletter ceasing nine years later. The long-running MediaWest Con ended 2018, and the Arundel Affair, held annually by UK fans since 1997, met for their last weekend in 2019.

The main interaction in U.N.C.L.E. fandom has shifted to Facebook, particularly on the Inner Circle, which lists almost five thousand members. Like other Facebook groups and pages, this community is moderated by male fans. As a result, the current gender ratio has nearly equalized, with 52 percent reporting female, 46 percent male, and 2 percent nonbinary or undetermined.[28] Several LiveJournal communities still survive, chiefly for fan fiction writers and readers, both gen and slash. These are predominantly, if not exclusively, populated by women fans, a mix of First Cousins and those who encountered the original series in some form after its initial run.

BUT IS IT U.N.C.L.E.?

In August 2015, several dozen fans got together in Burbank, California, to attend an evening screening of the new Guy Ritchie–directed feature film. The project had followed a long, complicated path to the screen with budget cuts and revolving casts and production teams. The original release date of January 2015 was delayed by Warner Bros. until August in hopes of attracting a late summer audience. The U.N.C.L.E. movie received mixed to good reviews from critics and audiences, but it only managed to earn $109.8 million worldwide with a budget of $75 million.[29] As a prequel and a reboot, the film filled in Solo and Kuryakin's back stories, complicating and darkening the characters. As an international thief working for the CIA, Henry Cavill's Solo was still smooth, suave, and urbane. However, Armie Hammer's Illya, now a KGB spy from a disgraced family, repressed an explosive temper under his boyish exterior. Not so incidentally, he was much taller and more physically formidable than McCallum's character had been. Still, more than one critic noted the film's overall style and 1960s vibe.[30] A fan-edited video on YouTube compared the film and the TV versions side by side, showing the various callbacks scattered throughout the film.[31]

In the 2014 survey a year before the film premiered, U.N.C.L.E. fans revealed their feelings toward the project. While a third said they dreaded it or expected to be disappointed, 60 percent of respondents were hopeful, even optimistic. The remaining fans were neutral, content with at least owning the complete series on DVD. Male fans were considerably more enthusiastic than female fans. After the film's release, only 5 percent said they hated the film while 11 percent refused to even see it. On the positive side, 43 percent enjoyed it, recognizing the details that linked it to the original series. Nearly as many, however, said that while the film was a well-done and entertaining spy romp, without the organization, the communicators, Thrush, and especially the easy-going friendship between the partners, it wasn't really U.N.C.L.E. Surprisingly, female fans liked it better than male fans by a ratio of 50 percent to 37 percent. The reason may be that the women, used to fan fiction, accepted the film as simply another interpretation of Solo and Kuryakin's partnership. The film featured a strong female presence, an innocent named Gaby (Alicia Vikander), who serves as a love interest for Illya and is recruited as an agent by the end of the film. A number of long-time fans said they hope the film might attract more new or younger fans as the rare appearances of U.N.C.L.E. had done previously. Unfortunately, judging by the fan pages on Tumblr dedicated to Cavill, Hammer, and the 2015 film (including interestingly enough, young Russian fans), there does not seem to be too much link-up between the new film fans and the older, established community.

One point that almost everyone seems to agree on is that there should be a sequel. The frustration, expressed in comments from Twitter to YouTube, has been palpable. For a time, Armie Hammer, who became something of a fan himself, also pushed for it.[32] Unfortunately, in early 2021, allegations against Hammer for physical and emotional abuse and sexual assault of several women began to appear in the media. The controversy led to the Los Angeles Police Department opening an investigation in March 2021, and Hammer was subsequently cut from several film projects and dropped by his agent and publicist.[33] Once again, fans whispered about the "U.N.C.L.E. curse."[34]

Of course, a sequel could still be filmed with Henry Cavill and someone else playing Illya. Or perhaps an entirely new project with a different cast might find success on cable or a streaming service. If any new effort contained more recognizable elements, like the New York headquarters, the communicators, and Thrush villains, it might provide the older community and the newest generation of cousins with more in common. Right now, the relationship is, as one fan described it, like two branches of the same tree. Will the branches ever grow toward one another and ultimately intertwine? Considering that it took fifteen years after the end of the original series before a movie was made, another twenty-four years before a DVD set was released, and still another eight years after that for a feature film, anything is possible. After all, if the several generations of U.N.C.L.E. fandom have anything in common, it's that they know how to wait.

Fans of Female Film Stars in Turkey
THE CASE OF TÜRKAN ŞORAY

Yektanurşin Duyan

Why Türkan Şoray? Why does an eighteen-year-old woman tattoo an image of Türkan Şoray on her arm? Why is an eighty-year-old man still archiving Türkan Şoray photos? Fans are the most important element of stardom in Turkish cinema. Some writers in Turkey believe that a star's immortality depends on his or her fans; a celebrity's stardom dies with these fans. Do fans make a star timeless and immortal? This study investigates the transgenerational qualities of the fan base of a seventy-five-year-old female movie star who has not acted for twenty years yet remains a timeless star of Turkish cinema.

Although Türkan Şoray first appeared on the big screen in *Köyde Bir Kız Sevdim* (Türker İnanoğlu, 1960), the first sparkle of her stardom emerged with *Aşk Rüzgarı* (Nevzat Pesen, 1961). When lead actor Göksel Arsoy's character chose Suna Uslu over the dark-featured Şoray, the audience reacted by shouting, "Choose the brunette! Choose the one with black hair!" It seems that the audience felt that Şoray deserved to be both the protagonist and star of the movie. Şoray thereafter became the protagonist of most of her movies. So began her climb to stardom.

"Yeşilçam" refers to not only a period of time (1960–1989) but also a system of film production and a narrative, star-driven cinema at that time. The golden years of Yeşilçam were between 1960 and 1975. The Yeşilçam film production system has four dynamics: regional film management (*Bölge işletmeciliği*) (production), movie theaters (distribution), producers (screening), and audience/fan and stars (consumption), the common goal of the previous three. If a producer wants to show a film in a big theater, they must get an advance from the regional film manager for that film. To support the film being made, the regional film manager wants a specific star to play in that film. Stars have to work with producers who have connections with important movie theaters to reach a large audience. As you can see, these dynamics are interconnected, and the focus is on the audience/ fans and the stars.

The poor economic conditions and strict rules of Turkish cinema in the Yeşilçam period challenged most of the producers, filmmakers, and actors to lead huge protests against the film industry. Despite the inhospitable climate, Şoray became the highest-earning actress in Turkey, with top billing in more movies than any other actress at the time. Her fans' seemingly endless love, protection, and support distinguished Şoray and her rise to stardom. She became the first female star to emerge in Turkish cinema through having been chosen by her audience.

After 1990, Şoray started to appear on TV series rather than in feature films. Although she did not appear on the big screen for about seventeen years before her most recent movie, *Suna* (2007), her fans never gave up on her. In 2010, they organized on social media and began meeting periodically with Şoray. This study uses an interpretive phenomenological analytic research method to investigate Şoray's fandom through interviews and archived materials. Before starting this study, I attended and took notes on a Türkan Şoray fan meeting in Istanbul on September 28, 2018. Based on their demographics, Şoray's fans are quite heterogeneous by age. There is also a significant difference between the actress's age, seventy-five, and the mean age of her fans, thirty.

This study concentrates on film stars' fandom, looking at the case of Şoray, and investigates the question of whether Şoray's fans are transgenerational or multigenerational.

THE FANS OF FILM STARS IN TURKEY

The beginning of Turkey's fan culture can be found in letters written by readers to certain newspapers and magazines. The era of Yeşilçam cinema saw Turkish films produced exclusively from box office revenue. A particularly successful film meant that additional, similar films could be made. As a result, the audience of this time was "spoiled" by having their preferences perpetually catered to.[1] Because Yeşilçam cinema was made with the audience in mind, it was from these audiences that film studios derived their power and money.[2] For audiences, going to the cinema was more than just watching a movie. They often chose a movie solely for the actors in it. Part of being a cinemagoer meant being a fan of a certain star. Audiences watched their favorite star's movies, consumed all available information about them, and often reached out in hopes of a personal connection with the object of their fascination. The most important means of communication were cine-magazines; apart from helping establish and develop Turkish cinema culture, these magazines shaped Turkish fandom.[3] The contents and writers of cine-magazines functioned as bridges between the stars and their fans.

According to Dilek Kaya-Mutlu, the star-fan relationship existed in a framework of imaginary social relations, essentially functioning as a means to social intimacy with otherwise unobtainable stars.[4] Of particular interest is Kaya-Mutlu's notion that fans, instead of trying to escape into the glamorous world inhabited by stars, tried to bring these stars into their homes.[5] To test this relation, called "bringing home," she examines fan letters published in popular film magazines.[6] In a follow-up study, she confirmed that fans did attempt to bring the glamorous stars into their own more modest worlds. Note that the word *home* does not primarily refer to a physical space fixed in space and time but to an imaginary space in a continuous process of becoming.[7] In other words, fans brought stars into their own fantasy worlds.

To tighten the bond fans felt with stars, *Ses* magazine organized the "Your Favorite Star on the Phone" event. Every fifteen days, fortunate fans got to speak on the phone with a star; the magazine later published the conversation. Fans asked stars about every detail of their lives, from private matters to their relationships with other stars. *Ses* followed up these successful contests with the 1968 "Your Favorite Star in Your Home" event, which brought stars into some lucky fans' homes for a visit. Cine-magazines provided an intimacy and emotion that films could not, making stars accessible to their fans and transforming parasocial interactions into parasocial relationships. Despite Donald Horton and R. Richard Wohl's definition of parasocial relation, it is often more two-sided than it appears, because fans can often speak and interact with stars.[8] Cine-magazines literally bridged the gap by bringing stars into fans' homes, weddings, and broader lives.

Cine-magazines of the Yeşilçam period functioned as the first bridges between film stars and their fans. In this sense, we can say that Turkish fan culture originated during this time. These magazines allowed audiences to experience film stars more intimately than their larger-than-life silver screen images allowed. Magazines reflected emotions and feelings that films could not. The screen only presents the star as an image to fans, whereas magazines allow the audience to touch, hear, and even eat with them. These activities are different and stronger than the emotions given by the films. Although fans may identify with a character in movies, magazines allow fans to share something "in reality" with a star. By arranging phone conversations, home visits, and Christmas gift exchanges, cine-magazines brought the stars down to Earth; they appeared more "real."

Fans of Female Film Stars in Turkey 103

The Yeşilçam period began to wane in 1990, eventually leading to the collapse of the Turkish star system. Movie stardom changed, though the most famous Yeşilçam stars maintained their celebrity status.[9] The advent of television, the internet, and social media fundamentally changed the star-fan dynamic, precipitating a shift to a new generation of fan activities and the emergence of a new generation of fans.

As internet access proliferated in the late 1990s, online fan communities became steadily more popular. The spread of social media further encouraged this trend. In bringing people together through new media, this innovation played an important role in film stars' fandoms. Fans used social media to find and interact with others like themselves, bringing together people who were otherwise disconnected.

TURKISH CINEMA'S TIMELESS STAR: TÜRKAN ŞORAY

Since the 1960s, Şoray has been one of the most influential female movie stars in Turkish cinema. In addition to her nearly ubiquitous presence in Turkish films, especially as a leading actor in Yeşilçam melodramas, her representation as a Turkish woman in public media (television and press) constituted a complementary offscreen persona. This section examines Şoray's image and the response to this image from her transgenerational fans.

As the "sultana of Turkish cinema," Şoray was cast as the honorable virgin or faithful woman in her films, which through the 1960s and 1970s were mostly love stories. She was a woman with whom everybody could fall in love, and many tried to imitate her. According to Agah Özgüç, Şoray became a fetish, piquing the interest of audiences through her puerile, feminine roles.[10] According to Serpil Kırel, Şoray became famous for two reasons: her acting and her swarthiness. In the period of black and white films, a good female character was always swarthy.[11] Seçil Büker notes that Şoray satisfied a latent audience desire for a relatable, Middle Eastern, rural face on the big screen.[12] Similarly, sociologist Nilüfer Göle notes that Şoray possessed a beauty "special to those lands," an *alaturca* beauty.[13]

Şoray's star image is reflected in her fans' letters. Kaya-Mutlu's research into letters published in cine-magazines has revealed that many audience members did not perceive Yeşilçam stars as untouchable elites but more like friends and family. Many letters address the star in familial terms, like sister/brother or *yenge* (a brother's or friend's wife) and were often similarly signed. This changed in later generations; no one calls Şoray *yenge* or sister anymore, but she is still considered a member of her fans' families.

Although she is now referred to as Türkan Hanım (Mrs. Türkan) or Türkan, her fans' feelings toward her and the way she has been positioned in their lives indicate that she remains a family member. She is an archetype: the missing mother, the unattainable lover, and so on. New generations of her fans say that she is a "part of our family."

Şoray herself has said that, over the years, she has tried not to leave a single letter from her audience unanswered. She recognizes many of these letters from the shape of the envelopes and their penmanship. She keeps most of these letters, although today's social media channels have replaced them. The audience shares their feelings for her there, and she becomes happy as she reads the messages. Even so, she still has fans who haven't stopped sending letters. She explains this love from her fans: "The love given by the audience is the most valuable award. . . . I can only meet with my audience at galas, festivals, and special nights or events. This is the most meaningful award for me. In these ceremonies, while introducing me onstage, they used to say: 'The crownless queen of cinema wearing an invisible crown from the love of the audience.'"[14] She remains the first name that comes to mind when Turkish audiences are asked to name the brightest star of Turkish cinema. She is timeless, and through their admiration, fans share in her success.

THE FANS OF TÜRKAN ŞORAY

After the Yeşilçam period, Şoray transitioned to television and did not appear in a feature film for nearly seventeen years. After the 1990s, Turkey's film production system changed dramatically. The popularity of Yeşilçam stars waned. In Şoray's case, this was primarily because she had not received a film offer suitable for her star image. The other, broader reason is that commercial cinema showcased TV celebrities while arthouse cinema employed unknown actors. Despite these setbacks, Şoray's fandom did not decrease. Instead, her fans grew in number.

In 2010, Şoray's fan base organized a series of events. Six people, who define themselves as the core fan group, met frequently and became friends at events organized for Şoray. Metin Şamdan, known as *Şoraykolik* (the addict of Şoray), has a very large archive of Şoray memorabilia. Şamdan and Şoray met during the 1970s. He was an artist who painted Şoray's portrait and presented it to her at the Altın Kelebek (Golden Butterfly) award ceremony in 1974. Şoray liked the painting, so he has continued painting for her and gives one to her at every award ceremony. Thus began a friendly relationship between them. Şoray receives her pictures, news about her, and magazine coverage that she needs from Şamdan because he has a huge archive. This close interaction has continued over the years.

After each of Şoray's events, always attended by most of the fan group, Şamdan arranges a gathering with Şoray. He has become a sort of gatekeeper between Şoray and her fans. They eventually decided to organize these meetings, modeling them on events similar to those for pop singers Gülben Ergen and Demet Akalın. The first of these fan meetings took place at Şoray's home in 2015, then at a café, and then at a hotel. Now Şoray regularly meets with her fans under Şamdan's organizational control. Şamdan also invites fans who reach out to him through social media, thus gaining influence among the fandom as the first point of contact for someone who wants to reach Şoray. He claims that Şoray gives her fans love and that this, combined with her humility, is what makes her special.

The venue of the most recent fan meeting was the Kavacık Limak Hotel in Istanbul on September 28, 2018. Şoray described this gathering as a "love meeting" because she does not accept the word *fan*. She stated, "These are people who love me. They do not admire me; they just love me. So they are not my fans; they are dear friends."

Examining the demographics of the fan meeting in 2018 reveals that this community is surprisingly heterogeneous. Although Şoray was seventy-five years old at the time, the average age of her fans is thirty. This disparity marks her as a transgenerational star with transgenerational fans. A mother and daughter, both avid fans, attended the meeting together. The love for Şoray passes from generation to generation. Older fans tend to be archivists and, having spent more time as a fan, seem more passionate than her younger fans. Some such older fans may define their feelings for Şoray as passion, some recognize it as an obsession, and others may recognize their feelings as love. In any case, all admit that she is important to their lives.

There are archivists among the younger fans as well. One spent nearly all his money obtaining some of Şoray's personal belongings, such as photographs. Fans in this younger demographic reveal that they share postcards, photographs, posters, and more from their collections among themselves. From these fans' social media accounts, it is apparent that they often engage in friendly competitions of who has the largest archive or is the biggest fan.

The relationship between fans and their idol could be interpreted as becoming lost in the melodramatic narrative of the star's public life as presented by various forms of media, such as interviews, articles, gossip, and the films themselves. Fans may thus sympathize, empathize, or even

TABLE 1. The number of followers and fan pages of film stars in Turkey

	Türkan Şoray	Fatma Girik	Filiz Akın	Hülya Koçyiğit
Followers of Instagram account	572,000	N/A	386,000	167,000
Fan pages on Instagram	52[a]	8[b]	5[c]	2[d]
Followers of Facebook account	N/A	80,303	9,207	10,483
Fan pages on Facebook	58[e]	8[f]	15[g]	12[h]
Followers of Twitter account	N/A	1,824	N/A	N/A
Fan accounts on Twitter	23[i]	N/A	1[j]	6[k]

[a]The most popular page has 18,800 followers.
[b]The most popular page has 27,200 followers.
[c]The most popular page has 2,075 followers.
[d]The most popular page has 18,800 followers.
[e]The most popular page has 9,600 followers.
[f]The most popular page has 4,000 followers.
[g]The most popular page has 1,500 followers.
[h]The most popular page has 1,500 followers.
[i]The most popular account has 13,095 followers.
[j]The most popular account has 346 followers.
[k]The most popular account has eight followers.

identify with the star.[15] Analysis of the fans' social media accounts can be instrumental in better understanding how their relationships with stars affect their everyday lives (see Table 1).

Lucy Bennett notes that through social media, public figures can speak directly to their fanbase without news or management filters, revealing "intimate" information and creating a sense of authenticity with frequent updates on their daily lives.[16] Some even directly respond to fan messages. The richness of fan creativity is on full display in the form of songs, artwork, and fiction, with the internet and social media circulating these works more easily and quickly than ever before. Communication with other fans has always been an important aspect of fandom. The internet and social media allow for further development and fragmentation of such fan communities.

Fans of Female Film Stars in Turkey 107

Social media has a particularly strong effect on some online forums, with members connecting via platforms like Facebook, Twitter, Tumblr, and Instagram to communicate and share news.[17]

Fans of movie stars use social media effectively in Turkey. Şoray's fans go to all the events that she attends by organizing on social media and WhatsApp groups. To join these groups, fans must reach out to existing group members and to those who are perceived as her biggest fans, creating an entrenched community and often instigating power struggles. Şoray's fan community has written about and sometimes interviewed her, showing that sharing these works on one's social media accounts garners prestige in the community. There is even competition among fans who claim that Şoray prefers those whose content she shares and upvotes. Even so, her fans discover an identity through their fandom. By posting pictures with Şoray on social media and sharing feedback, they win a place in the fan community and associate themselves with her success.

For the fans who have never seen Şoray in person, their first reaction on meeting her is often a surprised, "She saw me!" When asked about her magic, fans cite her humility and resemblance to them as middle-class people. This explains why fan impressions often emphasize traits and lifestyles that resonate with their own experiences, ideals, dreams, and desires. This strengthens their emotional attachment to the star as a "genuine person." Through ongoing introjection and projection, fans come to feel they intimately know the star.[18] They closely follow the star's career and life choices, likening it to the arc of a fictional character in an ongoing melodramatic narrative.[19] This feeling of personally knowing a celebrity—including their private thoughts, feelings, and lifestyle—can become strong enough to elicit feelings of personal friendship or love.

For some of Şoray's fans, the love that is lacking from their parents is instead found from her. According to her fans, Şoray's love replaces missing love; some even liken it to the love of nature—the more you care about a plant, the more it will flourish. Likewise, if you give attention to Şoray, she will give you love in return.

Sibel, a young fan, explains what this love means to her: "My mother is jealous of my fandom for Türkan Şoray. I would do anything for her. She embraces everyone. She hugs her sweaty fans. She is not like other actors and actresses. Her motherhood and relationship with her daughter are very beautiful. Loving a person unrequitedly is the most beautiful and special love."[20] Yağız Yılmaz, who is eighteen years old, explains what Şoray means to him: "Beyond being a famous movie star, it was her sincerity, sacrifice, and innocence that struck me. A love like that cannot even be found from one's mother and father! Türkan Şoray became a shelter for me, a port! Şoray is the troubling partner of my long nights, a napkin that wipes away my tears on sleepless evenings."[21] Burak and Hasan are both twenty-five-year-old men who have romantic feelings for Şoray's characters.[22] Burak loves Azize from the film *Karagözlüm* (*My Black-Eyed*, Atif Yilmaz, 1970) for her natural beauty. Hasan loves Leyla from the movie *Tatlı Meleğim* (*My Sweet Angel*, Mehmet Dinler, 1970) because of her femininity. Both want partners who resemble Azize and Leyla, projecting their desires onto these characters as readily available objects of love. Şoray's physical appearance and public persona closely match their idealized woman; their impression of her personality is a projection of their own unfulfilled desires and hopes, essentially reflecting their image of an ideal, everyday romantic relationship. Their parasocial relationship with Şoray is cathartic in that it is not constant but develops and recedes as a direct psychological response to their real-life relations with women.

Most of Şoray's fans of various ages describe their feelings toward her as love, explaining it as receiving attention from the person they love or admire. Once a fan feels that she notices them, they feel as if they should pay more attention to her as well. In fact, this definition of love invokes the double meaning of "chasing dreams": following the person they admire and following their own dreams.

Even Şoray's perfume is a point recognized by her fans, who explain that once you inhale her fragrance, you become addicted. There is peace and happiness in her scent, doubly so when combined with her eyes and voice. These descriptions evoke a kind of addiction and a way of getting closer to Şoray. Her fans claim that their relationship with her is different from typical fandom because they believe there is an unresolved bond between them. Their fandom is romantic love, passion, motherly love, and sometimes even sexual love.

One female fan believes that there is a difference between the men and women who admire Şoray. "Male fans say that Türkan Şoray is their love, but we women fans call her Mrs. Türkan. We prefer addressing her formally. The fandom of a woman for a woman espouses love without jealousy. A woman can learn everything from Şoray; she is a role model. The fandom of men for a woman is different because their love includes sexuality; ours does not."[23] Yet most male fans express that their admiration is a sublime love that precludes sexuality. They believe that theirs is an asexual relationship, although they do not stop calling her "my love." In this relationship between

Fans of Female Film Stars in Turkey 109

fan and star, most fans—male and female—prefer to hide their sexual desire for her. There could be many reasons for this, including rejection of homosexuality or a desire to not cheapen the love they feel for Şoray with base sexuality. Whatever the reasons, they prefer to disassociate their love for her from references to age, sex, gender, and sexuality. They believe that she embraces endless compassion, mercy, and love. They may use their love for her and the love they feel from her as a substitute for a lack of love in their lives. Şoray herself even states that the love she feels from her fans helps compensate for the love she lacks in her own life.

Fans often compete over the questions "Who is the biggest Türkan Şoray fan?" and "Who is closest to her?" Such fandom also involves intracommunity competition, which can escalate to the formation of archrivals. For example, fans like Şamdan collect everything they can get their hands on, essentially transforming their homes into museums. A star's personal belongings not only bring the collector closer to their idol but act as a badge of honor in the fan community. These fans often see these personal archives as their most precious treasures, partly because of the prestige they grant among other fans. The extensiveness of their collection indicates the sincerity of their fandom.

There also exist important collectors among Şoray fans. According to them, some who call themselves Şoray fans are actually just Yeşilçam fans; real Şoray fans live their whole lives just for her. Fans claim there is a difference between being a Şoray fan and being a Yeşilçam fan. This distinction helps fuel their desire to collect their star's memorabilia; when a fan sees something related to Şoray, the desire is to add it to their collection. When asked why they collect everything they can, their answer is twofold: love for her and competition with other fans. They have an ambition that everything belonging to Şoray should be theirs.

In the fan club, Ulvi Cemil Sulaoğlu is considered the oldest Şoray fan. He is sixty-eight and describes himself as having been her fan for six decades. Sulaoğlu has collected photos, posters, newspaper articles, and books about Şoray over the years, eventually opening an exhibition with all of his materials. Yağız Yılmaz is the youngest member of the club. He opened his Şoray exhibition at only sixteen years old. Age does not affect the attitude and behavior of fans toward each other. They say that what binds them together is their love for Şoray. There is thus no age-based respect or mentoring relationship among fans. When young fans compare themselves to their older counterparts, they claim to be bigger fans because of their posters and photo collections. They don't take age into account, though they may not realize that the contents of their archives are drawn from earlier generations. Fans of various ages interact across the generational gap; this is what makes Şoray's fans transgenerational, not multigenerational.

Archiving and collecting are one of the most important elements allowing transmission of Şoray's fandom from generation to generation. Collecting has an economic and an amorous dimension. The prices of the memorabilia purchased by fans and collectors increase daily, and the most expensive movie posters and photographs in bookshops are of Şoray. In other words, Şoray—who had the highest box office yields during the Yeşilçam period—retains her high-earner status in terms of her merchandise. This is an important indicator of her longevity as a transgenerational movie star and in classifying her fans as transgenerational. In addition to their admiration and collections, her fans suspend her in her glory years, rendering her timeless.

CONCLUSION

When we look at Şoray's transgenerational fandom in Turkey, we see two core drivers: the transfer of the fandom across generations and a strong emotional attachment to Şoray. The first driver represents the preservation of value. In Turkish culture, the family heirloom is left as a legacy to the person who will value it. Şoray is seen by her fans as a legacy passed down from generation to generation. Fans are the intermediaries who carry Turkish cinema from the past into the future. They also immortalize their favorite stars, preserving them for future generations.

Second, her fans display an immense emotional attachment to Şoray. It is commonly presumed that one's stardom ends when one's last fan dies. The timelessness of Şoray's stardom is seen in the agelessness of her fan base. Some may truly be in love with her—the notion is not as absurd as it may seem, as romance and sexuality are likely what initially caught her fans' interest. Nonetheless, they usually insist that their love for her is spiritual, not sexual. Şoray fills several emotional gaps in her fans' lives, including motherly love and a desire for beauty, fame, and creative expression. In the end, the most important reason for her fans' devotion is that Şoray is the ideal woman in their eyes.

Fans of Female Film Stars in Turkey III

"I Named My Daughter Ripley"

FAN GIFTING AND INTERNAL HIERARCHIES IN THE ALIEN FANDOM

Janelle Vermaak-Griessel

There is, in the *Alien* scholarship, a strange absence of work on audience. Given the recent growth of reception studies and the way in which acknowledged audience demands for more instalments have kept Ripley and the Aliens alive— indeed, have brought about their resurrection from the dead—this seems odd.[1]

The experience of being a fan is based on an emotional or intellectual connection between the viewer and the text that encourages the individual to explore their engagement with the specific object of interest.[2] In the case of the Alien film franchise, this connection is created by the fans being introduced to the films at a young age, often by an older sibling or parent: "in the course of everyday interactions with significant others, the authoritative positioning of the parent can be used to heavily influence momentary and future actions of the child."[3]

Limited research on fan gifting, self-perception, and hierarchies in the Alien film franchise has been conducted, which explains the rationale behind this chapter. Studies on fandom in the Alien film universe consist of work by Pamela Church-Gibson, Martin Barker et al., and myself.[4]

The purpose of this chapter is to explore the transition, or gifting, of the Alien fandom from one person (the fan) to another person (the nonfan). This gifting often takes place through friendships or familial relationships, and this study focuses on the connection between the film franchise and its fandom. The Alien franchise has been in existence since 1979, which means that its fandom consists of different generations of fans who wish to share their love for the films with their siblings, children, or friends. The connection between the film franchise and its fandom, which consists of different generations, is the locus of the study. The reason that fans of the Alien franchise were chosen (and not just anyone who liked the films) was because this study focuses on fan gifting and fan hierarchies and identity. If someone simply enjoyed the films and was not a fan, there would be less chance that this person would share their fandom with someone. This study is also focused on the exploration of fan identity and fan hierarchies and how Alien fans self-identify differently than more mainstream fandoms.

RESEARCH METHODOLOGY

Fans of the Alien franchise are able to construct their own reality and knowledge regarding their experiences and identity. Through this lens, fan gifting, identity, self-perception, and internal hierarchies are analyzed to understand generational fandom in the Alien film universe. The principal methodology is qualitative, and the specific texts are analyzed through textual analysis. The methods used to generate and collect data were online focus groups administered through a Facebook group interaction and online surveys conducted with Google Forms and Survey Monkey. These data generation methods were chosen because they were found to be the most appropriate means of discovering elements that reflected fans' relationship with the franchise and their opinions around their fan identities. The content and meaning of the texts were also analyzed, and they were deconstructed to understand how they created meaning. The first part of this study consisted of two online focus groups through Facebook, with specific focus on the fans of the selected online fora or Facebook pages.

I hope to identify how fans of the Alien franchise share their fandom and develop hierarchies to create new fans and new knowledge around this specific fandom. In this way, Alien fans' institutionalized knowledge, language, and representations can be analyzed to understand their current gifting and hierarchy practices and enable researchers to possibly set new practices into play.

The primary purpose for choosing the internet as the tool for data gathering is that it allowed me to witness communication between fans and observe meaning being created through interaction.

The selection of the Alien franchise, which encompasses the science fiction and horror genres (also known as speculative fiction) would mean tapping into the fan base that these genres tend to attract, and there appears to be little research that indicates that Alien fans have been analyzed in terms of their willingness to share their fandom, as well as self-identifying into hierarchies. Science fiction and horror tend to attract loyal, engaged fans.

For ease of reference, the responses have been coded according to the data collection method, with the participant number added:

"I Named My Daughter Ripley" 113

- Facebook Alien Franchise Fandom PhD Study Group—FGP
- Survey Monkey Questionnaires 1 and 2—SM1 and SM2
- Google Forms Questionnaire—GF

GIVING THE GIFT OF ALIEN

The practice of fan gifting "occurs within fan communities where elements of fan cultural production are circulated and exchanged between fans like gifts."[5] Fan gifting runs against the general discourse regarding competitive "othering" in inter-fan relations, as discussed by Mark Jancovich and Nathan Hunt, Leora Hadas, and Rebecca Williams.[6] Fan gifting is not controlled by aspects such as knowledge or level of participation.[7] Instead, it is an example of an activity that surpasses hierarchical or power levels.[8] Hellekson defines fan gifting as an exchange that is made up of three elements: "to give, to receive, and to reciprocate . . . the tension and negotiation between the three result in fan creation of social relationships that are constructed voluntarily on the basis of a shared interest, [such as a film franchise or] fandom itself."[9]

The Alien franchise, according to the respondents, has many lifelong fans. Many of them were introduced to the Alien films through an older family member or friend, such as a cousin, parent, older sibling, or grandparent. Barker et al. echo these responses, stating that "the significance of the Alien viewing is intensified when attached to a memory event shared with a close friend or family member."[10] The respondents were exposed to the fandom of their family members, which was passed down to them and which could possibly be passed down to the respondents' children; this could be theorized as heirloom fandom. Barker et al.'s study on Alien audiences echoes these results, as the viewing is a "generational experience," in which the experience of watching is more important than the film itself: "It is this sharing of the filmic experience—the packaging of Alien as a filmic rite of passage—that [we] categorize as a distinctive and significant fannish activity surrounding the film. For many of [our] participants, the introduction of Alien itself was an integral part of the viewing experience."[11]

These responses speak to "the possibility that one's fandom might be constructed by significant others and then unconsciously adopted as though it is an inherent component of one."[12] The respondents in this study speak of their most memorable moments regarding their first Alien film viewing, and they were introduced to at least one of the films from the franchise at a relatively young age—between the ages of eight and fifteen. This film acted as a "hook" (FGP33) into the Alien film universe. The first film, *Alien* (Ridley Scott, 1979), gave one of the participants nightmares; the film was frightening but also fascinating, and more exciting than scary, according to this respondent. The film kept another participant on the edge of their seat, "trying to discern more details of the monster, marveling at the set/costume detailing, or just awe-struck by the sheer beauty of the film" (FGP02). *Aliens* (James Cameron, 1986) "totally blew my mind" (FGP01), and *Alien 3* (David Fincher, 1992) was "dark, beautiful and poetic with a fantastic score" (FGP15).

Examples of respondents' exposure to a film include illicit viewing at a friend's house or being exposed to part of the Alien extended universe by viewing an image from the film that appeared in a book or magazine or as part of a cartoon. The Alien comics from Dark Horse or the Kenner toys could have acted as a bridge into the fandom. The film franchise entered the respondents' lives when they were young and has had a lasting effect on them: "*Alien* is unlike other horror cinema, possessing an unspecified factor—a 'something'—that makes it stand out, and implying that this might be connected to a visceral impulse: of it getting under [respondents'] skin."[13] For some respondents, they can relate life experiences to the films, and the franchise has become part of their own "life mythology" (FGP29). Media (and in this case, films) "are largely seen as channeling memories and funneling history rather than as involved in the construction of our lifeworlds."[14] We can link our memories with media to specific moments in our lives. The lasting impact of the Alien films on respondents and the way they have incorporated the films and their fandom into their lives are indicative of how cinema and popular culture have a place in people's everyday lives, through life stages, memories, and life narratives.

Watching one of the Alien films for the first time as a child could arguably be terrifying and could cause nightmares. However, one could overcome this fear to deal with life and watch the films again, each time being less afraid. The respondents experienced an adrenaline rush as fear set in, and their reactions to the films evolved from being frightened to being fascinated and enthralled by the creature and its life cycle, as well as experiencing a deep admiration for H. R. Giger's artwork and his contribution to the Alien universe. These responses indicate that there is a performative cultural elevation of the fan object. The fear factor of the films was attractive and possibly a rite of passage, as it "forced" respondents to confront their fears: "I was a kid when *Aliens* came out, I saw it by accident and it scared the living shit out of me. But as with all things scary, I always have to overcome the fear, so I forced myself to rewatch it" (FGP32). These rites of passage

"I Named My Daughter Ripley" 115

can be likened to Roger Aden's symbolic pilgrimages and promised lands in that "we create our own symbolic promised lands as a means of making sense out of the disorientations—material and otherwise—we routinely experience. . . . Our personal promised lands can . . . encourage a spiritual sense of communion with others and offer a transcendent perspective of the cultural terrain."[15] It could be theorized that Alien fans feel a "sense of communion" with others because they have all experienced and overcome the fear of their first Alien experience, which links them to each other.

FAN IDENTITY

According to the respondents, fans devote their time and money to their fandom, allowing it to become part of their lives and lifestyles. A fan is an "enthusiastic devotee" (GF14), someone who is emotionally invested in their fandom. Should this person spend a disproportionately higher amount of time and money on their fandom, they are considered to be a "bigger" fan. Sandvoss defines fandom as "the regular, emotionally involved consumption of a given popular narrative or text."[16] It is interesting to note that his definition does not imply any form of fan community.

The respondents believe that the level of knowledge, insights, and invested research one puts into understanding the theories within the franchise are important. Jenkins states that knowledge of films (what he calls spoilers) can be compared to prestige, reputation, and power.[17] The more knowledge fans have regarding the franchise, the more influential and authoritative they are perceived to be. These are "fans who seek to explain their fan culture to and for itself, and who also criticize and analyze the media industry. These . . . fans are . . . very knowledgeable, and . . . committed to accumulating further fan knowledge."[18] A fan, according to the respondents, needs to enjoy introducing their fandom to others and sharing their love for their fandom and fandom object. However, a fan does not need to "love" all the films in the franchise. Commonly, a fan will have a least favorite, a favorite, and perhaps a movie that they feel compromises the franchise: "In the case of the *Alien* series, oftentimes *Alien: Resurrection* and *Alien 3* are seen as inferior to the first two films, but people still consider them canon, for now anyway" (FGP09). These responses can be linked to Wilson's in that fans are emotionally committed to their fandom, and it can be theorized that fans are prone to love their first Alien film experience, regardless of whether the film is accepted into the fandom canon.[19] Newer fans initially exposed to the less popular films may need to defend their choices to older fans. Jenkins also mentions that popular culture is shaped by emotional intensification, which is evident in the responses gathered here.[20]

FAN LEVELS IN THE ALIEN FANDOM

When asked how important the Alien fandom was in their lives, the respondents of the Survey Monkey survey were clearly divided between three opinions: very important, semi-important, and not important. Of the responses, 43 percent described their fandom as being very important in their lives, 43 percent as being semi-important, and 14 percent as not being important. The respondents of the Google Forms survey were split between stating that their fandom was "very important" to them (43 percent) and "somewhat important" to them (46 percent). Eleven percent of respondents indicated that their Alien fandom was not at all important to them, and one respondent stated that their fandom was both very and somewhat important to them.

The respondents who stated that their fandom was "very important" can be theorized as "high-level" fans. Those who said their fandom was somewhat important to them can be theorized as "mid-level" fans, and those who stated that their fandom was not important can be theorized as "low-level" fans.[21]

These levels echo Barker et al.'s account "that the most committed audiences are the ones who work hardest to remember, make sense, make comparisons and connections across films, and examine their own reactions to the film [or franchise]."[22] These results link to Bourdieu's work on the "habitus," in that these fandom levels are based on "the principle of division into logical classes which organize the perception of the social world."[23] The works of Grossberg and Brower can also be linked to the responses regarding fan identity.[24]

TYPES OF FANDOM

The respondents described two types of film fandoms, which link to Hills's work on the differences between consumers and fans, and they indicated there is a difference between the "forms of expertise and knowledge" each group has.[25] De Certeau speaks of taste distinctions, which can be applied to these two types of film fandoms and can be theorized as follows:

1. Fast-Burner: These fandoms start up fast and hard over a short period, only appealing to part of one generation, have a single strong

"I Named My Daughter Ripley" 117

core theme, but are generally limited in scope. These fandoms are highly commercialized. The fast-burner film fandoms usually appeal to younger audiences and have preestablished followings through books or comics on which the films are based. Targeted and extensively aggressive marketing approaches administered through various online channels and social media platforms further help develop fast-burning film fandoms. Fast-burner fandom can be linked to Grossberg's popular culture audiences, the "cultural dopes who passively consume the texts of popular culture," and Hills's "consumers."[26]

2. Slow-Burner: These film fandoms grow slowly over many years and appeal to different parts of successive generations. The slow-burner fandoms can be linked to Grossberg's popular culture audiences "who actively appropriate the texts of specific popular cultures, and give them new and original significance," and Hills's "fans."[27] Slow-burner fandoms allow for a broad scope and often offer more adult/complex themes.

The Alien franchise fandom, according to the respondents, is definitely a slow-burner, as it has been in existence since 1979 and has an expansive and growing fan base attracted by its mysteriousness, provoking open-endedness, and various thematic elements in the films: "*Alien*'s plot is traditional for the sci-fi/horror genre, but its concerns are contemporary—it focuses on feminism, anti-institutional individualism, ecology, and technology—and its success may be attributable to this combination."[28] While the first film is over forty years old, the issues raised in the films are still relevant, and fans of the franchise can link film themes to issues in society today. Each Alien franchise movie is a different genre, and three were by different directors, allowing for the franchise to attract a diverse fanbase. These fans, according to the respondents, are primarily fans of the Alien films, but due to their diversity, they are usually fans of other film franchises as well.

Respondents who discussed fast-burner film fandoms indicated that there is a devaluing of other fandoms based on age. This perception and discrimination on age is highly problematic and fits in with Bourdieu's work on why fans of film franchises such as Twilight are dismissed and stereotyped according to their gender or age. Comments that the noted examples fit into the fast-burner category demonstrate that these respondents are othering and stereotyping other franchises in an attempt to bolster the value and uniqueness of their chosen fandom. Busse speaks on fan "border policing," which is the act of "protecting one's sense of fan community and ascribing positive values to it while trying to exclude others."[29]

Other highly commercialized fandoms, such as Star Wars, have also persisted across generations and many years. The respondents are constructing meaning that needs to be challenged and critiqued, as they are positioning themselves via an art-versus-commerce binary that is homologous to enduring-versus-faddish. The Alien franchise is and has always been commercial, so the fan distinction is highly problematic. Also, "fad" fandom could be a code for devalued and negatively stereotyped fandom from which the Alien fandom disassociates. These responses are indicative of a discourse of "enduring" pop culture as art (slow-burner, cult fandoms) versus pop culture as commerce (fast-burner fandoms). The fast burn (commercialized) versus slow burn (noncommercialized art) binary valorizes the fan object and the Alien franchise. Alien fans see their franchise and themselves as superior to other fans, as smarter, more intellectual, and "deeper" (a word used by several respondents). It can be theorized that if "art" tends to be slow burner, perhaps it has a more cross-generational appeal and can have more staying power in the individual fan's life.

ALIEN AND THE FEMALE FAN

Some respondents stated that fans of the Alien franchise are diverse with regard to race and sexuality but that there is a stigma attached to being a fan of the Alien films, particularly regarding female fans. Busse states that "when women act according to stereotype, their behaviors get dismissed as feminine; when they act against stereotype, their behaviors get dismissed as aberrant or get reinscribed negatively as feminine nevertheless."[30] According to the respondents, it is "not feminine" (FGP17, male) to be a fan of the Alien films. It is interesting that a male-identified fan stated this, as it could be theorized that he sees "feminine" fandom as something negative. He wants to celebrate Alien and Ripley because she is physical, muscular, and a high-ranking officer, features usually associated with the male lead in a movie. It can also be theorized that perhaps male fans are reclaiming Alien as a masculine fandom, despite its woman-centered story.

The respondents feel that Ripley is not sexually objectified and subjected to the male gaze as is typically the case in action and sci-fi films. One female participant stated that she "wouldn't be surprised at meeting a female [Alien] fan" (FGP05), but that she "encountered some stigma attached to [being an Alien fan]." Two male participants stated that they would not be surprised by

"I Named My Daughter Ripley" 119

meeting female fans. The female respondent said she finds that "people are surprised at female [Alien] fans" (FGP05). She understands that stereotypes such as "space is for men" and "women don't enjoy sci-fi" (FGP05) are still prevalent. She further stated that she has often been told that she doesn't look like an Alien fan and that "apparently I should exchange my stilettos for combat boots and shave my hair," referring to Sigourney Weaver's look in *Alien 3* (FGP05). The female respondents' answers link with Cherry's work on female fans of horror films and how some women watch horror films as an act of defiance.[31] One male participant stated that "horror is not a women's genre" (FGP27). Barker et al.'s study indicates that fans of Alien "are certainly more likely to be male."[32] However, some participants believe that the Alien fandom is "balanced" (FGP02, male) according to gender, as more women are playing Alien-related computer and console games and the fandom appeals to all genders on different levels. It could be theorized that as the franchise has evolved, fans' perceptions have changed. Fans' own identities beyond gender, such as age and race, might be connected to their perception of fan gender.

The respondents perceived fans of the franchise as primarily older men, more mature, more in control of their emotions, less obsessive (though very devout), more relatable, resistant to stereotyping, and able to be fans of multiple fandoms in comparison to fans of other franchises. These responses echo Busse's work on fandom and gender, in that "at every level of dismissal gender plays a central part. . . [and]. . . gender discrimination occurs on the level of the fan, the fan activity, and the fannish investment."[33] The strong female lead should suggest an appeal to female fans, but the respondents did not engage with that at all.

Busse examines the gender bias that pervades much cultural conversation surrounding fan discourses and links her analysis to Hills's concept of "interfandom stereotyping."[34] She points out that Twilight fans "are ridiculed in ways fans of more male-oriented series are not."[35] Respondents believe that gender discrimination is mostly aimed at female fans, and their fan interests are easily mocked. Hinerman critiques the stereotype of women/female fans as somehow more vulnerable to the effects of fandom because of stereotypes surrounding their emotional behavior.[36] This corresponds to respondents who stated that the Alien fandom is for intelligent, deep, serious fans, excluding the stereotypical hysterical female fan. Gender relations play a pivotal role in the Alien films, specifically in the depiction of a female lead (Ripley) and the significant role assigned to the Alien Queen as Other. One way of expanding the discursive formation to other franchises

120 GENERATIONS OF ENDURING FANDOMS

would be to focus on the feminist subtext underpinning the Alien franchise. Slack's notion of "cultural acupuncture" is apposite in this regard: "a conscious rhetorical strategy mapping fictional content worlds onto real-world concerns."[37] Ripley is seen as an embodiment of a nonconformist type of femininity and as such could serve as a symbol of transforming patriarchal assumption and stereotypes of what femininity entails.

In this regard, see the following remark by Maloney:

> Weaver's portrayal of Ellen Ripley, the warrant officer who uses massive guns and major smarts in order to triumph over a seemingly endless parade of giant, terrifying, body-snatching aliens, was and continues to be a major leap for science fiction. It subverted gender roles in a stunningly logical fashion—by casting a mostly gender-neutral role with an actor who just happens to be a woman—and proved beyond doubt that women could play beleaguered, tough-as-nails action heroes just as men had for decades.[38]

Perhaps this has to do with the date of the film and the connection to generations—of the films, of the fans, and of feminism. More recent action movies with female leads have emphasized femininity and sexuality in a postfeminist way.

CONCLUSION

It is important to note how my respondents drew on stereotypes and how these stereotypes are and are not challenged. The respondents in this study have already stereotyped other fandoms without any critical reflexivity but deny there is any pattern to their own fandom. This behavior can be described as "inter-fandom," which Hills defines as "relationships between different media fandoms, whereby one fan culture defines itself against and negatively stereotypes another."[39] How and why are these respondents critical of stereotypes? When they do draw on these stereotypes nonreflexively, it is crucial to understand why. Presumably, a discourse of diversity creates a sense of Alien fandom as eclectic and discerning. One needs to ask why these respondents would be invested in a "nonstereotype stereotype" of their own fandom. Perhaps this works to downplay any notion of subcultural conformity. Subcultures rarely position themselves discursively as conformist or inauthentic, as they will always construct their own authenticity.

"I Named My Daughter Ripley" 121

There is a powerful connection between the Alien franchise and its fandom, especially when examined from a generational standpoint. Alien is passed down through generations, and the films have had a lasting impact on fans. Returning to the title of this chapter, there is something beyond an individual fan showing their love for Alien by naming their child after the main character. Now, whether the child likes it or not or fully understands, she is also part of that generational fan legacy.

"The Power of the Jane Austen Fandom"

BRIDGING GENERATIONAL GAPS WITH
THE LIZZIE BENNET DIARIES

Meredith Dabek

Although she received little recognition and praise for her work during her lifetime, Jane Austen is now considered "a commercial phenomenon and a cultural figure" whose literary accomplishments are consistently ranked among the best in English literature.[1] Austen has become so ubiquitous in contemporary pop culture that fans can find her likeness on everything from T-shirts and greeting cards to a 10£ bank note.[2] Most Austen scholars agree that the 1870 publication of James Edward Austen-Leigh's *Memoir of Jane Austen* helped spark what Johnson calls "Janeiteism" or "the self-consciously idolatrous enthusiasm for 'Jane' and every detail relative to her."[3] Austen's influence extends into the field of adaptation, with one of the earliest transformations of her novel debuting in 1895 as a stage show based on *Pride and Prejudice*.[4] In the years since, Janeites have had an abundance of adaptations to choose from, varying from the faithful (1995's *Pride and Prejudice* mini-series) to the more creative and interpretive (2016's *Pride and Prejudice and Zombies*, for instance).

Adaptations of Austen's novels have occurred with such "stunning frequency" in the twentieth and twenty-first centuries that it is "increasingly possible to gain exposure to [Austen's] plots and characters not through her novels, but through other media."[5] This chapter explores the Janeite fan community through the lens of a print-first/screen-first dichotomy, where generational divides coalesce not around age but around a fan's first encounter with Austen: print (text) format or screen (film/television) format. Moreover, as later sections will show, it is possible that Austen screen adaptations can serve as what Leitch calls "entry-level adaptations" or gateways to the source material, prompting screen-first Janeites to discover the novels for the first time and encouraging print-first Janeites to rediscover a longtime favorite.[6]

GENERATIONS OF JANEITES

While we trace the origins of the Austen fandom to the eighteenth century and Austen-Leigh's biography, Devoney Looser highlights one specific adaptation for "single-handedly transform[ing] Austen's cultural stock" and renewing Austen fervor among Janeites in the late twentieth century: Andrew Davies's 1995 six-part mini-series of *Pride and Prejudice* for the BBC.[7] The now famous (and entirely noncanonical) scene in which Colin Firth's Darcy jumps into a lake at Pemberley triggered a wave of "Darcymania" among Austen's female fans. The release of Joe Wright's 2005 *Pride and Prejudice* adaptation stirred up tense debates in the Janeite fan community, as Janeites endlessly debate who is the "best" Darcy, Firth or Matthew Macfadyen.[8] Of course, Janeites discuss more than which actor is the best Darcy. Fandom topics can include queries such as: should Austen's novels be considered social commentary or romance? Does Austen reveal herself as liberal or conservative through her writing? Which underappreciated heroine deserves more attention, Fanny Price or Catherine Morland? Even as they unite over a shared love of Austen and her novels, Luetkenhaus and Weinstein propose: "Among fans there is never going to be an agreement on which novel is best, which heroine most dear, or which hero most appealing because . . . Austen and her works mean different things to different people."[9] Prominent Austen scholar Juliet McMaster suggests this is because many Janeites "want to think of Jane Austen as their special private friend," while Claire Harman contends that Austen's legacy is ultimately one that is "so intimately connected with our sense of ourselves."[10]

For many Janeites, their personal feelings about how and when they became an Austen fan help shape their sense of generational belonging. Harrington and Bielby point out that "popular media are . . . thoroughly implicated in life course processes and transitions" while "media texts and technologies help unite cohorts, [and] define generations and cross-generational differences."[11] Bolin argues that "many people can probably testify about the moment at which they discovered a cherished artist, film star, or novel that would make a lasting imprint on their lives."[12] These "generational media experiences" act as "a structuring element in how fans establish and maintain a sense of generational belonging" through their fandom.[13] Many Janeites can recall their first introduction to Austen, whether it came in childhood or adulthood, from reading one of her novels or viewing a specific film or television adaptation. Bolin contends that these "smaller, much more personal events" can have a powerful, resonant "impact that can be revived and returned to later in life."[14] Furthermore, while these generational media experiences "more generally create a specific personal bond between the admirer and the cherished object," Bolin suggests that "some experiences will also extend between generations and can thus be the basis for inter-generational shared experience."[15]

Given that "at least one new Austen screen adaptation has appeared in every decade" since the early 1990s and that "Austen fans are continually reviving old or finding new ways to interact with each other," we could therefore organize the Janeite community into different groups not based on sociological or demographic characteristics, but rather different "media generations," as proposed by Bolin.[16] A print-first generation of Janeites who discovered Austen in text format may develop based on discussions of the author's writing style or clever use of free indirect discourse. In contrast, a screen-first generation, whose members first encounter Austen through a screen adaptation, might form around comparisons of character portrayals or visual appeal. Despite their differences, the two generations are nevertheless linked by a transgenerational love for and appreciation of Austen.

DIGITAL AUSTEN: *THE LIZZIE BENNET DIARIES*

One specific adaptation of *Pride and Prejudice* combined elements of text and audiovisual content by offering Austen fans a new kind of experience: *The Lizzie Bennet Diaries* (LBD), a contemporary version of the story told through YouTube videos, Twitter feeds, and Tumblr posts where fans could "talk" to Lizzie on Twitter, pin and share Jane's fashion photo sets on Pinterest, and comment on Lydia's vlogs. With its modern updates, clever use of social media, and additions to the *Pride and Prejudice* story, LBD introduced new fans to Austen while enabling longtime fans to rediscover a favorite author. Consequently, LBD serves as "entry-level adaptation" that "makes prescriptive cultural touchstones widely accessible."[17] As this chapter shows, both print-first and screen-first Janeites enjoyed and appreciated LBD, which helped bridge the gap between different generations of Austen fans by providing a shared, common experience.

Initially released in real time through biweekly vlogs in 2012 and 2013, LBD centered on modern-day graduate student Lizzie Bennet's YouTube channel. Her videos offered an ongoing narration of her life and provided details of different events as they occurred, such as her first encounter with William Darcy or her trip to VidCon.[18] Beyond YouTube, LBD had multiple accounts on different social media platforms. These accounts enabled fans to participate in the narrative by sharing the content with friends, conversing with fictional characters, and creating original fan art.[19] These opportunities for engagement helped drive the development of a specific LBD fandom, a subset of the larger Janeite fandom where print-first fans and screen-first fans came together to enjoy this multimedia adaptation. LBD also coincided with the two hundredth anniversary of *Pride and Prejudice*'s publication: the January 2013 celebration of Austen's best-loved novel took place while Lizzie's stay at Pemberley Digital unfolded on social media.[20]

Linda Hutcheon asserts that adaptations "have an overt and defining relationship to prior texts" and that "recognition and remembrance [of the prior text] are part of the pleasure of experiencing an adaptation."[21] LBD enabled fans to remember Austen's novel and previous adaptations by offering "digital breadcrumbs" or little hints and nods to well-known plot points in *Pride and Prejudice*. These breadcrumbs foreshadowed events that had not yet occurred or provided alternative perspectives on events discussed in Lizzie's videos. In early April 2012, for example, the characters Bing Lee, Caroline Lee, and Darcy exchanged messages on Twitter, which indicated they were attending a party of some kind:

> @bingliest: @wmdarcy put your phone down and go dance with somebody.
> @wmdarcy: @bingliest not likely.
> @that_caroline: @wmdarcy nice catch! #awkward
> @bingliest: @wmdarcy I take it back. you should definitely stay off the dance floor.[22]

The tweets imply that Darcy danced with someone rather unsuccessfully. A week later, LBD provided additional context when Lizzie shared via her vlog that she was at the same party and was the person involved in "the most awkward dance ever" with Darcy.[23] Although reading the Twitter conversation was not necessary to understand or enjoy Lizzie's video, doing so added extra meaning for Janeites already familiar with *Pride and Prejudice*. Fans of Austen's novel likely would have recognized Lizzie and Darcy's dance as their infamous first meeting, which is a crucial part of the narrative and vital to the development of their relationship. Screen-first fans, meanwhile, could compare Lizzie's biased re-creation of the first meeting with Darcy's tweets, thereby gaining a more complete sense of the events than the ones provided by the video or Twitter exchange alone.

As other chapters in this volume illustrate, adaptations do not merely retell a story but translate the original material into "something new" to "fit new times and different places" while retaining a link to the source text.[24] In addition, Leitch explains that entry-level adaptations eschew strict fidelity to the source material and instead "involve numberless choices concerning which elements of [the] story . . . to be faithful to."[25] Accordingly, LBD co-creators Bernie Su and Hank Green "strongly felt that [LBD] needed to have other races in our series to accurately represent our setting of contemporary America," which resulted in updating Austen's Charles and Caroline Bingley into Asian American siblings Bing and Caroline Lee, while Lizzie's good friend Charlotte Lucas was reimagined as Charlotte Lu.[26] LBD also included an openly gay character, Fitz Williams. According to Su, Fitz's sexual orientation was primarily about incorporating into the narrative "a guy . . . that wasn't a 'romantic/pairing' interest to any of the women" while simultaneously furthering LBD's accurate presentation of contemporary America.[27]

LBD's connections with and references to *Pride and Prejudice* were an important part of the reading and viewing experience for many Janeites, including both print-first and screen-first fans. This theme emerged from a survey of LBD readers and fans conducted over four weeks in fall 2017. The mixed methods survey, which I created and administered, asked LBD fans to reflect on their individual narrative experiences with Lizzie's story. Three hundred sixty-one people completed the survey, 95.5 percent of whom identified as female (2.5 percent identified as male and 2 percent identified as gender-fluid or nonbinary).[28] The majority of respondents (46 percent) were between the ages of twenty-five and thirty-four, and 33 percent were between eighteen and twenty-four years. The thirty-five to forty-four years category accounted for 12 percent of respondents, and the forty-five years and older category totaled 9 percent. The dominance of female respondents generally aligns with the broader Janeite fandom. Meanwhile, the age breakdown and preponderance of younger respondents was likely due in part to my recruitment of participants from an LBD fan group on Facebook and the use of snowball sampling methods through the social media networks of LBD's production team.[29]

The print-first and the screen-first generations of Janeites include fans of all ages, as the survey results show that age was not a significant factor in categorizing the survey respondents. There were roughly equal numbers of print-first fans and screen-first fans in each age bracket. In addition, age did not appear to determine a survey respondent's enjoyment of Austen's novel or LBD and its social media components.[30] There were some small differences worth noting. Older respondents (thirty-five and older) were more likely to have read Austen's novel before viewing LBD and describe themselves as "extremely familiar" with the story. Meanwhile, the younger respondents (those between eighteen and thirty-four) were more likely to indicate that their experience with LBD motivated them to reread *Pride and Prejudice* and that some degree of participation was "extremely" or "very" important to their individual narrative experience. One aspect that transcended the various generational divides was the pleasure many participants found in LBD because of their appreciation for Austen's novel, with nearly all (97 percent) of the survey respondents indicating they had read *Pride and Prejudice* at some point. One fan commented that LBD was an opportunity to "watch my favorite book unfold in real time." Another fan said the LBD story "was both real and new and yet still familiar." As these comments suggest, many Janeites felt that LBD helped fans "unlock a lot of Austen's social commentary" and "increase the accessibility of the story." LBD achieved this through updates and creative interpretations of the Bennet family's financial circumstances, Charlotte's acceptance of Mr. Collins, and Lydia's scandal.

Financial Instability and Student Loans

In episode 19 of LBD, Lizzie struggles to stay awake as she relates the tale of going grocery shopping with her mother at four o'clock in the morning because Mrs. Bennet "decided she doesn't want any of the neighbors to see us using coupons."[31] Later in the video, Lizzie mentions overhearing her parents talk "about a second mortgage and the falling value of the house" before confessing "there's a reason we all still live at home and Jane isn't paying back her student loans." These glimpses into the Bennet family's financial troubles and Lizzie's mentions of her "mountain of student loans" provided a contemporary update of Austen and helped LBD fans identify with Lizzie. One survey respondent explained that "it's easier to relate to a girl trying to get a degree and struggling with what she's going to do with the rest of her life" because *Pride and Prejudice*'s theme of marrying for financial security does not hold the same importance in the twenty-first century. Another fan pointed out that LBD's Lizzie felt more recognizable because "it's more of a leap to say that I identify with a woman from a few hundred years ago than to say that I identify with a grad student paying back her student loans." In transforming "nineteenth-century female disinheritance" into the "cultural anxieties of emerging adulthood in a looming recession," LBD offered

Janeites characters that "were relatable and tangible in a way the original novel wasn't," with one survey participant suggesting that "Elizabeth Bennet felt like a novel character; Lizzie could be a real person."[32]

From Marriage of Convenience to Business Partnership

For many contemporary Janeites, LBD proved particularly helpful in understanding Austen's relevance, especially when it came to the character of Charlotte Lucas/Charlotte Lu. In *Pride and Prejudice*, Charlotte decides to marry Mr. Collins, a man she does not love and does not know very well, "making a clear choice for financial security over romance."[33] This choice can be confusing to twenty-first-century readers who have other options for independence and self-sufficiency. LBD addressed this confusion by having its version of Mr. Collins propose a business partnership and offer Charlotte a job. By reworking Austen's plot to better reflect contemporary trends and social mores, LBD "made it a bit easier to relate" to Charlotte and "added depth to the understanding of the original character and [her] choices," according to one survey respondent. Similarly, another LBD fan maintained that "taking a job that might not be your dream in order to afford taking care of yourself and your family is absolutely something many people can relate with today."

Furthermore, LBD's use of multiple social media accounts allowed Charlotte to "speak" for herself through her Twitter feed and Tumblr blog. Doing so, one fan said, provided the secondary characters with "opportunities to speak about their background and goals," which enabled fans to "draw [their] own conclusions about the characters." For another Janeite, LBD gave her "a deeper appreciation for characters [like Charlotte] that [she] didn't totally love" when first reading *Pride and Prejudice*. With the updates to Charlotte's specific narrative, LBD took a plot point that one survey participant claimed "always felt crazy in the book" and transformed it into a modern equivalent that "made it easier [for readers] to connect with *Pride and Prejudice*."

The Redemption of Lydia Bennet

LBD's depiction of Lydia, Lizzie's younger sister, was perhaps the most significant departure from Austen's novel while also being the clearest expansion of the *Pride and Prejudice* plot. The book describes Lydia as "self-willed and careless . . . ignorant, idle, and vain" but does not provide many details or insight into her thoughts or feelings.[34] In contrast, LBD reimagined Lydia as a more complex and complicated person. She retained the bubbly and energetic nature of her print counterpart, but thanks to her own Twitter feed and YouTube channel, fans also saw her grow and evolve as her vulnerabilities emerged. As one fan observed, "you could understand why Lydia fell for Wickham a lot better" thanks to her videos and tweets, which "added a layer of credibility" to the story. Another Janeite explained that the expansion of Lydia's character "allowed you to reach beyond what we know as canon and further interpret who the characters are and what their motivations might be." The updates to Lydia's story provided readers with content that was not present in Austen's novel, thereby creating an enhanced experience of LBD and contributing to the rich corpus of *Pride and Prejudice* adaptations, continuations, and retellings. Moreover, Lydia's plotline was incredibly popular with LBD fans. LBD co-creator Hank Green confirmed that the writers expanded Lydia's role in the narrative "entirely . . . due to viewers' reaction to her."[35] Although readers did not have any influence over the course of events in Austen's novel, LBD presented fans with an opportunity to at least partially help shape the narrative. As a result, Janeites "got to see things that didn't happen on the page in *Pride and Prejudice*," according to one fan, and another declared that LBD "was the first adaptation I'd seen that made me think about Lydia differently, and question Austen's judgements."

THE SYNERGY OF PRINT AND DIGITAL

LBD transformed Austen's static text into a dynamic text with which fans could engage, providing new avenues for Janeites to "react and interact with their favorite stories and characters as time processes and societal and cultural norms shift and grow."[36] One fan reported that she felt like she "was no longer a reader or audience member, but part of one of my very favorite stories in a way I never was before." Another fan specifically pointed to Lydia's expanded role as evidence that LBD benefited from "draw[ing] on the enthusiastic Jane Austen fan base" since her "arc was changed due to the love given to her character by myself and others."[37] LBD became, as one fan described it, "a safe space to re-discover a classic and find many people who were fans of Austen and bond with those who had not read her works before."

Unlike previous works, LBD did not fit neatly into the screen adaptation category, nor did it exist as a solely print adaptation. It was both—a hybrid of digital media and analogue literature—making it the ideal middle ground for screen-first and print-first Janeites. One print-first fan explained that "re-reading *Pride and Prejudice* after watching LBD made me appreciate LBD creators and Jane Austen's original characters even more . . . [because] LBD provided more insight into each individual character." Another print-first fan said, "rereading the novel is a . . . comforting thing for bedtime" while LBD "surprised me time after time, keeping me fully invested even though I actually knew . . . how the overall plot would have to go." Meanwhile, among the screen-first survey participants who had not read *Pride and Prejudice* before their experience with LBD, all but one (nine out of ten) said LBD motivated them to read the book for the first time. For these screen-first fans, LBD served as an "entry-level adaptation" by "assuming the elements that make a book a classic can be made available to viewers who have limited interest or ability to enjoy the book itself."[38] LBD became a gateway into Austen's novels, using the digital to complement and supplement the analogue. One screen-first fan confessed that "when I first attempted to read *Pride and Prejudice*, I found the language too hard to understand, so I gave up." After watching LBD, however, she tried again: "knowing the plot of what was happening helped me get into the language a lot easier and I finished the book in two days."

LBD's relative success in helping print-first Janeites reconnect and screen-first Janeites connect with Austen's novels arose from two seemingly contradictory factors. First, in adapting *Pride and Prejudice*, LBD strove to focus on the "universal elements" that capture "something of the literary classic's quite distinct units of cultural capital."[39] At its core, LBD told the familiar story of first impressions, misconceptions, and two people coming together after learning and growing. One fan explained that "Austen's original story has a lot of excellent social criticism," and LBD "handled many of these issues well, in their modern forms." Another fan pointed out that LBD "helped boil down the essential parts of the story [and] why it's remained a classic" before sharing that "LBD helped me identify why the story still managed to resonate with me." In updating *Pride and Prejudice*, LBD provided print-first fans with the comfort and familiarity of Elizabeth and Darcy's story and reminded them of why they enjoyed Austen's novel in the first place. Screen-first fans were able to appreciate the "timelessness of the story" because LBD offered a pathway for "bringing new readers to old texts on those readers' terms," according to one fan's comments.

At the same time, LBD's creators crafted the adaptation as an intentionally contemporary story, which necessitated adjustments and variations to fit within a twenty-first century setting. The multiple social media platforms used to distribute the story required some expansion and extension of the novel with new content. Many fans emphasized that the contemporary setting and added narrative components helped reinforce "the relevance of

Austen's work to modern life" while "making it more accessible to an audience that might have not enjoyed the novel." One fan even admitted that she "did not enjoy my first experience" with *Pride and Prejudice* but eventually attempted another reading because LBD "made me love and appreciate the original source material a lot more." Thus, for this fan and many others, LBD succeeded because it did "not try to compete with Austen's tale, but rather honored it," allowing them "the freedom to enjoy LBD for what it is."[40]

CONCLUSION

The widespread prevalence and general awareness of Jane Austen in contemporary popular culture suggests that "we [now] live in a time when cult-like activity around [Austen] has a far greater reach than in previous eras."[41] In addition to new print editions of Austen's novel and a seemingly endless stream of film and TV adaptations, Janeites also have the opportunity to experience Austen in digital format through transmedia narratives like *The Lizzie Bennet Diaries*. Although Janeites of all varieties continue to find innovative and unexpected ways to celebrate their love of Austen, hybrid media-literature narratives like LBD can provide common ground for print-first and screen-first Janeites. For older Janeites who were more likely to be a part of the print-first generation, LBD was a way to revisit a familiar story from a new perspective. For younger Janeites who were more likely to actively engage with the story on social media, LBD served as an entry-level adaptation, giving them a pathway to Austen's novels for the first time.

The print-first and screen-first generational divide outlined here can extend beyond the Janeite fandom to other media fandoms, particularly transmedia franchises. As more comic books, graphic novels, and fiction series are adapted for screens, fans will continue to encounter these stories in a variety of ways, expanding the boundaries of the print-first and screen-first media generations while providing shared narrative experiences for fans. After all, LBD helped bridge the generational gap by offering Janeites "a sense that there is a common emotional world available" to them through their Austen fandom "that promises a certain experience of belonging."[42] The result, as one fan explained, was that LBD succeeded in "creating a community of new and old Austen fans to interact and participate from all over the world in the adaptation of a classic story." Another fan admitted to being bored by previous attempts to read Austen's novels or watch the older films. Thanks to the *Lizzie Bennet Diaries*, however, this fan realized "it was the first time I felt like Austen was really meant for me."

PART THREE

GENERATIONAL TENSIONS

Star Wars Fans, Generations, and Identity

Dan Golding

Star Wars pulled the same move twice. "Every generation has a legend," began the trailer for the final Skywalker film, *The Rise of Skywalker* (J. J. Abrams, 2019), in a conscious repeat of the first title card for *The Phantom Menace* (George Lucas, 1999) trailer twenty years earlier. *The Rise of Skywalker* was here to conclude a legend for a new generation of Star Wars fans, just as *The Phantom Menace* had opened Star Wars up to a previous one. "It's like poetry, it rhymes," said Star Wars impresario George Lucas in an often mocked line in a making-of documentary for *The Phantom Menace*. He was pointing out the similarities between Anakin Skywalker destroying the Trade Federation battleship and his son Luke destroying the Death Star in the original film, but "rhyming," or pulling the same move twice, might as well describe the logic of the whole franchise: enemy bases are infiltrated, hands are chopped off by lightsabers, the plucky underdog's plan succeeds despite the overwhelming odds, Skywalkers confront Palpatines. This is any generation's Star Wars legend. Yet such intergenerational rhyming was not invented by Lucas for the prequels and has been the defining logic of the series since 1977. Generations are forged in the fires of media and memory, and from the beginning Star Wars has been adept at wielding these tools.

This chapter explores how Star Wars is understood as generational and the implications and conclusions that can be drawn from framing the franchise as a text and associated fan practices and identities as generational. Star Wars as an entire undertaking has always been concerned with providing contemporaneous entry points for new and returning media consumers alike. The very first Star Wars film (George Lucas, 1977) was a deliberate attempt from Lucas to "reinvent the feel and shape of characteristic art objects of an older period," in the words of Fredric Jameson, and to "show people it was all right to become totally involved in a movie again," in the words of 20th Century Fox producer Alan Ladd Jr.[1] For viewers of Lucas's age (thirty-three in May 1977) or older, Star Wars recalled the affective appeal of the rough, quick, and exciting movie serials like Flash Gordon and Buck

Rogers that Lucas had encountered on television as a child growing up in Modesto, California. For younger viewers, such nostalgic associations were replaced by the appeal of a contemporary entry to those affective mediated experiences, complete with cutting-edge special effects. In 1977, Star Wars either welcomed you in or it welcomed you back.

This is how Star Wars began and is how it proceeded, continuing with various logics of the new and the return until the current, Disney-owned era of Lucasfilm. After more than four decades, there have been several distinct and not-so-distinct generations of Star Wars fans and their association with franchise eras, objects, taste, politics, gender, representation, and identity. When it came time for Disney-owned Lucasfilm to revive the Star Wars brand in the mid-2010s, a new generation of texts and fans were created. This time, there was a new twist to intergenerational rhyming in the form of the legacy film. The legacy film, which I have written about elsewhere, is usually a sequel to a dormant franchise that augments the appeal of renewal associated with the model of the reboot while maintaining a level of continuity for nostalgia or related purposes.[2] These films are renegotiated, usually late-franchise entries (in the sense they follow some years after the previous film) that aren't about starting over again but about reviving a franchise and passing it on to the next generation. Under this model, franchises no longer need to end: they can be bequeathed from generation to generation, across characters, cast, crew, audiences, and fans. Since about 2010 and in the context of Disney's Star Wars, this type of film has become almost ubiquitous: from early films like *Star Trek* (2009) and *Tron: Legacy* (2010), to 2015, which served as a critical year for the legacy film (including *Creed, Jurassic World, Terminator Genisys, Vacation,* and of course *The Force Awakens*), to more recent attempts like *Blade Runner 2049* (2017), *Halloween* (2018), *Mary Poppins Returns* (2018), *Ocean's 8* (2018), *Terminator: Dark Fate* (2019), *Bill and Ted Face the Music* (2020), and more. As overtly intergenerational projects, each has a complex relationship with questions of nostalgia, fandom, and gender.

It should come as no major surprise that Star Wars became one of the central pillars—if not *the* central pillar—for the legacy film phenomenon and of this moment in franchise time. In the eyes of Disney, who purchased the franchise along with Lucasfilm in 2012, Star Wars represented the keys to a dominion of popular culture that sat alongside their other culturally dominant evergreens like Mickey Mouse, Marvel, Pixar, and their live action remakes (such as *Aladdin* [2019] and *The Lion King* [2019]). Already, much has been written about Disney's plans for a renewed Star Wars to be created

136 GENERATIONAL TENSIONS

for a new generation of fans.[3] Yet in this context, Star Wars was redesigned to become, as *Wired* put it, "the forever franchise," a franchise that doesn't just extend into the future for endless financial returns and endless new generations of fans but that actively communicates with the past and with older generations, too.[4] In this chapter, I am interested in the legacy film as the essence of the present moment for Star Wars, where intergenerational exchange—and sometimes conflict, particularly along political and representational lines—has become central.

Although Hollywood and filmmaking in general have long been concerned with the past, the legacy film represents a moment where that concern has become concentrated beyond any real precedent and almost codified into a franchise subgenre. Legacy films are films in conversation with other films released decades ago and with audiences and their memories of those earlier films. Legacy films are made with an awareness of the intergenerational possibilities of fandom and an eye to stimulating and authorizing a moment of renewal and generational transference across multiple levels of narrative, production, and reception. Thus, audience members can encounter the same legacy film through different yet coherent perspectives: perhaps as an "original" fan, eager to revisit and renew their fandom with new franchise entries; perhaps as a newcomer to the franchise, too young to have much familiarity with the originals, but interested in being initiated into franchise fandom and now provided with an entry point; or perhaps as something in between. Although the reboot, prefiguring the legacy film, provides moments of franchise initiation for new fans, Urbanski makes the crucial distinction that this is less a singular model than a continuum of "increasing separation from their inspiration franchises."[5] These new films, in contrast, can be so close to the "inspiration franchise" as to be literally minutes of franchise narrative time apart (as in *Rogue One*, Gareth Edwards, 2016) while providing initiation for new viewers. This lack of separation is not a symptom of a Hollywood whose creative well has run dry—it is the point.

However, Star Wars has been transferred intergenerationally well before the present moment and the model of the legacy film, as a franchise and as a presence in the lives of fans. To be a Star Wars fan has often meant being concerned with fandom passed down through families and friends, informally and ritualistically. This has happened partly as the result of deliberate cultivation on behalf of Lucasfilm and as the result of everyday fan practices and a culture well beyond the limits of official product plans and marketing strategies. This tension, along with shifting expectations around gendered fandom, were summed up by J. J. Abrams, who argued that Star Wars had always been "a movie that dads take their sons to" but that "I was really hoping this could be a movie that mothers could take their daughters to as well."[6] The implications for who, in public discourse, is "authorized" as a Star Wars fan to perform this intergenerational transference are clear. (Of course, women, mothers, daughters have always been Star Wars fans.[7])

For more than four decades, with periods of particular concentration, Star Wars has been at the heart of popular culture. Necessarily, this ongoing popularity, combined with the relative distinctiveness of eras when it comes to franchise texts, has produced a sense of "generationing" among fans. The simple passing of time between major Star Wars films means that someone who was ten years old when the first film was released was thirty-two when *The Phantom Menace* came out and forty-eight when *The Force Awakens* was released. From age ten to almost fifty is a significant span of a lifetime: careers, relationships, and children may well have filled the intervening period. Few individuals have been better placed to observe this lifelong phenomenon than the objects of fan affection—the Star Wars cast—at fan conventions and promotional events and in their correspondence with fans. In her memoir, *The Princess Diarist*, Carrie Fisher notes that Star Wars fans have "a common language that runs from five to eighty-five," a language that is bequeathed across generations.

> In a way, it's as if they know they have this great gift to bestow, and they want to bestow it as perfectly as possible—the perfect time, the perfect place, the perfect situation for passing on this life-defining experience. And the kids will always remember for their entire lives how they first felt when they first saw their now favorite movie. And they were given this gift from their parents, and can now share it together. Truly a family affair.[8]

If only to illustrate the divergence between generations of Star Wars fans and their indelible association with the franchise media of their own entry points, debate continues to flow surrounding the correct formula for what Fisher identifies as "the perfect situation for passing on this life-defining experience." As a Star Wars fan, do you show the next generation the films in the order of their release? The numerical order of franchise narrative? What to do with the new, Disney-era standalone films? What about the Ewok Adventure films (1984, 1985), the 1978 Holiday Special (perhaps not), or the more recent TV series, both animated and live-action? Where do they fit in?

What about the layering of special editions? Perhaps the correct initiation rite lies beyond the obvious in a fan vernacular concoction like the "machete order."[9] The presence of Disney-era films that do not have the same authorial blessing of creator George Lucas complicates things further: should fans treat Lucas-era Lucasfilm as genuine, with recent entries reduced to something like very expensive fan fiction, as is sometimes claimed? Which generation of Star Wars texts have authoritative power?

Generations of Star Wars texts produce generations of fandom. "I can tell what generation you are by what you call this character," tweeted writer Scott Weinberg, accompanied by an image of the unfortunate alien who meets a grisly fate in the Mos Eisley cantina at the wrong end of Ben Kenobi's lightsaber in the original *Star Wars* film. "Generation X calls him Walrus Man," he continued, while "younger nerds call him Ponda Baba, which is just silly" (@scottEmovienerd, Twitter, August 3, 2020). Fan fondness for the more wooden moments in the often mocked prequel trilogy perhaps began ironically but eventually morphed into a semi-coherent community, with online outposts like the subreddit r/prequelmemes developing a playful and ironic sense of validity for the 1999–2005 trilogy. The subreddit is notably sometimes placed in mock conflict with its more contemporary counterpart, r/sequelmemes, which focus on the 2015–2019 films, with the resulting meme wars between subreddits playing out across generations, representation, and a kind of fan-led reclamation of franchise texts viewed popularly as bad taste, bad quality, controversial, or perhaps all three.

A clash of generational fandoms, however ironic, is not without its own complex politics, particularly when played out across memes and online communities. Questions of representation and gender complicate this kind of fan practice even further. The three central trilogies of Star Wars have their own unique relationships to representation and politics, and setting up even ironic conflicts between fans of each has implications for how key questions of gender and race are articulated. What does it mean to have some Star Wars fans circulate memes that reclaim a sense of fun for *Revenge of the Sith* (George Lucas, 2005), a film that gives dialogue to only one woman (Padmé) and depicts the rise of a brutal fascist dictatorship?[10] What can begin in irony can end in sincerity. Alternatively, what does it mean to have other Star Wars fans propagating memes that mock Rose Tico (Kelly Marie Tran), perhaps still the most prominent woman of color in the Star Wars cinematic universe (even now a very narrow field)? Ironic humor can be its own pleasurable end, but it can also be used as a barrier against progressive criticism or to conceal sincere regressive politics. Star

Star Wars Fans, Generations, and Identity 139

Wars fan spaces like r/sequelmemes and r/prequelmemes are arenas where generational taste is established and sticky questions of representation are pushed back and forth across decades. Following the vicious reception of *The Phantom Menace* in 1999, Jar Jar Binks actor Ahmed Best contemplated suicide; in 2018, Kelly Marie Tran deleted her social media accounts following similar harassment.[11] Yet in 2019, Best and Tran both received standing ovations and had their names chanted by crowds at Lucasfilm's Star Wars Celebration fan event.[12] Evidently, even clearly identifiable generations of Star Wars fans contain multiplicities.

Some perspective is then needed on media generations. Göran Bolin argues that nostalgia underpins generational gaps, often appearing between parents and children through insurmountable differences in their respective media landscapes.[13] As a serialized franchise, there are plenty of insurmountable differences for *Star Wars* fans, and prime among them is the irreplaceable encounter with the "new" of Star Wars, the sense of what franchise texts are emerging in the moment they are first encountered. Today, one can never again encounter the original Star Wars trilogy at the moment it was new, regardless of some fan practices, such as showing the films in release order to newcomers, which seem to reinforce if not the newness of the original trilogy then at least its textual primacy. Indeed, despite the franchise's continual backward glances, one can only encounter Star Wars in the perpetual present. To watch the original films, or even the prequels, is to encounter them as historical media texts. This distance is an essential part of what Bolin describes as the "process of generationing," that is, the delineation of generations as distinct identities through which nostalgia and memory "actualize the relation between the present and the past."[14]

Media generations are also infused with technology. Elsaesser draws out different "takes" on cinephilia across cinema history in part based on technological changes across history and film culture: the first "take" concerned with the celluloid image and the big screen, the city and its movie houses; and the second with the DVD and the internet, a division between scarcity and ritual, plenty and mobility.[15] Indeed, technology similarly shapes generations of Star Wars fans as much as the media texts themselves and has long been a preoccupation of the franchise and its creators. Seeing the first Star Wars film in celluloid in a dark theater in 1977, writing to fan magazine *Starlog* after witnessing the conclusion of *Return of the Jedi* (Richard Marquand, 1983), downloading *The Phantom Menace* trailer on dial-up internet in 1999, discussing the prequel trilogy's failings on fan forums, retweeting a superlative appearance from Carrie Fisher (and her dog, Gary)

TABLE 2. A broad outline of Star Wars fan generations

Generation	Key Texts	Auxiliary Texts	Broad Demographic	Technologies
1	Original trilogy (1977–1983)	Toys and merch, fan magazines, soundtrack records, early comics, Star Tours ride	Born before 1983	Multiplexes, merchandise, magazines, records, game arcades, early consoles
1.1	—	The "dark times" and extended universe special editions (1997), *Shadows of the Empire* (1996)	Born after 1983, early 1990s	VHS, CDs, novels, video games, fan magazines, forums
2	Prequel trilogy (1999–2005)	Video games (*Battlefront* series, 2004; *The Force Unleashed*, 2008), CD soundtracks, novels	Born mid-1990s to early 2000s	Forums, DVDs, video games (including online play), torrenting
2.2	—	*The Clone Wars* (2008–2014, 2020 revival), *Legacy* novels	Born late 1990s to early 2000s	Forums, social media, torrenting, streaming
3	Sequel trilogy (2015–2019) and stand-alone films	TV: *Rebels, The Mandalorian,* and *Resistance; Journey to Star Wars* publishing, Galaxy's Edge theme park area	Born after 2005, franchise latecomers	Streaming, Blu-Ray, social media, YouTube, memes

on a morning talk show to promote *The Force Awakens*—all of these are Star Wars fan memories hewn by media texts, technology, and generations.

Broadly speaking then, we could think about generations of *Star Wars* fans by the logics (many of which are shared with how fans actually distinguish themselves) outlined in Table 2.

Of course, this delineation can hardly be taken rigidly and must immediately be countered with nuance. It is easy to imagine any number of people who do not fit neatly into such a taxonomy: someone who loved the first Star Wars movie in 1977 but then lost interest until seeing *The Last Jedi* by chance in 2017; a person who felt the gender and racial politics of the Star Wars universe excluded them until the coming of the Disney-era films; or even someone who feels no particular attachment to any generation and enjoys all eras of the franchise. Actual individuals are too complicated to effectively theorize in cross-sections, but taken exclusively as caveated and qualified massed groups, we can start to make some sense of things.

Although it is possible to imagine individual exceptions to the generations drawn in Table 2, or of "latecomers" to each period in terms of demographic (that is, someone born in 1940 might have ignored Star Wars until the era of the sequel trilogy), what is not possible to disregard are two key points. First, the ascendant key texts for each period also define each generation of fandom that encountered them as entry points to the franchise. Second, the overarching intergenerational engagement with Star Wars has thickened to become the franchise's central strategy in the sequel trilogy era, following the logic of the legacy film. These generations recognize each other—"what Star Wars did you grow up on?"—and are reified through intergenerational play as meme wars between subreddits, franchise nostalgia, and the interpolation of marketing campaigns (which generation's is this legend?). They are also sometimes a defining source of friction for Star Wars texts and the culture that surrounds it: Proctor and McCulloch argue that Lucas "failed to predict a backlash of waves of diehard first-generation fans who balked at the way in which Lucas tinkered with the original films and added new CGI elements."[16] In an episode of the sitcom *Spaced*, an adult character played by Simon Pegg (a celebrity Star Wars fan who later appeared in *The Force Awakens*) tells off a child for buying a Jar Jar Binks figure: "You so do not understand—you weren't there at the beginning!" he screams. Indeed, the figure of the irascible, betrayed generation 1 *Star Wars* fan is by now familiar to the point of parody. Despite Disney's marketing of *The Force Awakens* carefully conjuring up memories of the original trilogy and not the prequels, generation 2 fans not only exist but have now come of age and are well into adulthood, a fact acknowledged by *The Last Jedi* and *The Rise of Skywalker*'s cautious inclusion of prequel elements (the name Darth Sidious, the fan favorite line "The Dark Side of the Force is a pathway to many abilities some consider to be unnatural," and the many prequel trilogy Jedi who make voice cameos at *Rise*'s climax).[17]

Far from isolating fan generations into separate strata, contemporary Disney-era Star Wars strategy seems to be providing multiple paths through their texts. This can be seen most directly in the finale of the animated series *The Clone Wars* (2020), which premiered on Disney's streaming service and included plot threads potentially appealing to generation 1 (the finale episode's Darth Vader epilogue), generation 2 (the story parallels the events of *Revenge of the Sith*), generation 2.2 (the long-awaited conclusion to the 2008–2014 era *The Clone Wars*), and generation 3 (revealing the backstory of *Rebels* characters Ahsoka, Rex, and Maul, as well as the Black Sun crime syndicate). This is an evolution of the logic of the legacy film—which targets old and new generations alike—and can increasingly be seen across Disney's Star Wars works (generation 1.2 favorite from key extended universe novels, Thrawn, became a villain in the generation 3 series *Rebels*; generation 3 series *The Mandalorian* has associations with Boba Fett [generation 1] and Jango Fett [generation 2], while also bringing in the Darksaber [generation 2.2]). These are not just points of interest for different fans seeking a reason to engage with new material but further proof that although the texts and their fans can be broken into broadly discrete generations, contemporary Star Wars texts are increasingly intergenerational. The growing blend of Star Wars eras in the Disney era can be seen in Table 3. Beginning with *The Force Awakens* in 2015, we see a strong reliance on the legacy film model through the invocation of the original Star Wars trilogy but with very little interrelation with the prequels or the *Clone Wars* era. Moving forward to Lucasfilm's most recent productions, the difference is striking in its reference to elements across all generations (with the notable exception of 1.1, which is perhaps less surprising given that all texts of this period were proclaimed noncanon by Lucasfilm shortly after the Disney takeover).

Finally, I touch on how Star Wars fans are appraised in the public domain, beyond the confines of fandom, and in particular, the relationship between the notional Star Wars fan of each generation and politics. Across these forty years and more, the image of the Star Wars fan has been discursively constructed and reconstructed in various domains by scholars, journalists, the Star Wars industry, and fans themselves. A full survey of the politics of Star Wars or even of the various identities of those who have claimed Star

TABLE 3. The growing intergenerational elements in Disney's Star Wars texts

	1	1.1	2	2.2	3
The Force Awakens (2015)	Sequel to *Return of the Jedi* in cinematic series time; numerous returning characters	Broad similarities	—	—	A constituent part of the third trilogy
The Mandalorian season 1 (2019)	Boba Fett association, *Return of the Jedi*-adjacent setting, Mos Eisley cantina, IG droid	—	Jango Fett association, live-action *Clone Wars* flashbacks, pit droids	The Darksaber, Mandalorian lore and history	The Force can heal wounds, Death troopers
The Rise of Skywalker (2019)	Luke lifts his X-wing, a medal for Chewbacca, numerous returning locales and characters	—	"The Dark Side of the Force is a pathway" quote, Jedi voices: Qui-Gon, Obi-Wan, Anakin, Mace Windu	Jedi voices: Ahsoka Tano, Adi Gallia, Aayla Secura, Luminara Unduli	The Ghost from *Rebels* appears, Jedi voices: Kanan Jarrus A constituent part of the third trilogy
The Clone Wars season 7 (2020)	Darth Vader epilogue	—	Story parallels and incorporates events of *Revenge of the Sith*	Direct conclusion to 2008–2014 *The Clone Wars*	Backstory of key *Rebels* characters Ahsoka, Rex, and Maul, as well as Black Sun

Wars fandom is neither possible nor desirable here, such is the breadth and well-trodden nature of the topic.[18] But I do want to take the opportunity to highlight how Star Wars fans have been understood with regard to ideology and what we might call "acceptable fan behavior" over the years.

Most obviously, and as already discussed, Star Wars fans as a group have recently been understood as the perpetrators of everything from hate speech and bigoted harassment to social media trolling of popular figures, including Star Wars creatives. In 2018, *Esquire* journalist Matt Miller assessed the situation: "Whereas the vocal majority of *Star Wars* fans were once simply passionate people who cosplay and debate the logistics of a Kessel Run, they've now been overpowered (on the internet, at least). *Star Wars*, and a loud section of *Star Wars* fans, have tragically become synonymous with hate, bigotry, and pervasive assholeness."[19] Miller is hardly alone in this contemporary assessment. There is a lot of anxiety about the state of Star Wars fandom, whether it is regarding racism and sexism toward particular characters and their actors, or a generalized critique of Star Wars fans as overly nostalgic and beholden to the Disney corporate behemoth. Anxiety about Star Wars fandom, however, is far from a recent development and is instead new in its contemporary inflections, rather than its overarching construction of the Star Wars fan as regressive. Indeed, from a generational point of view, the discursively constructed Star Wars fan is not particularly unusual. In Robin Wood's assessment from 1986, for example, first-generation Star Wars fans were "only comprehensible when one assumes a widespread *desire* for regression to infantilism, a populace who wants to be constructed as mock children."[20] Wood (and others like him) pinioned Star Wars and its fans as presaging the Reaganite politics of the 1980s: simple, nostalgic, and ultimately uncritically regressive. When fan generation 2 arrived with the prequels, the public equation was colored by George Lucas's blunt political allegories embedded in the films, including his skewering of the language of George W. Bush, and the horrible harassment of Ahmed Best and Lucas himself.[21] In perhaps a genuine break from the Lucas era, the Disney-led sequel trilogy is political not in its intended allegories of US wars in Vietnam or Iraq but in its casting, storytelling, and representation of gender and race. In other words, the sequels are seen as political by those who find the central presence of women and people of color in the films objectionable. In this sense, the sequel trilogy is of its progressive historical moment as much as the earlier trilogies were in their critique of American empire. Few political issues dominated the 2010s in American popular culture as roundly as that of gender, race, and representation.[22]

It is hardly surprising that Star Wars fandom should become a site of political struggle. As Stuart Hall memorably wrote, popular culture "is the arena of consent and resistance. . . . That is why 'popular culture' matters."[23] The stuff of Star Wars is the stuff of politics: allies, antagonists, war, belief, ideology, mysticism, individualism, martyrdom. It would be wholly reasonable to return to Table 2 and insert something like what we see in Table 4.

These are the political issues frequently ascribed to generations of Star Wars texts and fandoms and also some of the broader political issues of these moments in US history. The problem only arises when we consider the generations of Star Wars fans to be definable entities acting in coherent and specific ways. In other words, Star Wars fandom is not political because it is a distinct community or milieu, removed in precise ways from other forms of popular culture. It is political because it is popular culture and is therefore "the arena of consent and resistance." Fandom is a site of conflict. It is a venue for the circulation and articulation of politics and identities; it is hard to imagine any generation of Star Wars fandom that is not concerned with the major issues of its time. Indeed, the strangest thing about Miller's assessment of contemporary Star Wars fans is his nostalgic description of "passionate people who cosplay and debate the logistics of a Kessel Run." Is there a generation of Star Wars fandom that meets that description, and that description alone, without also being associated with politics? Ahmed Best and even George Lucas were pilloried well before the sequel trilogy and social media era.

Understanding Star Wars fans through the framework of generations needs to be met with a healthy dose of nuance and the acknowledgment that individuals are always more complex than any analytical diagram. However, taxonomizing generations helps track discourse surrounding perceived attributes of Star Wars fans as well as aiding in a necessary unhinging of assumptions about how easy it is to identify and categorize who it is that we are studying when we study fandoms. "Every generation has a legend," as they say. Yet given the centrality of the key Star Wars texts to each fan generation and the relative distance between each set of trilogies, it is also possible to come to a greater understanding of various factors, like technology, in the creation of each, as well as the occasional friction between generations and the accessibility of new points of entry.

Star Wars fandom has always been intergenerational. From the first film's appeal to young cinemagoers at the tail end of New Hollywood and adults nostalgic for old adventure serials in the 1970s, to the legacy film approach to *The Force Awakens* from a Disney-owned Lucasfilm, the pattern

146 GENERATIONAL TENSIONS

TABLE 4. Star Wars generations and political issues

Generation	Key Texts	Political Keywords
1	Original trilogy (1977–1983)	Reaganite politics, nostalgia, Vietnam War, empire
2	Prequel trilogy (1999–2005)	George W. Bush and the War on Terrorism, online fandom, the second Iraq war
3	Sequel trilogy (2015–2019) and standalone films	Representation and diversity, gender, race, sexuality, social media fandom, Trump and the rise of far-right politics

of welcoming in and welcoming back is as central to Star Wars as ever. However, what has changed has been the transition from catering to two audiences—one returning generation and one generation of newcomers, a past and a present—to catering to a present and multiple returning generations who may otherwise clash on issues of both textual primacy (which films are the "real" Star Wars?) and also representation and politics (is Rey a "Mary Sue"? Is it a problem that Padmé is the only woman with a speaking role in *Revenge of the Sith*?). This is a far more difficult balancing act, and it complicates claims that a simple nostalgia for Star Wars is at the heart of the franchise's Disney-led revival. It is illustrative that, following the logic of the legacy film, Disney has increasingly included elements familiar to multiple generations of Star Wars fans in their films and TV series. Indeed, as I write this, the Star Wars fan world is reacting to the appearance of Temuera Morrison as an aged, post–*Return of the Jedi* Boba Fett in season 2 of *The Mandalorian*, a move that tantalizingly revisits key elements of original and prequel trilogies in one Disney-era package.

This is a different kind of fandom, one that illuminates the intergenerational politics that come with nostalgic franchise models like the legacy film and the kinds of multigenerational franchising and fandom that will follow in its wake. As franchising consolidates its dominance over the entertainment industries, and as the most popular and long-running media

Star Wars Fans, Generations, and Identity 147

franchises age, intergenerational models like the legacy film will give way to multigenerational models. The Disney project of Star Wars today leads this move, but it is also instructional as the blueprint of a new and developing intergenerational model. This might look like films and TV series that are not just in conversation with the past, but with multiple texts, multiple generations, and the multiple and sometimes incongruent fan politics that accompany each and every element. Following Disney's Star Wars franchise, fandom is now generationally thick.

148 GENERATIONAL TENSIONS

Roads Go Ever On and On

FAN FICTION AND ARCHIVAL INFRASTRUCTURES AS MARKERS OF THE AFFIRMATIONAL-TRANSFORMATIONAL CONTINUUM IN TOLKIEN FANDOM

Maria K. Alberto and Dawn Walls-Thumma

Even those who haven't read J. R. R. Tolkien's books will probably recognize the hobbits, elves, and orcs they helped popularize, but Tolkien's work also draws fans "who attend to a text more closely than other types of audience members" and use chosen text(s) to identify their shared community.[1] Moreover, this long-lived fandom differs both from other book fandoms (such as those surrounding literary texts like Jane Austen's) and media fandoms (which often develop around films, TV shows, video games, etc.). Instead, much of Tolkien fandom's transgenerational appeal stems from its relationships with a complex canon or the "authoritative collection of central texts" that guides fan practices.[2]

In this chapter, we focus on Tolkien fan fiction authors, a subset of Tolkien fandom whose work and community mores reveal telling shifts. We define Tolkien fandom "generations" around the releases of major texts that drew in large numbers of new fans, while also noting that each release both coincides with other factors (such as growing home internet access or fandom migrations) and also influences shifts along an affirmational-transformational continuum of fan works and fan attitudes. To date, the initial *Lord of the Rings* books (1954–1955), Peter Jackson's *Lord of the Rings* trilogy (2001–2003), and Jackson's *Hobbit* trilogy (2012–2014) each demarcate distinct generations of Tolkien fandom, at times even prompting intra-fandom distinctions between "book-firsters" and "film-firsters."[3] That is, each text inducted a major influx of fans—and fan fiction authors—who brought to bear their own interests in Middle-earth.

Drawing on a fandom-wide survey Walls-Thumma conducted in 2015 and a second iteration we launched in August 2020, we note that Tolkien fan fiction authors engage with their canon in interesting ways that become especially visible with treatments of gender, sexuality (particularly queerness), and sexual content—topics this canon itself often seems to foreclose. Such treatments exemplify how the fan fiction–focused side of Tolkien fandom has spanned those three generations, benefiting from multiple entry points into the canon and fandom infrastructures that fostered distinct fan cultures.

SKETCHING OUT TOLKIEN FANDOM

Most definitions of the term *fandom* emphasize its social connotations, and we build from this to define Tolkien fandom as the communities that engage with any part of Tolkien's fiction and/or any of its adaptations.[4] We open here because relatively little scholarship focuses on Tolkien fandom, creating what Walls-Thumma has identified as a "lacuna" in fan studies.[5] When Tolkien fans are discussed, it is often by way of Jackson's films, considering blockbuster marketing or anticipations and reactions.[6] Rarer examples note fan works, including fan fiction and fan films, but otherwise, Tolkien fandom is typically discussed as a market niche or creative force rather than a community.[7]

Another key concept stems from the concepts of affirmational and trans-formational fandoms, as introduced by Dreamwidth user obsession_inc in 2009. Briefly, affirmational fandom celebrates canon as is, locating the authority to interpret a work with its producers, while transformational fandom invests fans with the authority to interpret and transform canon. Thus, transformational fandom is often regarded as how female, BIPOC, queer, disabled, and other marginalized fans can see their own interests represented in canons that initially exclude them.

While obsession_inc discusses affirmational-transformational practices as a continuum, not a binary, fan studies has tended to describe fan fiction as transformational.[8] Tolkien fan fiction writers, however, offer a particularly clear example of that affirmational-transformational continuum, since they draw from both types of practice—collecting details from canon (affirma-tional) but then using that scrutiny to inform writing that pushes against it (transformational). Then too, Tolkien fan fiction subcommunities often form based on the text(s) their members write about most (*The Hobbit, The Lord of the Rings* [*LOTR*], or *The Silmarillion*), but also in terms of shared values along that continuum.[9]

The majority of this chapter focuses on a broad overview of fan fiction–writing Tolkien fandom, and later sections revisit data collected through the 2014–2015 Tolkien Fanfiction Survey.[10] This survey collected voluntary responses from 1,052 participants, asking about how, where, and why they read and/or wrote Tolkien fan fiction. We collate survey findings on Tolkien-specific archives as they were used at different points and examine how these reiterate our schema of fandom generations.[11]

A TALE OF THREE GENERATIONS

It is difficult to gather comprehensive information about the first generation of Tolkien fandom in the pre-internet era, let alone the fan fiction produced during it. As in other early fandoms, Tolkien fans often published in amateur fanzines—few of which have been archived and many more irrevocably lost. (Marquette University has begun archiving the fanzine collection of collector Sumner Gary Hunnewell, but as of this writing, has made just over one hundred available online.) None contain exclusively fan fiction; in fact, most contain no fan fiction at all.

This early affirmational orientation is further evidenced in how these zines' few examples of fan fiction bear little resemblance to the stories described by Camille Bacon-Smith and Henry Jenkins in their foundational fan studies work, conducted closest to this era.[12] Instead, this early Tolkien fan fiction typically builds into ficto-historical periods beyond *The Hobbit* and *LOTR* (*The Silmarillion* was not published until 1977), drawing from hints in *LOTR* appendixes. There is little examination of relationships between characters, and there certainly isn't any sex.

This is not to say that discussions of sexual content were completely nonexistent; rather, such discussions differed from counterparts in media fandoms such as Star Trek or the Man from U.N.C.L.E. While contemporaneous reviews of Tolkien's books sometimes point to a lack of sexual content, Brenda Partridge opened the scholarly discussion in 1983, and Tolkien fandom waded in sometime in between—usually disapprovingly.[13] In a 1961 essay, Marion Zimmer Bradley—then a Tolkien fan fiction author whose thoughts we include only because they would have constituted a well-known example at the time—purports to champion "sexual realism" in genre fiction but also claims that in *LOTR* it "would be grotesque." Bradley also rejects a reading of same-sex desire between Sam and Frodo because their relationship is "innocent . . . unselfish . . . and devot[ed]," implying that overt same-sex desire would signify the opposite.[14] Similar attitudes pervaded the Tolkien fandom even through its first migration online: defining its values, predicting its internal conflicts, and shaping its infrastructure well into the early 2000s.

Roads Go Ever On and On 151

For more than a decade, this primarily society- and zine-based generation of Tolkien fandom coexisted with its online-oriented successor. The early 1990s saw the establishment of mailing lists and newsgroups such as rec .arts.books.tolkien (RABT) in 1993. Although this newsgroup's charter asserts that fan fiction was permitted "provided that it did not violate anyone's rights or copyrights," even a quick perusal reveals a pervasive unease with the very concept.[15] In true affirmational fashion, one 1994 discussion appeals to Tolkien's authority throughout, with multiple references to a 1966 letter in which Tolkien describes a fan wanting to write a *LOTR* sequel as a "young ass."[16] Another common, affirmationally oriented claim on RABT scorns the "disrespect" of fan writers, who supposedly positioned themselves on par with Tolkien as Middle-earth's creator.

Conspicuously absent here—especially given its centrality in later arguments—was any objection to sexual content in fan fiction. While RABT members regularly debated whether discussions of sex in Middle-earth were appropriate, early discussions never connected this with fan fiction.[17] The late 1990s, though, proved to be a watershed moment: Elwin Fortuna established the tolkien_slash mailing list in 1999, while on RABT, a small contingent calling itself the Tilde Club began posting "randy" content, often in the form of mildly sexual, sometimes homoerotic parodies.[18] More widespread internet usage appears to account for at least part of this change. Fortuna's mailing list could only have existed online, and in a majority-male fandom space, while the more vocal Tilde Club supporters appear to be mostly women.[19] Thus, although affirmational practices of collecting and explicating the canon continued to dominate Tolkien fandom, we can see the first intimations of increasingly transformational leanings that would intensify with the second generation.

It is also worth noting that the bar for entry remained high even as Tolkien fandom transitioned online. Would-be writers required the institutional knowledge necessary to locate fanzines, and at this point the fandom was still unequivocally a literary one, meaning that deep knowledge of the canon was needed to contend with a sometimes hostile readership that valued both getting the details right and also a more elusive "respect for Tolkien." Given the appeal of Tolkien's work, though, the fandom persisted for decades—albeit without any dramatic influx of new fans.

This changed in 2001 with the first release of Jackson's *LOTR* trilogy, which provided an entry point for fans to begin writing fan fiction about Middle-earth without committing to the books.[20] This release also coincided roughly with growing access to home internet, which curtailed much of the

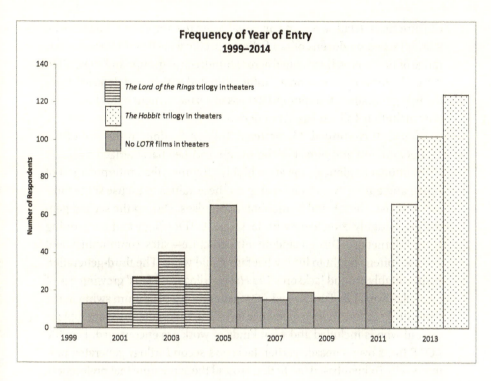

FIGURE 3. Frequency of year of fandom entry by Tolkien fan fiction authors, 1999–2014 (self-reported in 2014–2015 Tolkien Fanfiction Survey).

institutional and technical knowledge previously required to read and share Tolkien-based fan fiction. As Figure 3 shows, this confluence of factors produced a boom of interest.

However, the films also provoked an important and ongoing cultural shift: immediately following the *LOTR* trilogy, fan fiction authors began choosing "to take Jackson's artistic license [as] an invitation to produce their own ... based on Tolkien's work, yet free to stray from its storyline in original, unexplored directions."[21] Both versions of the Tolkien Fanfiction Survey have confirmed this: those who began writing fan fiction during one of Jackson's trilogy releases were less likely to identify Tolkien's perceived approval or morality as central influences.

Thus, growing internet democratization, rapid entry of new fans, and these fans' comparatively diverse values all sparked creativity and conflict during the early second generation. Within a few years, Tolkien fan fiction went from being a practice occasionally indulged in by fans willing to risk censure from detail-savvy, affirmational peers to comprising thousands of stories hosted on dozens of fan fiction–specific websites.[22] Moreover, this range of new voices fragmented across hundreds of groups and sites, often driven by differing views on a conflict initiated within and deferred from the first generation: the appropriateness of sexual content in Middle-earth, now including Tolkien-based fan fiction.

This shift continued. Mainstream Tolkien fandom at the end of the first generation and outset of the second can be characterized by heavy affirmational tendencies toward a highly circumscribed interpretation of canon and authority—often leaning on these values to excuse some fans' racist, sexist, ableist, and homophobic impulses. During the second generation, roughly coincident with Jackson's *LOTR* trilogy and burgeoning home internet use, Tolkien fandom infrastructure—sites, communities, and events—often sought to limit what fans could write. The third-generation maps roughly around Jackson's *The Hobbit* trilogy and fans' growing use of open platforms like Tumblr and AO3, generating a pendulum swing in the opposite direction: more general-use infrastructures supported attempts to expand who is included and what kinds of work are encouraged. Like the *LOTR* films over a decade earlier, Jackson's second trilogy generated new interest in Tolkien-based fan fiction around the same time that preferences for posting, reading, and discussing this work shifted away from journaling platforms and fandom-specific archives.[23]

These shifts also sparked tensions similar to the early second-generation conflicts between pre-internet (often affirmational) values and emerging online (increasingly transformational) values. Third-generation tensions, though, often concerned clashes between incoming fan practices and values (usually transformational, often from multifandom creators) on the one hand, and certain existing Tolkien fandom traditions on the other—which, although not limited to this arena, often included further normalization of writing about gender, sexuality, and sex. For example, kink memes—anonymous writing challenges frequently oriented around sexually explicit requests—originated in 2007 but did not become common practice in Tolkien fan fiction until *The Hobbit*'s release in 2012.[24] Also, as attrition from the second generation increased, new fans filled the vacuum with their own events, many of which opened Tolkien-based fan fiction to more diverse voices.[25]

However, even third-generation Tolkien fan fiction is not completely transformational. Instead, strong affirmational elements, such as high value on canon (particularly book canon), remain indicative of Tolkien fandom culture. Put differently, growing acceptance of transformational values does

154 GENERATIONAL TENSIONS

not necessarily mean wholesale rejection of affirmational ones. Often the latter are simply reshaped and applied to new contexts.[26]

MARY SUES (AND BALROG WINGS): THESE WERE A FEW CONTROVERSIAL THINGS

These three generations of Tolkien fandom, plus their respective fan fiction writers, have each engaged differently with sexual content and gender. We now turn to the 2014–2015 Tolkien Fanfiction Survey in more detail, given these themes' prevalence there.

Sexual Content

Obsession_inc locates writing about sex specifically in transformational fandom, and thus its near-complete absence and distinct notoriety in first-generation Tolkien fan fiction attests to a primarily affirmational orientation. As Tolkien fandom moved online, though, cross-pollination with more transformational media fandoms generated growing interest and acceptance. For instance, the first Tolkien slash archive, Least Expected, was inspired by conversations from Star Wars fandom.[27] Still, sexual content was seen as a marginal concern well into the second generation. As Ty Rosenthal observes in 2004, "For [only] *a substantial minority* of Tolkien fans, [the] martially proscribed libidos of Tolkien's Middle-earth seem . . . wrong, missing, childish, a marked absence."[28] Rosenthal, herself a prolific fan fiction author and early proponent of Tolkien slash, also identifies fan fiction as an important outlet for this "minority" of fans.

Suddenly part of a fandom visibly larger and more heterogeneous following Jackson's *LOTR*, second-generation Tolkien fans swiftly compartmentalized themselves—a division based largely on shared approaches to canon, such as whether to affix sexual content to what many preferred to see as a work without it.[29] Thus siloed with like-minded peers, Tolkien fans needed not encounter content or interpretations they found uninteresting or offensive—a system leveraged by both the more affirmationally minded, who didn't want depictions of sex and sexuality, as well as Rosenthal's "substantial minority," who could now explore such topics with less fear of harassment.

Tolkien fan fiction archives at the time were often delimited by their stance on sex and sexuality and distinct from one another in terms of how they navigated the fandom's various affirmational and transformational values.[30] Fans often perceived these large archives as operating in opposition and viewed authors on "other" archives negatively.[31] Meanwhile, those who wrote

Roads Go Ever On and On 155

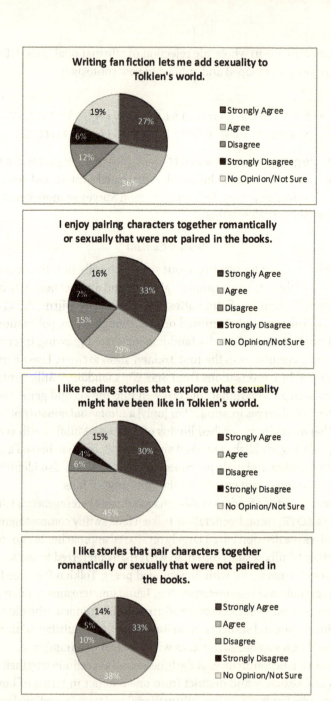

FIGURE 4. Author and reader views on sexual content in Tolkien-based fan fiction (2014–2015 Tolkien Fanfiction Survey, conducted by Dawn Walls-Thumma).

sexually explicit material—especially same-sex pairings like slash—were often treated viciously on archives hostile to such interests. However, this same compartmentalization also allowed distinct fan cultures to flourish since it created spaces where fan authors could explore once-taboo topics safely. Thus, irrespective of the generation during which they entered Tolkien fandom, fan fiction authors participated on the archives that best fit their values—a striking example of how polylithic fandom experiences are, rather than the monolith often assumed by community outsiders.

A decade after Rosenthal's observation that only a substantial minority of Tolkien fans were interested in sexual content, survey findings suggest that this has become a majority motive (Figure 4).[32] The sudden expansion of fandom infrastructure had created spaces in which Tolkien fans interested in writing about sex or outright sexual content could do so, as well as spaces where those opposed to this could remain shielded from it and were kept from leveraging their numbers to compel others into adopting this preference.

Gender

Although evidence suggests that the first generation of Tolkien fan fiction was not authored predominantly by women—another unusual departure from wider norms—this changed by the time online fandom eclipsed its society-and-zine predecessor.[33] The growing predominance of women, though, does not necessarily mean that stories about women were tolerated, much less encouraged, in Tolkien fan fiction. Much like the fandom's evolving attitudes on sexual content, attitudes toward women in Tolkien-based fan fiction generated conflict, compartmentalization, and eventually change.

As with many other pre-internet fandoms, the "Mary Sue" phenomenon initially exerted a chilling effect. The term "Mary Sue," originally coined in Star Trek fandom, describes an original female character—assumed to be styled after the fan-author—who exerts a disproportionate influence on canon characters or plot.[34] In Tolkien fandom, organized campaigns harassed writers deemed to have written Mary Sues, which then prevented others from exploring women's perspectives out of fear of the same treatment.[35]

Though often framed as an objection to poor writing, Tolkien fandom's early opposition to Mary Sue stories was equally about resistance to emerging transformational practices in a fandom retaining a strong affirmational orientation. Ika Willis illustrates the heart of common objections to fan fiction foregrounding original female characters as the question of whether the canon should "make room" for authors' own experiences, interests, and desires.[36] Indeed, this framing was antithetical to the strongly affirmational culture still lingering from first-generation Tolkien fandom.

In a canon where less than 20 percent of named characters are female, few are developed beyond a name, and many more are elided as merely relations of named male characters, it is hard not to see Tolkien fan fiction's centering of female characters as a feminist act.[37] Moreover, the strong disapprobation these stories drew demonstrates the troubling sexism endemic in early Tolkien fandom—where, in affirmational terms, exclusion of women could be conveniently framed as merely canonical—as well as fertile ground for increasing transformational leanings toward reframing that canon. Tensions grew between affirmationally oriented fans wanting "more of" the canon as it was and transformationally oriented fans who saw canon as something they could reshape.[38] As with sexual content, though, Tolkien fan fiction authors' treatment of women characters has undergone substantial shifts with each generation, further facilitated by the compartmentalized nature of online fandom infrastructures.

While 78 percent of Tolkien fan fiction authors surveyed in 2015 asserted their interest in stories about women characters, survey findings also reveal that gender is still a complicated topic. Figure 5 shows how many stories on two Tolkien-specific archives include female characters. Comparing Stories of Arda (which had the tightest content restrictions and required approval to post) and the Silmarillion Writers' Guild (SWG, which never had content restrictions or approval systems) reiterates this fandom compartmentalization based on affirmational-transformational values.[39] As the third generation progressed, the number of women characters tagged/named on Stories of Arda remained static, whereas those on the SWG surged, revealing again that certain spaces were more accepting of writing about characters or perspectives deemed missing from Tolkien's canon. Although some fans across generations may have been interested in fan works we would call transformational, fandom spaces were not always encouraging of either these works or those interested in them.

CONCLUSION

Although sexual content and gender are by no means the only contentious topics in Tolkien fandom—indeed, recent discussions have highlighted the need for more attention paid to white fans' treatments of race and to BIPOC fans' experiences of racism in fandom—they do provide themes by which we can delineate three main generations of Tolkien fandom.[40] Moreover,

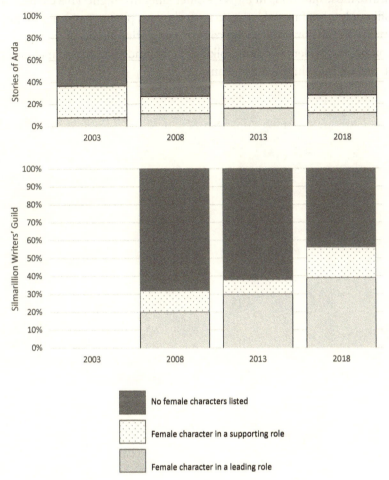

FIGURE 5. Percentage of stories on two major Tolkien fan fiction archives that include female characters.

looking at Tolkien-based fan fiction and authors across these generations reveals how, even today, Tolkien fandom occupies multiple loci on the affirmational-transformational continuum. Whereas fans of the current third generation are largely more accepting of exploring certain topics, this remains a fandom that highly prizes its canon and tends to use fan fiction to engage with it—endeavors that, while hardly exclusive of sexuality/ orientation, gender, and sexual content altogether, also do not always prioritize those questions in the ways other fandoms might. This chapter can offer only a brief introduction to such complex phenomena, and we hope we are not the only ones who continue exploring them, as they provide compelling evidence of how Tolkien's work, and Jackson's adaptations of it, remain meaningful for so many.

"Fannish Sensibilities"

FISSURES IN THE SHERLOCK HOLMES FANDOM

L. N. Rosales

A *Study in Scarlet*, the first Sherlock Holmes novel, appeared in *Beeton's Christmas Annual* for 1887. Sir Arthur Conan Doyle went on to publish fifty-six short stories and three other novels featuring the detective until 1927, by which time the oeuvre had inspired a vast following. Stage, radio, film, and television adaptations released over the subsequent ninety years were a result of this initial and continuing popularity and simultaneously ensured it by introducing the detective for new generations of fans. Indeed, as Sherlockian Al Shaw notes, "every generation chose their own Holmes as portrayed on film or television, and, if you knew who their favorite Holmes was, the odds were that you could guess their age better than a carnival con man could."[1]

Most recently, the BBC's *Sherlock* (2010–2017) and CBS's *Elementary* (2012–2019) have ushered a new generation of fans into the century-old fandom. Naturally, a fan community that has existed for such a chunk of history goes through a litany of shifts as it evolves, particularly in a century that saw such sweeping social changes and swift technological advancements. In this chapter, I offer a short history of the Sherlock Holmes fan community and its traditional practices. Although some of these traditions continue today, the evolution of online fan communities has created new fan practices; thus, members of a new generation often consider themselves fans without participating in the older traditions that are frequently less accessible to them. I will show how the fandom is resultantly fragmented despite calls for unity. Ultimately, I argue, it is not differing fan practices alone that cause these fissures; it is instead a desire to distance beloved tradition from contemporary stereotypes regarding "fangirls," with which these fan practices are largely associated. These stereotypes are inherently sexist and ageist. However, the history of the Sherlock Holmes fandom is itself troubled by a misogynistic past that informs its present.

Christopher Redmond defines the term *Sherlockian* as one who ascribes to a community passionate about Sherlock Holmes. But which Sherlock

Holmes? Only the original Holmes from Conan Doyle's tales? What about adaptations of Holmes? He muses: "are their admirers Sherlockians? We have to say yes, or we shall incur the charge of 'gatekeeping,' which is metaphorically used nowadays to mean an assumed right to decide who is, and who isn't, a member of a cultural group, including a fandom. (Is the Sherlock Holmes community a fandom? More definitions; let's not go there.)"[2] Redmond's tone hints at a bone of contention in the realm of Sherlock Holmes fans. Reluctant to admit that Sherlockians constitute a "fandom," he acknowledges against his will that admirers of Holmes in particular adaptations can be Sherlockians and mocks the idea of gatekeeping. Throughout the collection of essays, there are other hints, some less subtle, that something's rotten in the state of Denmark. In her contribution, Angela Fowler notes: "With new Holmes adaptations and new avenues of engagement, both in person and online, we're seeing a renaissance of Sherlockian fandom. It's tempting for older fans to get defensive, to try to test and exclude and critique those older fans' concerns: 'How can someone be a Sherlockian if they haven't read the original stories?' The thing is, they can."[3]

Fowler and others urge the Sherlockian community not to be gatekeepers. She implores, "A community . . . can only grow and thrive through new members. Each new Sherlockian brings with them their own voice, their own interpretation, and their own engagement, and it's essential that more experienced Sherlockians include rather than exclude."[4] Andrew J. Peck warns, "For the BSI [Baker Street Irregulars, a Sherlockian society] to survive into the future, it must always be accepting of new Sherlockians, even if they come to Holmes more from Cumberbatch than from the written Canon."[5] Wendy Fries insists, "Building on what *was* to create what *is* is the province of everything living. Nothing remains static, and so creation and recreation is what we fans *do*."[6] These examples identify a certain level of generational gatekeeping. Ashley Polasek classifies two seemingly opposing modes of fandom—affirmational and transformational—that are at work in Sherlock Holmes fan practices; she ties the former to traditional Sherlockian enterprises, such as playing "the Grand Game" via pseudo-scholarship and emulating Conan Doyle's Watsonian style in printed, published pastiche, and the latter to more transmedial work, such as publishing online fan fiction.[7] Polasek ultimately argues that there is overlap and bleeding betwixt the categories but finds they are useful in plotting community divisions.[8] Bearing these fissures in mind, let us dive into the history and development of this complex fandom.

THE SHERLOCK HOLMES FANDOM, HISTORICALLY

The earliest "fans" of Sherlock Holmes wrote letters to Sir Arthur Conan Doyle, sometimes mistaking Holmes for a real person, as in the case of the woman who offered the retired Holmes "her services as a housekeeper now that he had moved to a country cottage."[9] Others participated in contests sponsored by *Tit-Bits* magazine, like Mr. G. Douglas Buchanan, who composed a winning persuasive essay in 1894 on why "The Adventure of the Speckled Band" is the best of *The Adventures of Sherlock Holmes* series.[10] *Tit-Bits* also sponsored multiple contests for Sherlockian pastiche, inviting readers to submit original stories.[11] Some of these practices endured in various forms as the century chugged forward and organized fan communities emerged.

In his comprehensive social history of Sherlock Holmes, his afterlives, and the fan communities he inspired, Mattias Boström describes the context surrounding the birth of the first Sherlockian societies. Starting with a 1911 lecture republished by Ronald Knox in a book of essays in 1928, a domino effect occurred.[12] S. C. Roberts, while reviewing the essay collection, fell down a slippery slope investigating the chronological problems in the Holmes stories and published a series of pamphlets in 1931.[13] T. S. Blakeney followed with *Sherlock Holmes: Fact or Fiction?*, H. W. Bell with *Sherlock Holmes and Dr. Watson: A Chronology of Their Adventures*, and Vincent Starrett with *The Private Life of Sherlock Holmes*.[14] It is not surprising that amid the backdrop of this deluge of scholarship, the world's foremost Sherlockian societies were born. It is perhaps also not surprising that given the time required to put forth such scholarship, those who did so at this time were men of a particular social class.

As the legend goes, the Baker Street Irregulars (BSI) evolved out of Christopher Morley's lunch clubs. To celebrate the repeal of Prohibition as well as—by his tenuous estimation—Sherlock Holmes's birthday, Morley organized an extravagant lunch event at the Duane Hotel's restaurant for January 6, 1934. As a regular columnist for the *Saturday Review of Literature*, Morley printed information about the event, referring to it as the first meeting of the Baker Street Irregulars; under this heading he also published relevant texts from others, including a constitution for the club.[15] Morley's younger brother constructed an elaborate Sherlock Holmes crossword puzzle for use as an entry test into the club. Anyone able to successfully complete the puzzle within one month was considered eligible to join the BSI. Or almost anyone. Women, despite submitting perfectly solved crosswords, were not permitted entry.

"Fannish Sensibilities" 163

The BSI set the precedent for organized Sherlock Holmes fan practices in the United States. As some of the Victorian and Edwardian readership had done, the BSI treated Holmes as if he had been a real person. However, this practice was treated as more of a self-aware intellectual exercise, rather than the result of the errors of fancy or ignorance. The stories and novels were referred to as the "Sacred Writings," penned by Dr. John Watson, relegating Conan Doyle to the role of literary agent. Studying the Sacred Writings and attempting to resolve resultant conundrums (e.g., how many wives *did* Dr. Watson have?) or ameliorate relevant details came to be known as "playing the Grand Game." It became common practice for members of the BSI to write papers and give lectures in this vein—a tradition that continues. Unsurprisingly, given the quantity of such papers amassing as membership expanded, in 1946 Edgar W. Smith devised the idea of a quarterly publication.[16] Currently, anyone can purchase an annual subscription to the *Baker Street Journal*; for $41.95, one receives four quarterly issues and the Christmas annual.[17]

While the BSI is the flagship Sherlockian society in the United States, dozens of localized scion societies have popped up in the past seventy years, as well as independent sister societies around the world. The Bootmakers of Toronto are the original Sherlockian organization in Canada, and the United Kingdom is home to the Sherlock Holmes Society of London, the Deerstalkers of Welshpool (Wales), and the Crew of the S.S. May Day (Northern Ireland). Non-UK European societies include the Reichenbach Irregulars in Switzerland, the Magyar Club in Hungary, the Baskerville Hall Club in Sweden, and Circulo Holmes in Spain, as well as others in France, the Czech Republic, Italy, and Germany. Both Japan and India have Sherlockian societies, and Australia hosts various regional groups. Each society has its own traditions. For example, the Brothers Three of Moriarty based in Santa Fe, New Mexico, held the annual Unhappy Birthday You Bastard celebration at the Frontier Saloon in the nearby town of Moriarty. The climax of these festivities were the members' contributions to the "Moriarty Memorial Manure Pile, on which was deposited manure from horses, mules, donkeys, cows, geese, and one or two more exotic animals, such as camels and kangaroos, donated by Sherlockian societies from all over the world."[18] Different societies also have different traditions regarding ceremonial toasts given during their annual dinners. Drinking and toasting are integral to Sherlockian community traditions. The very by-laws of the BSI constitution contain detailed guidelines regarding the consumption of alcohol (in particular, who picks up the tab for a round).[19] Harrison Hunt recalls "the wives' group of the all-male Sons of the Copper Beeches in Philadelphia—affectionately known as the Bitches of the Beeches" whose purpose was that of "gathering together to drive their too-jolly husbands home."[20] Perhaps one reason women were so long excluded from these societies in the United States is that the members were concerned they would no longer have ready designated drivers on call for early morning transport.

Prior to the advent of the internet, participating in the Sherlockian fandom was largely limited to attending the meetings and events of nearby scion societies, publishing pastiche or pseudo-scholarship, collecting, and maintaining a written correspondence with other Sherlockians. The internet introduced new dimensions to these traditions and certainly made it easier for nascent Sherlockians to learn of and locate their local scion society, but it was not until the explosion of new adaptations hit screens after the turn into the twenty-first century that a new-new generation of fans would begin to popularize contemporary fan practices. As we witnessed in Redmond's introduction, "fandom" itself is a label that traditional Sherlockians frequently eschew. Andrew Solberg and Richard Katz elucidate, "In general, seasoned (i.e., old) Sherlockians must swallow before we admit that what we do for and with our love of Sherlock Holmes fully fits in the fannish domain. . . . We like to think of ourselves as aficionados or devotees."[21] The next section explores the realm of fandom—and why it may seem so antithetical to how traditional Sherlockians both see themselves and want to be seen.

SHERLOCK HOLMES FANS TODAY

On January 15, 2012, "The Reichenbach Fall" episode of BBC's *Sherlock* was broadcast, loosely adapted from the story "The Final Problem" in which Holmes allegedly dies. In the adaptation, Sherlock (Benedict Cumberbatch) jumps to his death off a rooftop after nemesis Jim Moriarty (Andrew Scott) artfully convinces the public that he is a fraud. Mika Hallor subsequently suggested on Tumblr that fans start a movement to clear Sherlock's name.[22] Within twenty-four hours, the number of responses reached over ten thousand.[23] The hashtag #BelieveInSherlock could be found on all social media platforms, and in the physical world messages such as "I believe in Sherlock" and "Moriarty was real" spread.[24] Such was the commitment of *Sherlock* fans.

This anecdote illustrates the explosive popularity of *Sherlock*. Though CBS's *Elementary* has its own fan base, and the Warner Bros. films *Sherlock Holmes* (Guy Ritchie, 2009) and *Sherlock Holmes: A Game of Shadows* (Guy Ritchie, 2011) are beloved by many, it is BBC *Sherlock* fans and their practices

"Fannish Sensibilities" 165

to which multiple scholarly tomes have been dedicated in recent years. The *Sherlock* fanbase is the most vocal and visible, in their online presence on such sites as Tumblr, as well as in person, crowding filming locations to the point of extreme interruption. In 2012 Louisa Ellen Stein and Kristina Busse's edited collection, *Sherlock and Transmedia Fandom: Essays on the BBC Series*, was published, and 2018 saw the publication of Jennifer Wojton and Lynette Porter's *Sherlock and Digital Fandom: The Meeting of Creativity, Community, and Activism* and Ann K. McClellan's *Sherlock's World: Fan Fiction and the Reimagining of BBC's Sherlock*.[25]

In her discussion of the internet archive's depths and *Sherlock* fans' use of that space, Rebecca Pearson cites a blog post and comment interaction to indicate "that *Sherlock*'s success stemmed from the text's deliberately engineered appeal to fannish sensibilities and networks."[26] Sean Duncan, the commenter, suggests that *Sherlock* is "easy to translate into common internetty fan practices (slash, 'squeeing,' fan vids, etc.)."[27] These "internetty fan practices"—and Duncan's condescending tone—are at the heart of contemporary forms of Sherlockian fan practice and the fissure, I suggest, in the Sherlock Holmes fandom.

In an article concerning female *Sherlock* fans over fifty, Line Nybro Petersen wrote about her emails with older women about their fandom engagement. She finds a common theme: the insistence of separating oneself "from that of screaming girls behaving hysterically."[28] Similarly, Martin Freeman (who portrays Dr. John Watson on *Sherlock*), comments, "I've got some great reactions to things I'm very proud of, but I don't think any surpass *Sherlock* in . . . just a general feeling that you're in a mini Beatlemania."[29] This image of screaming young women is perhaps exactly what the Sherlockian community combats in their reluctance to own the fandom label. In Steve Duncan's list of fannish activities, this image represents the "squeeing" with which Sherlockians do not wish to be associated: an impression that is very much aged and gendered.

Let's consider another item on the list. Slash fan fiction features a romantic pairing of two same-sex characters from a fictional universe; frequently, in BBC *Sherlock* fan fiction, that pairing is John Watson/Sherlock Holmes (Johnlock). Various websites host a frankly staggering amount of Sherlock Holmes fan fiction, much of which is slash, often giving readers the opportunity to browse fan fiction from separate Sherlock Holmes iterations, such as *Sherlock, Elementary*, the original canon, or even a 2013 Russian series. Is fan fiction an aspect of Sherlock Holmes fan practices that is unique to a new generation of Holmes fans, ones who grew up with internet? Duncan's comment leans heavily on this assumption. However, this assumption takes it for granted that before the internet, there were no fan-produced writings about Holmes.

Yet *Tit-Bits* magazine solicited stories featuring Holmes from its Victorian readers. In 1944, Ellery Queen edited an anthology featuring pastiche, *The Misadventures of Sherlock Holmes*. The collection was celebrated by BSI members and critics in the press.[30] Decades later, Nicholas Meyer's *The Seven Per-Cent Solution* (1974) became the second-best-selling book in the United States and remained on the *New York Times* best-seller list for forty weeks, after being reviewed glowingly by Sherlockian societies.[31] These two ventures, so well received and strongly endorsed by the most official of Sherlockian communities, seem to be merely separated in their reception from online fan fiction by medium (print versus virtual) and the ethos of a publisher's stamp on the title page.

Meyer writes of his motivations regarding *The Seven Per-Cent Solution*: "I wrote the book for my own pleasure and as a corrective to other Holmes imitations (chiefly films) that I couldn't abide. . . . Nor did I care for yanking Holmes out of period and a number of other (to me) unpardonable liberties."[32] Lyndsay Faye cites similar inspiration for her *Dust and Shadow: An Account of the Ripper Killings by Dr. John H. Watson* (2009), explaining, "it . . . rankles me when Holmes talks in relentless abstruse paragraphs, stringing clauses together *ad nauseam*. . . .What good would nitpicking do if I never sat down and attempted to channel Doyle's remarkable prose myself?"[33] Faye and Meyer, both invested members of the BSI, exhibit two impulses: to do Conan Doyle justice and to improve on previous adaptations or published pastiche. They are both participants in the traditional forms of Sherlockian fan practice embraced by earlier generations. In her study of *Sherlock* fan fiction, however, McClellan cites Parachute_Silks, who offers a particular motivation behind her story "Astronomy"; she writes the male characters as women "as a slightly desperate reaction to this show's female character problem."[34] Like Meyer in a previous century, Parachute_Silks wished to improve on an adaptation. Her story is published on the website LiveJournal rather than a physical book, which corresponds with Polasek's conception of "transmedial" rather than "traditional" fan practice.[35] The other main difference is stylistic; Meyer and Faye not only use Doyle's characters in their works, they emulate his style (Meyer "had even included a handful of deliberate continuity errors and other mistakes to make the text resemble the originals even more closely").[36] Each is portrayed as being written by Dr. Watson and at the beginning offers an explanation as to why the cases

"Fannish Sensibilities" 167

were excluded from initial publication. "Astronomy," on the other hand, is written with a third-person narrator in contemporary, colloquial language, reflecting its usage of the characterizations from *Sherlock*, not the canon. It is not interested, as traditional pastiche is, with establishing plausible explanations for how it can be inserted into the canon. There are more degrees of separation between "Astronomy" and Conan Doyle—perhaps one of the biggest hallmarks of a large percentage of online fan fiction.

Sanna Nyqvist writes about "hardcore imitation" pastiche, ultimately arguing that Sherlockian pastiche is more subversive than it might seem on the surface. She mandates that "their metafictiveness and playfulness indicate complexity. . . . Even the most reverent imitations bear traces of radical subversion in a manner that is typical to pastiche as a double-edged literary form."[37] Parachute_Silks explains that her motivation to write "Astronomy" as a gender-swapped narrative is to fix the problematic (and lack of) representation of women in *Sherlock*. Nyqvist's essay begs fan studies to remember that traditional published pastiche has the potential to perform a similar task. If traditionally published pastiche and online fan fiction have inherent subversive potential, and both are frequently written with similar motives, what separates them is more of a technicality. That and the prejudice resultant from generational stereotypes.

Lyndsay Faye describes her career: "I make my living . . . writing Sherlock Holmes fanfiction that also happens to qualify as pastiche. But allow me to begin this discussion from the heart rather than from any perceived intellectual distinction between the F-word and the P-word."[38] Faye immediately acknowledges the contentious debate of fan fiction versus pastiche, indicating a popular belief that fan fiction is not the intellectual equal of Sherlockian pastiche. In a blog post, she similarly parodies the discomfort the traditional Sherlockian community has with the "fandom" label:

> it falls to me to discuss certain disturbing tendencies on the part of new devotees to refer to that venerable institution, the Baker Street Irregulars, as a "fandom" when it is actually a literary society. . . . For the purposes of this intellectual exercise, the possibility that the BSI may potentially be a storied and erudite literary society *and* a happily thriving fandom simultaneously will be ignored. This decision was made in light of the fact that a noun cannot be two things concurrently, the way the Empire State Building is not both a functioning office tower and a tourist destination, and the way Bill Clinton is not both a former president and a saxophone player.[39]

168 GENERATIONAL TENSIONS

The post continues, glibly insisting that knowing the colors of Holmes's dressing gowns and other trivia are not the same as learning Klingon, nor is collecting Sherlock Holmes first editions identical to seeking rare comic books. With tongue in cheek, Faye hyperbolically debunks any self-righteous snobbery possessed by traditional Sherlockians—ostensibly, those of the previous generation. To be a card-carrying member of a scion society, who voraciously reads pastiche, collects Sherlockian knick-knacks, and can instantaneously rattle off obscure Sherlockiana is, in fact, to be a fan.

A STUDY IN GENDER

In 1968, six female college students protested the annual male-only BSI dinner in front of Cavanagh's Restaurant in New York with banners reading "We want in!" and "BSI unfair to women."[40] These women had created a Sherlockian discussion group at their college and begun corresponding with various BSI members to discuss Sherlockiana; finding that the Irregulars did not allow women to join, they traveled from Connecticut to demonstrate. The protest, however, was unsuccessful.

Julia Carlson Rosenblatt, one of the first women invested into the BSI in 1991, writes about her experience of exclusion from and subsequently inclusion in the society. In describing the exclusion of women from the BSI, Rosenblatt begs readers:

> Before rushing to judgment, bear in mind how times have changed since the 1930s. Today we can hardly imagine that women would not expect to pick up their share of the tab. BSI membership, in which the gentlemen shared the check for the ladies, would not only be expensive but would hardly be membership on an equal basis. In addition, the inclusion of women in these early gatherings was more flirtatious than serious. If the BSI were to be an ongoing club, the wives of the men might object to the presence of other women as Irregulars in an arguably frivolous setting.[41]

The Sherlock Holmes Society in London did not seem to suffer these same hesitancies, as they admitted female members from the beginning. Are wives less prone to jealousy in Britain than in the United States? Are the men less insistent on chivalrously paying for drinks consumed by ladies? Rosenblatt notes that the BSI "advanced a widely accepted myth that Holmes was a misogynist," whereas a prominent member of the Sherlock Holmes Soci-

"Fannish Sensibilities"   169

ety wrote of Holmes's appreciation of women.[42] Is the implication that the flagship society in each country merely took its cue from Holmes himself?

Rosenblatt describes the tradition of the BSI toasting a chosen woman as "The Woman" at the co-ed cocktail hour before the exclusively male dinner. In 1979, she was invited to be "The Woman," although she admits, "The idealistically feminist side of me questioned how I could possibly go along with such a sexist practice."[43] Ultimately, she accepted, reasoning, "This was not a time to isolate myself as some sort of feminist crank."[44] Yet when she met some of the previous Women, she noticed that none of them were Sherlockians; they were all wives of revered Irregulars. As the wife of a man who had been invested several years earlier, she pondered whether it was this position that won her the "honor" or whether it was her work coauthoring a Sherlock Holmes cookbook.

As a direct result of the sexist exclusion of women from the BSI, the Adventuresses of Sherlock Holmes were born. The Adventuresses, as described by Faye, "are not a 'scion' of the BSI, or 'a subgroup of likeminded merry fanatics under the BSI umbrella,' but rather the inevitable result of the fact that if you said no to women in the 1960s, they'd build their own clubhouse and invent their own secret handshake, thank you very much."[45] The Adventuresses held their own annual dinner in New York City at the exact same time as the BSI until admission of many of their number into the other dinner necessitated a schedule change. The Friends of Irene Adler is a society that was created specifically for women who were being excluded from an all-male Sherlockian group. Dan Posnansky founded the group for women in the Boston area who were denied membership into the scion society of the Speckled Band, which only began to admit women in 2017.[46]

Today, there are certainly young female members of the BSI and various scion societies who are active in the (now co-ed) traditional Sherlockian realm. Obviously, there is some transgenerational crossover between the two spheres. The Baker Street Babes are a group of young women who, via their podcast, conference events, and social media presence, "hope to help provide a bridge between the older and often intimidating world of Sherlockiana and the newer tech savvy generation of fans that are just discovering the Holmes stories for the first time."[47] Multiple members of the Baker Street Babes are invested members of the BSI, though Irregular Andrew Peck reveals, "some curmudgeons have grumbled about the Baker Street Babes."[48] The existence of these curmudgeons suggests that the overlap between the two spheres is not universally embraced. Baker Street Babes founder Kristina Manente recalls, "When I was told I wasn't serious enough to be a Sherlock Holmes fan, I felt a fire in my belly. Who had the right to say that to me? Just because I was a young woman, I was apparently invalidated as a Holmesian. I was told there was no 'body of work' that proved we were anything more than fleeting fan girls."[49] Fangirls squee; they write slash; they wax poetic over Benedict Cumberbatch's cheekbones—so goes the stereotype. Manente's righteous fury articulates the fissure in the Sherlockian community. Although there are some transgenerational efforts being made—the *Baker Street Journal* has recently pushed to publish more diverse voices, particularly those of young women—it is clear that the previous generation of Holmesians have a prejudice to overcome.[50] The ageist, sexist stereotype of the fangirl haunts the Sherlockian fandom like a specter, creating a division in the community between those who are ready to accept evolution and change and usher in a new generation of fans and those who cling to traditional practices, some of which were rooted in misogyny from the beginning.

"Fannish Sensibilities" 171

The Fandom Is a Welcoming Place Unless I Know More Than You

GENERATIONS, MENTORSHIP, AND SUPER-FANS

Mélanie Bourdaa

When it comes to defining fans and fandoms, the concept of generations is interesting because it includes notions of time, groups, and practices: "generation articulates temporalities, humanity and social changes, collective and individual life stories, individual and cultural profiles."[1] The concept also introduces life cycles, ages, and life trajectory. More importantly, Agnès Pécolo underscores that generations are a time landmark and a cultural marker that could reveal a collective consciousness.[2] In that sense, a media event or a TV show can shape a generation of audiences and fans and give them a collective identity that will be passed from generation to generation in a fandom. This also can lead to rejections in fandoms, especially when newcomers enter the fandom at a specific moment in time (for a reboot, for example, or when a franchise is discontinued and then changed).

This chapter focuses on time engagement in a fandom and how it structures mentorship and can sometimes lead to the outbreaks of super-fans in the community. Time is of the essence in the definition of fans, and there can be battles around the notion of authenticity. Mentorship is another important factor in fandoms because it allows the welcoming of new fans into a well-established space. On one hand, as I will show, mentorship is often a safe and reassuring practice in fandoms, and on the other hand, it can lead to hierarchy between fans when it is linked to the notion of authenticity and of the one true fan.

I created several questionnaires in English, using Google Forms. They were administered on social media, including Twitter, Facebook, and Tumblr, which allowed circulation through the phenomena of retweets and likes and within fandoms themselves and in the public sphere more broadly. I used specific hashtags from communities that seemed particularly active on social networks: #Sanvers (*Supergirl*, CW, 2015–2021), #WayHaught (*Wynonna Earp*, Syfy, 2016–2021), and #Olicity (*Arrow*, CW, 2012–2019). Those are the subcommunities I know the best and with which I have interacted at some point. The fan communities of *Hannibal* (NBC, 2013–2016), *Sherlock* (BBC, 2010–present), and *The Flash* (CW, 2014–present) took over and shared the questionnaires. I directly alerted influential fans who maintain blogs, podcasts, and fanzines about the questionnaires for them to share in their various networks.

The online questionnaire seemed to be the best tool for collecting data and quotes from fans on their identity, their affect, and their practices. The data were part of a much larger research aiming at analyzing fans in depth regarding their feelings of belonging to communities. In the questionnaires, I included questions on how long fans have been in one or many fandoms, on the notion of mentorship, and on affiliations and transmissions. I only offered open-ended questions to let fans express themselves fully and get enough answers to provide actionable analysis. I received 186 responses between October and December 2018.

I first define fans and their link with generations, ages, and life cycles. Relying on quotes I collected from the online questionnaire, I analyze how mentorship can be a useful and welcoming presence in fandoms. Finally, I emphasize how fans can consider themselves "true fans" and have toxic practices regarding new fans and reboots.

"I'VE ALWAYS BEEN A FAN": FANS, GENERATIONS, AND TIME ENGAGEMENT

The term *fan* is obviously not new, and from the first appearances of the word at the end of the seventeenth century in England, it took on a negative connotation and was closely linked to religious worship from the outset. It is the diminutive of *fanatic*, a word that highlights excess, devotion, and obsession, terms still often associated with fans of media or popular works to describe their marginal and extraordinary side in the press or in media reports and documentaries. The term was used in the United States first to qualify the passion of baseball spectators and finally passed into the common language to define a practice related to cultural and media works.

Today, it is extremely complex to define fans because the word covers a large number of definitions, tensions in academia, and popular beliefs, but also many practices and degrees of engagement. One of the most important pitfalls is that almost everyone today defines themselves as a fan of some-

The Fandom Is a Welcoming Place Unless . . . 173

thing without understanding the stakes that this term takes on regarding questions of identity, creativity, collective intelligence, and sharing. American cultural studies, thanks in particular to Henry Jenkins, have made it possible to change perceptions of fans and legitimize their practices in the academic world. In his foundational book *Textual Poachers*, Jenkins described fans as active audiences and content producers, working together in a common place, the fandom.[3] From this perspective, the fan is not only a "follower," a "collector," or an "enthusiast," to use the categories of Abercrombie and Longhurst, but above all is a producer of content and meaning.[4] Fans, in Jenkins's thought, are "consumers who produce, readers who write, viewers who participate."[5]

Likewise, for Sarah M. Corse and Jaime Hartless, "fans, and especially in the sci-fi community, can spend considerable sums, time, and energy on their cultural identities, getting to Comic Con in San Diego, making costumes, writing fan fiction or music, and participating in online communities to share their interests with other members who are similarly engaged."[6] These authors immediately underscore the notions of both emotional and material engagement in terms of money and time, which characterize the bond among fans in the community and between fans and the cultural and media work or works that fascinate them. But these definitions could easily limit the fan to a consumer, a prisoner of the capitalist system imposed on them by the media and contemporary media systems.

However, it is necessary that we do not consider fans as merely passive consumers of cultural products because their own productions can raise questions about sexual identity, racism, gender, or disability, for example. In addition, communities act as agents of empowerment and not as passive entities. This active dimension of fans makes it possible to understand how and how much fans create, write, or edit videos as well as also engage in politics or discuss important causes.

Paul Booth makes an important distinction between fans as individuals who acquire skills through practice and mentoring and fandom, this community, this collective of individuals. He explains that "Fans typically utilize their technological skills, their communal intelligence, their individual knowledge base, and their social interaction skills to investigate and explore media."[7] The fandom for its part "refers to the social grouping of individuals with shared interests, joined together through some form of mechanism of membership; the self-selected organization of a group of fans who both enjoy an extant media object, and who create additional content about that extant media object."[8]

174 GENERATIONAL TENSIONS

The individual who defines him- or herself as a fan joins a social group that will participate in forging his or her collective identity. In earlier research on fans of the *Battlestar Galactica* (Syfy, 2004–2009) sci-fi series, fans highlighted that they were happy to be part of a specialized social audience, the fandom, because it gave them a sense of belonging.[9]

Above all, these specific audiences have been fans for many years. Their commitment is anchored over a long time, and they manage to date each of their entries in a specific fandom: "My first experience in a fandom was made through the dedicated forums to *Daria, Darkwing Duck*, and cartoons in general, starting in 1999. I've been in a lot of fandoms since then, and right now my fan activities revolve around *Hannibal* and the Fullerverse (since 2013), the work of Terry Pratchett and Neil Gaiman (in several ways since 2000), Shakespeare (publicly since probably 2012), and *Queen Sugar* (summer 2017)" (Respondent 74). Respondent 10 is also very precise on the time spent in each fandom they are part of: "DW [Doctor Who]—since 1993, but in earnest since 2011; ST [Star Trek]—since c. 1990; HHGG [*Hitchhiker's Guide to the Galaxy*]—since 1993; SF [science fiction] in general—since c. 1990, but got fafiated [became inactive or left the community] in the 2000s. For a time I also edited an underground music fanzine from 2001 to 2004."

It is therefore a strong bond that crystallizes in a social group, marked by a commitment and a significant investment of time and personal resources, which takes place over a long time. In a sense, the very definition of a fan for those audiences relies on the time they have spent in a fandom, which gives them a legitimacy. Respondent 44 emphasizes that the degree of participation is as important as the time they have spent in the fandom to qualify their identity and practices: "Depending on the fandom and the intensity of my participation. For example, I have enjoyed Harry Potter and its paratexts for about 11 years but not at all as intensely as my much shorter (about 4 years) participation in *Hannibal* fandom." Often, we evaluate fan commitment by productivity and creativity, but longevity in the fandom is also an argument for commitment and engagement in the community.

I also investigated how fans learned about fandom. Two types of entry into the community appear in the responses given: through a family member or friend, or more often through the internet. For some fans, friends and family played a founding role in identity-building by sharing and conveying their media tastes. There is also a kind of legacy, handover, intergenerational transmission of taste when the fandom is presented by a family member. For example, Respondent 22 was introduced to science fiction by their family when they were a child.[10] Respondent 18 had a different introduction to the

The Fandom Is a Welcoming Place Unless . . .   175

fandom depending on the text: "my father introduced me to *Star Wars* & *LOTR*. I discovered Sherlock almost as soon as I could read and sucked up every detective mystery I could find. I found *Supernatural* because everyone on Tumblr and Pinterest kept posting about it. My cousin introduced me to *Doctor Who*."

Cultural taste and belonging to a social group are transmitted from one generation to another, functioning as a heritage that must be maintained, cultivated, and perpetuated.

MENTORSHIP AND SUPER-FANS IN FANDOMS

Fan communities are heterogeneous groups that welcome people of all social classes, genders, and ages. The issue of mentorship was asked in the questionnaire. I wanted to know if the "new" members were accepted in these communities and if they were helped by the "older" fans.

According to Jenkins, Ito, and boyd, one of the fundamental points of participatory culture is "an informal mentorship whereby what is known by the most experienced is passed along to novices."[11] The knowledge, the practices, the codes, and the rules held by the oldest fans in the community are transmitted to the new ones, who then hold them to welcome the next members. A community is never closed in terms of membership, and fans can join at any time depending on when they discover the cultural work. The oldest fans are the gatekeepers of the history and memory of the fandom and the common language, and they are responsible for the tradition. These mentors also possess a more encyclopedic knowledge of the series, which they happily share with others. When I asked about any form of mentorship in the fandoms they belong to, one fan answered: "I feel like this is a predominant trend in the *Hannibal* and Shakespeare fandoms. Both communities have a large number of older fans who have specific knowledge and skills to answer particular questions about the elements of storytelling" (Respondent 14). The oldest fans in the community are the most skilled and the ones people go to because of their cultural and time investment in the fandom. They welcome the new members and give them the cultural, historical, functional, and organizational foundations of the community. The oldest fans then play the role of historians of a cultural practice that is transmitted in the community through the creation of archives, texts, rules, and codes. "I guess sometimes older fans or people who have more experience in fandom tend to explain some of the history, culture. And people tend to encourage fans who want to create fic or art, I suppose proofreaders for fic could count depending on the situation" (Respondent 38). Another says that "older fans give advice to younger fans about life and how to behave properly in a fandom" (Respondent 66). There is a sense of policing in the fandom, something that is sustained by fans who have been in the fandom the longest and want to model the community a certain way. They feel entitled to do so, since they have been engaged in the community for the longest time.

Beyond this historical culture of fandom that is created, built, and consolidated over the generations of fans, older fans also guide the newest in the creation of content, not only by encouraging them but also by giving them advice and information. Respondent 28 tells us: "it's up to us to include the newbies so that they feel at ease and know the rules of fandom." Respondent 35 says, "In general, fans explain the basics to newbies when they ask (behavior, story, iconic content, jokes)." This sharing of technical knowledge both promotes and inhibits the creativity of fans. Mentoring is part of the creativity and facilitates exchanges and sharing, as Respondent 2 explains: "Most mentoring happens when the fans create something, and the rest of the fans offer feedback. A few fan artists have tutorials and video their creation process for new fans to watch."

This mentorship is obviously visible in many fan communities. It can also be visible across age generations, which could be qualified as a transgenerational relationship between fans. For example, young Harry Potter fans explain to the older ones the universe and the links between the characters, and the adult fans have tried to explain to the younger ones the concerns teachers have about this fiction. Rebecca W. Black analyzed the effects of mentorship around the practice of beta-reading (reading the first drafts of fan fiction) in fan fiction communities and how this practice made it possible to improve works.[12] Intergenerational barriers are broken through mentoring, and emotional and creative help is ensured in the community, with advice and tips shared between fans. "Fans help each other with drawing tips mostly, but also with beta-reading and editing fanfiction. When I was in the *Sims* fan community, there was a LOT of mentorship there. Fans would write many tutorials to help newcomers learn how to skin characters and create new assets for the game—these were very technical things. We also had forums where more experienced creators helped new creators. It was a really great experience" (Respondent 65).

However, these forms of mentorship are not all positive, since they create hierarchies in the communities (in terms of investment and time, knowledge, and possession of the cultural work), which do not please everyone.

The Fandom Is a Welcoming Place Unless . . . 177

As Jenkins, Ito, and boyd recall, "Old-timers and highly expert fans have developed new ways of signaling subcultural capital, to differentiate themselves from the newer, younger and less sophisticated fans."[13] Differences are then created and maintained by the fans themselves, highlighting hierarchies; these mostly popular fans are referred to as "super-fans" by other members of the community. But these hierarchies pose a problem because they jeopardize the merits of the community and the principles of belonging and harmony that maintain the coherence and cohesion of the social group. "There are users with big followings in every fandom. I've learned to be weary [sic] of them, however. Some let the small fame get to their heads—especially when they have fans of their own—and become problematic" (Respondent 22). These super fans can then become opinion leaders and split the community, as explained by this fan who has experienced this phenomenon in her fandoms: "I have noticed some phenomena that are repeated and in particular when someone has a large audience (so to speak) and expresses an opinion, some are quick to follow him and nod, and suddenly some fandoms are more divisive than others, and in particular because these strong voices like conflict more than the common interest of the fandom. Anyway, I try to get away from these people, because it weakens the fandom experience" (Respondent 110).

The welcoming of new fans into the community by the oldest ones is sometimes done in a violent way, especially when a reboot of a series or a film is involved. This is what happened with the science fiction series *Battlestar Galactica*, for which Ronald D. Moore and David Eick came up with a reimagined version for the Syfy channel. *Battlestar Galactica* (ABC, 1978–1979) had a solid fan base that did not hesitate to organize and send letters to try to save the series when ABC announced a cancellation after two seasons. The reimagined 2004 version, which deals with post-9/11 political, philosophical, and technological issues, angered older fans who coined it from the very first episodes as GINO (Galactica in name only). This version was for them a betrayal of the original on many levels—notably the fact that Starbuck, the flirtatious pilot of the original series, was portrayed by a woman, Katee Sackhoff, in the reimagined version. Dirk Benedict, who played the character in the first version of the show, issued a statement claiming that this casting choice was nonsense and that the character had been castrated.[14] For Ronald D. Moore, the gender change was an opportunity to dive deeper into the psychology of the character and explore new story arcs. In the reimagined version, even if Starbuck has masculine traits (short hair, muscles, attitude, and smoking cigars), she is in many ways a tortured woman with a heavy past. On forum boards, discussions between old and new fans around this reboot were more than inflamed.

Here, in these heated debates and online discussions, emerges the question of the "good" versus the "bad" fan. The good fan, in this case, is the one who has participated in the community from the beginning (again highlighting the notion of time) and appreciates the original version of the series more than the reimagined one. Fans may be perceived as "authentic" (in opposition to false fans) and, in this precise configuration, they act as the gatekeepers of the original (here authentic) work and its memory. The tensions that appear in fandoms when reboots are launched is a symptom of a fight between fans who keep the memory of a certain version of the media text and new fans who enjoy a reimagined and more modern version without denying what was before. Old fans invoke the time they have spent in the fandom as a marker of their authenticity as fans and as a generation of viewers.

Mentorship is a great part of any fandom that reinforces the idea of a welcoming space. In this concept, old generations of fans—that is, those who have been in the fandom the longest—are keepers of the history of the fandom, including its rules and good behaviors. They pass on this heritage to younger fans to keep the fandom alive. These older fans can use their time in the fandom as an advantage and instill some hierarchies by becoming super-fans. As such, they build vertical relationships in their fandoms, in a place where horizontal relationships between members are the norms. Indeed, these super-fans re-create a pyramidal structure in the community where they have some sort of power and cultural status over other fans. They sometimes build privileged relations with members of the production and acting crews because they have this cultural status in the community.

CONCLUSION

Fans and the notion of generations are intertwined for better or for worse in fandoms. On one hand, forms of mentorship can be built where old fans welcome newcomers in a safe online space. These older fans are the guardians of the codes, rules, and history of the fandom, which they pass on to the next generation of fans, even if it's a relatively new fandom. *Wynonna Earp* and its Earpers (as fans call themselves) have an example of true mentorship between old fans and newcomers. Here, old fans are those who have been involved and engaged in online fandoms for a longer time, and they welcome new fans with respect and benevolence. The Earper fandom is known for its acceptance and love for other Earpers, as well as their extreme, over-the-top obsessing over the show's cast and popular LGBTQIA+ couple known to fans as WayHaught. What is the most important for this "famdom" (family/fandom), as they call their community, is the inclusion of all members. Some answers to the questionnaire confirm that fans of the series do not engage in the toxic practices that may be experienced by other fandoms. "Twitter is a terrible place and there are so many things that can depress me . . . The Wynonna Earp community does nothing on this awful side, and that is what qualifies it for me" (Respondent 82).

On the other hand, the notion of time and generations can bring resentment from older fans toward newcomers in the community. At stake here is the very notion of authenticity that older fans claim because they have been a fan for longer and thus they know the rules, the philosophy, and the media text better. Moreover, when they feel that their favorite media text is tainted, they can use toxic fan practices and discourses to attack producers and casts and other fans. These practices show the dark side of fandoms and that fandoms can sometimes be broken and most of all divided.

According to Andrew Slack, cultural acupuncture is locating the psychological energy in the culture, and moving that energy toward creating a healthier world. Alongside cultural participation, this could be the answer to safer fandoms with positive mentorships. For example, the Harry Potter Alliance (now Fandom Forward) welcomes all fans to take actions around cultural, social, and political matters. For example, they organize training camps, "a place where fans, creators, organizers, and academics of all ages come together to tap into our collective imagination as a powerful force for good."[15] The will to be civically engaged in these actions leads to practices of mentorship in the community and outside of it and advice on how to spread the word. After Lexa was killed in *The 100* (CW, 2014–2020), fans from all generations, whether or not they were still in the community, turned their anger and disappointment into something positive and raised money for the Trevor Project, an association that helps prevent suicide in young LGBTQIA+ people.[16] Fans created a movement called "LGBT Fans Deserve Better" to crystallize and explain their actions. They also wrote a production document, called the Lexa Pledge, intended for the industry. This document listed important points for having better representation on screen and in TV shows and movies. This all-generation fan initiative was directly aimed to influence the industry and the narrations.

Those are examples of how generations can be a lever for calls for actions.

Contributors

MARIA K. ALBERTO is a Ph.D. candidate at the University of Utah, where her research interests include digital media, popular culture, adaptation, and transformative fan works. Her recent work has included essays in *Mythlore*, *M/C Journal*, and *Transformative Works and Cultures*, as well as forthcoming book chapters on Tolkien's mythic cities and queer readings of the Legendarium. Her dissertation explores how audiences and adaptations of fantasy texts use the term "canon."

MÉLANIE BOURDAA is associate professor of communication and information sciences at the University of Bordeaux Montaigne. She analyzes the new television environment and cultural convergence, particularly American TV series and fandom in the digital age. She is the head of the MediaNum research program, which examines the valorization of cultural heritage via transmedia storytelling strategies. She is the coordinator of the Design and Media Lab at the University of Bordeaux Montaigne.

MEGAN CONNOR is a Ph.D. candidate at Indiana University and a teaching fellow at Indiana University Northwest. Her research interests include girls' media studies, celebrity, and fandom, and her dissertation examines 2000s-era teen magazines as a site for the construction and maintenance of celebrity girlhood. Her work has been published in *The Black Girlhood Studies Collection* and *Spectator*.

MEREDITH DABEK was most recently a lecturer in media studies at Maynooth University. Her research focuses on digital literature (specifically the genre of literary web series), fan cultures, social media storytelling, and digital storytelling in general. She earned her Ph.D. in media studies from Maynooth University in 2020. She also holds a M.A. in digital humanities (Maynooth University), a M.S. in public relations (Boston University), and a B.A. in English literature (Fordham University).

SIMONE DRIESSEN is lecturer (with senior qualifications) and researcher in media and communication at Erasmus University Rotterdam. In 2017, she earned her Ph.D. in popular music fandom. Her research interests entail mainstream pop, long-term fandom, and reunions. She has published articles in *Participations* and *Popular Music and Society* and has contributed to a variety of edited collections on fandom and popular music.

YEKTANURŞIN DUYAN is assistant professor in the department of radio, television, and cinema at Mardin Artuklu University in Turkey. She completed her dissertation on gender and stardom in Turkish cinema. She has published widely in the field of Turkish cinema and its star system.

DAN GOLDING is associate professor in media and communication at Swinburne University and hosts *Screen Sounds* on ABC Classic. He is an award-winning writer, author of *Star Wars after Lucas*, and a video essayist. He presented *What Is Music* for ABC iView and Triple J. He co-wrote *Game Changers*, composed the soundtracks to *Push Me Pull You* and *The Haunted Island*, and from 2014 to 2017 was director of the Freeplay Independent Games Festival.

BETHAN JONES is an independent scholar whose research primarily focuses on gender, anti-fandom, and popular culture. Her work has been published in *Sexualities*, *Intensities*, and *Transformative Works and Cultures*, among others, and she has written extensively on *The X-Files*, popular culture, and new media. She is coeditor of *Crowdfunding the Future: Media Industries, Ethics and Digital Society*, published by Peter Lang, and is a founding board member of the Fan Studies Network.

BRIDGET KIES is assistant professor of film studies and production at Oakland University. Her research examines gender and sexuality in television and fan communities. She has previously published articles in *Transformative Works and Cultures*, *Intensities*, *Journal of Popular Romance Studies*, *Science Fiction Film and Television*, and *Feminist Media Histories*. She is currently working on a book examining the fear of Satan in historical popular television and is co-host of the *Cabot Cove Gazette*, a podcast about *Murder, She Wrote*.

SIOBHAN LYONS is an independent scholar in media and cultural studies. Her books include *Ruin Porn and the Obsession with Decay* and *Death and the Machine: Intersections of Mortality and Robotics*. Her work has appeared in *Understanding Nietzsche, Understanding Modernism*, *Westworld and Philosophy*, and *Philosophical Approaches to the Devil*. Her research looks at media theory and technology, as well as the intersections between popular culture and philosophy.

L. N. ROSALES is an adjunct instructor at Southeast Community College in Lincoln, Nebraska. She earned her Ph.D. from the University of Iowa in 2018 and since then has published on such topics as Sherlock Holmes and the gothic and Shirley Jackson's fiction. Her research interests include detective fiction and crime television series and gothic literature, television, and film.

ANDREW SCAHILL is assistant professor of English at the University of Colorado Denver. His work focuses on genre and reception studies with particular interest in representations of youth rebellion. His book *The Revolting Child in Horror Cinema: Youth Rebellion and Queer Spectatorship* examined the monstrous child as a potent metaphor for queer youth and uncontrollable futurity.

JANELLE VERMAAK-GRIESSEL is senior lecturer in media and communication at Nelson Mandela University in South Africa. She teaches in a range of disciplines including scriptwriting, film studies, communication studies, and written communication. Her research interests include fan studies, film studies, and television studies. The topic of her dissertation was understanding fans of the Alien film franchise, and she is currently writing several works for publication.

CYNTHIA W. WALKER is professor emeritus of communication and media culture at Saint Peter's University in New Jersey. A fan of *The Man from U.N.C.L.E.* series, she has written a number of U.N.C.L.E., spy, and fandom-related articles, including entries for the Museum of Broadcast Communication's *Encyclopedia of Television*. She delivers onscreen commentary for *The Man from U.N.C.L.E.* DVD set released by Time/Life and Warner Home Entertainment. Her book, *Work/Text: Investigating The Man from U.N.C.L.E.*, proposes a new dialogic model of mass media.

DAWN WALLS-THUMMA founded the Silmarillion Writers' Guild in 2005. Her curiosity about the fan communities she loved led her to the 2015 Tolkien Fanfiction Survey. She has presented at Mythmoot, the New York Tolkien Conference, the Tolkien in Vermont Conference, and the Popular Culture Association Conference and has published her scholarly work in the *Journal of Tolkien Research* and *Mythprint*. She works as a humanities teacher in a rural Vermont school.

Contributors 183

NETA YODOVICH is a postdoctoral researcher at the University of Haifa, studying cultural policy in a research project funded by Horizon 2020. She earned her Ph.D. in sociology from the University of Manchester in 2020 after studying women's reconciliation of science fiction fandom and feminism. Her previous studies about female fans and representation of singlehood in popular culture are published in *Sociology*, *Feminist Media Studies*, *Women's Studies in Communication*, and *European Journal of Women's Studies*. Her academic interests include fandom, feminism, identity, and belonging.

Notes

INTRODUCTION

1. Margaret Lyons, "What the Critics Said about the 1994 Debut of 'Friends,'" *Vulture*, January 2, 2015, https://www.vulture.com/2014/09/friends-1994-critics-review-roundup.html.

2. Edmund Lee, "Netflix Will Keep 'Friends' through Next Year in a $100 Million Agreement," *New York Times*, December 4, 2018, https://www.nytimes.com/2018/12/04/business/media/netflix-friends.html.

3. Ellie Woodward, "21 Times 'Friends' Was Actually Really Problematic," Buzzfeed, March 16, 2018, https://www.buzzfeed.com/elliewoodward/times-friends-was-actually-really-problematic.

4. "Courteney Cox: I Was Too Thin on Friends," CelebsNow, May 13, 2007, https://www.celebsnow.co.uk/latest-celebrity-news/celebrity-gossip-courtney-cox-i-was-too-thin-on-friends-233950.

5. Geraldine Ruiter, "The Tragedy of Monica Geller," Everywhereist, May 14, 2019, https://www.everywhereist.com/2019/05/the-tragedy-of-monica-geller/.

6. James Poniewozik, "'Friends' Reunion: The One with the 'Remember the One With ...?,'" *New York Times*, May 26, 2021.

7. Linda Holmes, "The 'Friends' Reunion That Lost Its Nerve," NPR Pop Culture Happy Hour, May 27, 2021, https://www.npr.org/2021/05/27/1000519295/the-friends-reunion-that-lost-its-nerve.

8. Alexandra Saizan, "Millennials Kill Everything," Pudding, September 2019, https://pudding.cool/2019/09/millennials/.

9. Joshua Bote, "Why Are Gen Z and Millennials Calling Out Boomers on TikTok? 'Ok, Boomer' Explained," *USA Today*, October 31, 2019, https://www.usatoday.com/story/news/nation/2019/10/31/why-gen-z-millennials-using-ok-boomer-baby-boomers/4107782002/.

10. Pew Research Center, "The Whys and Hows of Generational Research," People-Press, September 3, 2015, https://www.people-press.org/2015/09/03/the-whys-and-hows-of-generations-research/.

11. Derek Johnson, *Transgenerational Media Industries* (Ann Arbor: University of Michigan Press, 2019), 9.

12. C. Lee Harrington and Denise Bielby, "A Life Course Perspective on Fandom," *International Journal of Cultural Studies* 13, no. 5 (2010): 434.

13. Göran Bolin, "Media Generations: Objective and Subjective Media Landscapes and Nostalgia among Generations of Media Users," *Participations* 11, no. 2 (2014): 128.

14. Matt Hills, "Introduction: Fandom from Cradle to Grave?," *Journal of*

Fandom Studies 7, no. 2 (2019): 88.

15. Johnson, *Transgenerational Media Industries*, 57.

16. Johnson, *Transgenerational Media Industries*, 57.

"I AIN'T AFRAID OF NO BROS": THE GENERATIONAL POLITICS OF REBOOT CULTURE

1. Jayme Deerwester, "Leslie Jones on Milo: Stop Feeding the Trolls," *USA Today*, February 21, 2017, https://www.usatoday.com/story/life/books/2017/02/21/leslie-jones-advice-milo-yiannopoulos-stop-feeding-trolls/98190810.

2. C. Lee Harrington and Denise D. Bielby, "A Life Course Perspective on Fandom," *International Journal of Cultural Studies* 13, no. 5 (2010): 431.

3. Harrington and Bielby, "A Life Course Perspective on Fandom."

4. For an industry-focused approach, see Philip M. Napoli, *Audience Economics: Media Institutions and the Audience Marketplace* (New York: Columbia University Press, 2003).

5. Heather Urbanski, *The Science Fiction Reboot: Canon, Innovation and Fandom in Refashioned Franchises* (Jefferson, NC: McFarland, 2013), 8.

6. Ross Garner, "The Mandalorian Variation: Gender, Institutionality, and Discursive Constraints in Star Wars Rebels," in *Disney's Star Wars: Forces of Production, Promotion, and Reception*, ed. William Proctor and Richard McCulloch (Iowa City: Iowa University Press, 2019), 118.

7. Crazylegsmurphy, "Ghostbusters 2016: Childhood Ruined," Reddit, July 10, 2016, https://www.reddit.com/r/ghostbusters/comments/4s4vx3/ghostbusters_2016_childhood_ruined/.

8. Kelly McClure, "Real Men Confirm the New Ghostbusters Didn't Ruin Their Childhood after All," *Vanity Fair*, July 15, 2016, https://www.vanityfair.com/hollywood/2016/07/real-men-confirm-the-new-ghostbusters-didnt-ruin-their-childhoods-after-all.

9. This line was quoted in a number of digital media outlets but was first reported in an interview with *Variety*. See Jenelle Riley, "'Spy' Director Paul Feig on Backlash to Female 'Ghostbusters,'" *Variety*, March 13, 2015, http://variety.com/2015/film/festivals/sxsw-spy-director-paul-feig-on-response-to-female-ghostbusters-1201451451.

10. Ernie Hudson, "The Painful What-If That Haunts Ernie Hudson," *Entertainment Weekly*, November 5, 2014, http://ew.com/article/2014/11/05/ghostbusters-ernie-hudson.

11. OceanCyclone, comment on thread, Reddit, https://www.reddit.com/r/movies/comments/8p4l8t/opinion_oceans_8_is_doing_right_what_ghostbusters/.

12. Richard Jenkins, *Social Identity* (New York: Routledge, 2004).

13. Matt Hills, "Psychoanalysis and Digital Fandom: Theorizing Spoilers and Fans' Self-Narratives," in *Producing Theory in a Digital World*, ed. Rebecca Ann

Lind (New York: Peter Lang, 2012), 114.

14. William Proctor, "'Bitches Ain't Gonna Hunt No Ghosts': Totemic Nostalgia, Toxic Fandom, and the *Ghostbusters* Platonic," *Palabra Clave* 20, no. 4 (2017): 1120.

15. Proctor, "'Bitches Ain't Gonna Hunt No Ghosts,'" 1122.

16. PuppysPanties, "I Fixed the TERF Post as Requested," Reddit, January 28, 2020, https://www.reddit.com/r/GatekeepingYuri/comments/ev17sw/i_fixed _the_terf_post_as_requested/ffxa3yr/?context=3.

17. Serriaplays, "Me_IRLGBT," Reddit, June 7, 2019, https://www.reddit .com/r/me_irlgbt/comments/by1ml1/me_irlgbt/eqenz7q/?context=3; Crazylegsmurphy, "Ghostbusters 2016: Yes, I Admit It. It Is Because of Women," Reddit, July 11, 2016, https://www.reddit.com/r/MensRights/comments/4sd2yd /ghostbusters_2016_yes_i_admit_it_is_because_of/.

18. Crazylegsmurphy, "Ghostbusters 2016."

19. Ryan Milner, "FCJ-156 Hacking the Social: Internet Memes, Identity Antagonism, and the Logic of Lulz," *Fibreculture Journal* 22 (2013): 62–92, http://twentytwo.fibreculturejournal.org/fcj-156-hacking-the-social-internet -memes-identity-antagonism-and-the-logic-of-lulz/.

20. Adrienne Massanari, "#Gamergate and the Fappening: How Reddit's Algorithm, Governance, and Culture Support Toxic Technocultures," *New Media and Society* 19, no. 3 (2015): 333.

21. Matt Zoller Seitz, "Women's Work: The New *Ghostbusters*," RogerEbert, July 16, 2016, http://www.rogerebert.com/mzs/womens-work-man-babies-and -the-new-ghostbusters.

22. This is not to say that BIPOC, queer people, and girls/women cannot identify with or idolize cis white heterosexual male heroes, for indeed they often do, perhaps in the absence of other characters. The point is that the options for identification with characters of the same race, gender, or sexual identity are fewer.

23. Haley Goldberg, "Here's Kristen Wiig at the 'Ghostbusters' Premiere, Destroying Someone's Childhood," *Self*, July 14, 2016, http://www.self.com/story /heres-kristen-wiig-at-the-ghostbusters-premiere-destroying-someones -childhood.

24. Geena Davis Institute on Gender and Media, "Portray Her: Representations of Women STEM Characters in Media," SeeJane, 2019, https://seejane.org/wp-content/uploads/portray-her-full-report.pdf.

25. 21st Century Fox, Geena Davis Institute on Gender in Media, and J. Walter Thompson Intelligence, "The 'Scully Effect': I Want to Believe. . . in STEM," SeeJane, 2018, https://seejane.org/research-informs-empowers/the-scully-effect -i-want-to-believe-in-stem/.

26. Crispin Long, "The 'L Word' Reboot Seeks to Absolve the Original's Sins," *New Yorker*, December 11, 2019, https://www.newyorker.com/culture /on-television/the-l-word-reboot-seeks-to-absolve-the-originals-sins.

27. "Can Our Favorite Lesbians Rule TV Again?," *The Advocate*, December 2019/January 2020, 20–23.

28. Kim Parker and Ruth Ignielnik, "On the Cusp of Adulthood and Facing an Uncertain Future: What We Know about Gen Z So Far," Pew Research Center, May 14, 2020. https://www.pewresearch.org/social-trends/2020/05/14/on-the-cusp-of-adulthood-and-facing-an-uncertain-future-what-we-know-about-gen-z-so-far-2/.

29. Jeffrey M. Jones, "LGBT Identification Rises to 5.6% in Latest U.S. Estimate," Gallup, February 24, 2021, https://news.gallup.com/poll/329708/lgbt-identification-rises-latest-estimate.aspx.

30. Naomi Gordon-Loebl, "'The L Word: Generation Q' Is a Queer Soap Opera, and There's Nothing Wrong with That," *The Nation*, February 12, 2020, https://www.thenation.com/article/culture/l-word-generation-q-tv-review/.

31. Gordon-Loebl, "'The L Word.'"

32. Comments on Keith V, "One Day at a Time. I Hate It but I Can't Stop Watching (Discussion of 2017 Reboot Added at Page 5)," Steve Hoffman Music Forums, August 20, 2015, https://forums.stevehoffman.tv/threads/one-day-at-a-time-i-hate-it-but-cant-stop-watching-discussion-of-2017-reboot-added-at-page-5.454622/page-2.

33. Comments on Keith V, "One Day at a Time."

34. Comments on Keith V, "One Day at a Time."

35. ElSaborAsiatico, "Any Younger Fans of One Day at a Time?," Reddit, January 30, 2018, https://www.reddit.com/r/netflix/comments/7u19ht/any_younger_fans_of_one_day_at_a_time/.

36. As quoted in Kayla Cobb, "Pop TV President Brad Schwartz Explains Why They Wanted 'One Day at a Time' Despite It Not Being the 'Best Deal,'" Decider, August 20, 2019, https://decider.com/2019/08/20/pop-tv-one-day-at-a-time-schitts-creek-brad-schwartz-interview/.

37. CompleteMuffin, "Is the Show Preachy/Corny?," Reddit, March 14, 2019, https://www.reddit.com/r/odaat/comments/b14j5f/is_the_show_preachycorny/.

38. In 2019, for instance, 16 percent of cis LGBTQ people in the United States were living in poverty, compared with 29 percent of trans people. M. V. Lee Badgett, Soon Kyu Choi, and Bianca D. M. Wilson, "LGBT Poverty in the United States," Williams Institute, October 2019, https://williamsinstitute.law.ucla.edu/publications/lgbt-poverty-in-the-united-states/.

39. The poverty rates for American trans people cited in a 2015 study were also around 29 percent. See Jillian Edmonds, "Transgender People Are Facing Incredibly High Rates of Poverty," National Women's Law Center, December 9, 2016, https://nwlc.org/blog/income-security-is-elusive-for-many-transgender-people-according-to-u-s-transgender-survey/.

40. Cael Keegan, "In Praise of the Bad Transgender Object: *Rocky Horror*," *Flow*, November 28, 2019, https://www.flowjournal.org/2019/11/in-praise-of-the-bad/.

41. Sarah Banet-Weiser, *Empowered: Popular Feminism and Popular Misogyny* (Durham, NC: Duke University Press), 2.

REOPENING *THE X-FILES*: GENERATIONAL FANDOM, GENDER, AND BODILY AUTONOMY

1. Patrick Munn, "'The X-Files' Revival Nears Greenlight at Fox; Network Eyes Short Order, Gillian Anderson & David Duchovny to Return," TV Wise, March 20, 2015, http://www.tvwise.co.uk/2015/03/the-x-files-revival-nears-greenlight-at -fox-network-eyes-short-order-gillian-anderson-david-duchovny-to-return/.

2. Heather Urbanski, *The Science Fiction Reboot: Canon, Innovation, and Fandom in Refashioned Franchises* (Jefferson, NC: McFarland, 2013), 7.

3. S. E. Smith, "The Transphobia Is Out There," Bitch Media, February 5, 2016, https://www.bitchmedia.org/x-files-transphobia-transgender-character-weremonster-reboot; Michael O'Connell, "When 'The X-Files' Became A-List: An Oral History of Fox's Out-There Success Story," *Hollywood Reporter*, January 7, 2016, https://www.hollywoodreporter.com/features/x-files-became-a-list-852398.

4. David Lavery, Angela Hague, and Marla Cartwright, "Introduction: Generation X—*The X-Files* and the Cultural Moment," in *Deny All Knowledge*, ed. David Lavery, Angela Hague, and Marla Cartwright (London: Faber and Faber, 1996), 1–21.

5. Rhiannon Bury, *Cyberspaces of Their Own: Female Fandoms Online* (New York: Peter Lang, 2005).

6. There were variances on a survey-by-survey basis. In my April 2018 survey, Gen Z accounted for 57 percent of those who said that they had been fans for less than ten years, compared to 33 percent who were aged twenty-six to forty-five. However, as I suggest later, there may be another way of troubling the distinctions between fannish generations and generational identifiers by drawing on the concept of fannish ages.

7. Robert Bogdan and Sari Knopp Biklen, *Qualitative Research for Education* (Boston: Allyn and Bacon, 1992).

8. Bethan Jones, "The Fandom Is Out There: Social Media and *The X-Files* Online," in *Fan CULTure: Essays on Participatory Fandom in the 21st Century*, ed. Kristin M. Barton and Jonathan Malcolm Lampley (Jefferson, NC: McFarland, 2012), 92–105.

9. Thomas Austin, *Hollywood Hype and Audiences: Selling and Watching Popular Film in the 1990s* (Manchester: Manchester University Press, 2002), 30.

10. Brian Lowry, *The Truth Is Out There: The Official Guide to The X-Files* (New York: Harper-Collins, 1995), 239.

11. Tony Maglio, "Inside 'The X-Files' Revival's 201-Day Marketing Plan," The Wrap, January 24, 2016, https://www.thewrap.com/the-x-files-fox-marketing -plan-cmo-angela-courtin/.

12. Facebook and Twitter were the most used platforms among all groups, but

31 percent of the eighteen to twenty-five age group used Tumblr, with Reddit and Instagram also being used (11 percent and 2 percent, respectively), compared to 15 percent of the twenty-six to thirty-five age group and 8 percent of the thirty-six to sixty-five age group. Five percent of the twenty-six to thirty-five age group used Instagram, with 9 percent using Reddit. Two percent of the thirty-six to sixty-five age group used Instagram, and 6 percent used Reddit.

13. Teresa Bridgeman, "Time and Space," in *The Cambridge Companion to Narrative*, ed. David Herman (Cambridge: Cambridge University Press, 2007), 52–53.

14. Bridgeman, "Time and Space," 54.

15. Urbanski, *The Science Fiction Reboot*, 71.

16. C. Lee Harrington, Denise D. Bielby, and Anthony R. Bardo, "Life Course Transitions and the Future of Fandom," *International Journal of Cultural Studies* 14, no. 6 (2011): 570.

17. Matt Hills, "'Twilight' Fans Represented in Commercial Paratexts and Inter-Fandoms: Resisting and Repurposing Negative Fan Stereotypes," in *Genre, Reception, and Adaptation in the Twilight Series*, ed. Anne Morey (London: Routledge, 2006), 113–30.

18. Leora Hadas, "The Web Planet: How the Changing Internet Divided *Doctor Who* Fan Fiction Writers," *Transformative Works and Cultures* 3 (2009), https://doi.org/10.3983/twc.2009.0129.

19. Kristina Busse, "Geek Hierarchies, Boundary Policing, and the Gendering of the Good Fan," *Participations* 10, no. 1 (2013): 84.

20. For a copy of the interview and a transcript, see https://akiplo.tumblr.com /post/71339449399/interview-with-chris-carter-gender-types-the.

21. Lisa Parks, "Special Agent or Monstrosity: Finding the Feminine in *The X-Files*," in *Deny All Knowledge*, ed. David Lavery, Angela Hague, and Marla Cartwright (London: Faber and Faber, 1996), 122.

22. Urbanski, *The Science Fiction Reboot*, 7.

23. Christine Geraghty, *Now a Major Motion Picture: Film Adaptations of Literature and Drama* (Plymouth, MA: Rowman and Littlefield, 2008).

24. Quoted in James Hibberd, "*The X-Files* Creator Defends Shocking Premiere Twist," *Entertainment Weekly*, January 3, 2018, https://ew.com/tv/2018 /01/03/x-files-creator-season-11-premiere-interview/.

25. Emily Regan Wills, "The Political Possibilities of Fandom: Transformational Discourses on Gender and Power in *The X-Files* Fandom" (presentation at the Midwest Political Science Association conference, Chicago, IL, April 2–5, 2009).

26. The depiction of a trans character in season ten's "Mulder and Scully Meet the WereMonster" was roundly criticized for perpetuating negative stereotypes of trans people as well as using the fact that a significant number of trans people are forced into sex work to make a "joke" work, despite the episode as a whole generating positive reviews.

27. Denise Petski, "Gillian Anderson Speaks Out on 'X-Files' Lack of Female Writers," Deadline, June 29, 2017, https://deadline.com/2017/06/gillian-anderson-x-files-lack-of-female-writers-1202122314/.

MISSING TIME: *TWIN PEAKS*, *THE X-FILES*, AND THE RISE OF AGING FANS

1. C. Lee Harrington and Denise D. Bielby, "Aging, Fans, and Fandom," in *The Routledge Companion to Media Fandom*, ed. Melissa A. Click and Suzanne Scott (New York: Routledge, 2018), 406.

2. Anne Jerslev and Line Nybro Petersen, "Introduction: Aging Celebrities, Aging Fans, and Aging Narratives in Popular Media Culture," *Celebrity Studies* 9, no. 2 (2018): 160–61.

3. Hanif Abdurraqib, "Aging Out of Diehard Fandom Is Bittersweet," Buzzfeed, September 18, 2017, https://www.buzzfeednews.com/article/hanifabdurraqib/why-we-stan; emphasis added.

4. Bob1, "Passing Twin Peaks to the Next Generation," Twin Peaks Gazette, March 13, 2011, https://www.twinpeaksgazette.com/community/topic-topicid=5986.cfm.html.

5. Olga Hughes, comment on C. S. Hughes, "It's Happening Again—David Lynch's *Twin Peaks* to Return in 2016," Nerdalicious, October 8, 2014, https://nerdalicious.com.au/filmtv/its-happening-again-david-lynchs-twin-peaks-to-return-in-2016/.

6. Matt Hills, "Cult TV Revival: Generational Seriality, Recap Culture, and the 'Brand Gap' of *Twin Peaks: The Return*," *Television and New Media* 19, no. 4 (2018): 315.

7. Tasha Robinson, "Agent Cooper in *Twin Peaks* Is the Audience: Once Delighted, Now Disintegrating," The Verge, May 31, 2017, https://www.theverge.com/2017/5/31/15720780/twin-peaks-showtime-david-lynch-dale-cooper-kyle-mclaughlin-audience-avatar.

8. E. C. Flamming, "See Familiar Faces and Feel Old: The New *Twin Peaks* Trailer Is Here," *Paste Magazine*, May 4, 2017, https://www.pastemagazine.com/tv/twin-peaks-/see-familiar-faces-feel-old-the-new-twin-peaks-tra/.

9. Noel Murray, "'Twin Peaks' Season 3, Episodes 1–2: Back in Style," *New York Times*, May 22, 2017, https://www.nytimes.com/2017/05/22/arts/television/twin-peaks-season-3-episodes-1-2-recap.html.

10. Peter Ormerod, "Who Do We Most Need in Reactionary Times? *Twin Peaks*' Dale Cooper," *The Guardian*, April 18, 2017, https://www.theguardian.com/commentisfree/2017/apr/18/twin-peaks-dale-cooper-david-lynch.

11. Sabrina Qiong Yu, "Introduction: Performing Stardom: Star Studies in Transformation and Expansion," in *Revisiting Star Studies*, ed. Sabrina Qiong Yu and Guy Austin (Edinburgh: Edinburgh University Press, 2017), 5.

12. Jerslev and Petersen, "Introduction," 159.

Notes to Pages 32–36 191

13. Comments on Xxgreenhornet, "Just Finished All the Seasons. Going Back to Where It All Started!," Reddit, June 1, 2020, https://www.reddit.com/r/XFiles/comments/fc402d/just_finished_all_seasons_going_back_to_where_it/.

14. Brandon, comment on John Squires, "First Images of 'The X-Files' Season 11, Which Has 8 Monster of the Week Episodes," Bloody Disgusting, September 29, 2017, https://bloody-disgusting.com/tv/3461961/first-images-x-files-season-11-8-monster-week-episodes/.

15. Nick Person, "Where *The X-Files* Went Wrong," Trouble City, October 10, 2017, https://trouble.city/articles/2017/10/10/where-the-x-files-went-wrong.

16. Yu, "Introduction," 5.

17. Yu, "Introduction," 5.

18. Kirsty Fairclough-Isaacs, "Celebrity Culture and Aging," in *Routledge Handbook of Cultural Gerontology*, ed. Julia Twigg and Wendy Martin (New York: Routledge, 2015), 363.

19. Fairclough-Isaacs, "Celebrity Culture and Aging," 363.

20. Fairclough-Isaacs, "Celebrity Culture and Aging," 363.

21. Sarah Rainey, "Ageless Gillian and the BotoX Files: Actress Said Plastic Surgery Had 'Crossed Her Mind'—So Is Her Youthful Look Down to Injections, Peels and Fillers . . . or Just Clever Make-up?," *Daily Mail*, February 11, 2016, https://www.dailymail.co.uk/news/article-3441577/Ageless-Gillian-BotoX-Files-Actress-said-plastic-surgery-crossed-mind-youthful-look-injections-peels-fillers-just-clever-make-up.html.

22. Siofra Brennan, "'The Botox Is Out There': *X-Files* Fans Claim the Biggest Mystery of the New Series Is How Mulder and Scully Haven't Aged a Day," *Daily Mail*, February 9, 2016, https://www.dailymail.co.uk/femail/article-3438742/X-Files-fans-question-Mulder-Scully-haven-t-aged-series-returns-TV.html.

23. Brennan, "'The Botox Is Out There.'"

24. Siobhan Lyons, "From the Elephant Man to Barbie Girl: Dissecting the Freak from the Margins to the Mainstream," *M/C Journal* 23, no. 5 (2020), https://doi.org/10.5204/mcj.1687.

25. Matt Prigge, "'Twin Peaks' Has a New Trailer in Which Everyone Looks Old," Metro, May 4, 2017, https://www.metro.us/twin-peaks-has-a-new-trailer-in-which-everyone-looks-old/.

26. Dave Schilling, "Interview: David Duchovny: 'I Can't Play Mulder the Way I Did. That Would Be Obscene,'" *The Guardian*, February 5, 2016, https://www.theguardian.com/tv-and-radio/2016/feb/05/david-duchovny-xfiles-mulder-gillian-anderson.

27. Hills, "Cult TV Revival," 314.

28. Dhani Mau, "The Real Reason Agent Cooper Doesn't Look Much Older Than He Did in the Original *Twin Peaks*," Fashionista, May 22, 2017, https://fashionista.com/2017/05/twin-peaks-kyle-maclachlan-young-anti-aging-routine.

29. "Kyle MacLachlan Is in Excellent Shape for a Man of His Age," Welcome to Twin Peaks, July 18, 2017, https://welcometotwinpeaks.com/discuss/twin

-peaks-part-10/kyle-maclachlan-is-in-excellent-shape-for-a-man-of-his-age/.

30. Ditch Carpenter, comment on Gillian Anderson, Facebook, February 29, 2016, https://m.facebook.com/952678361446981/photos/a.952678648113619 /955029061211911/?type=3.

31. Eric Jones, "Love This Picture, They've Aged Better Than I Have," Pinterest, https://ar.pinterest.com/pin/445504588118409069/ (accessed July 27, 2021).

32. Sezin Koehler, "'What Happened to the Women of Twin Peaks?': Twin Peaks Is Aging Against the Machine," *Bitch Media*, September 8, 2017, https:// www.bitchmedia.org/article/twin-peaks-women-aging.

33. Liz Shannon Miller, "Review: 'The X-Files' Season 10 Episode 3, 'Mulder and Scully Meet the Were-Monster' Is a Treat to Be Treasured," IndieWire, February 1, 2016, https://www.indiewire.com/2016/02/review-the-x-files -season-10-episode-3-mulder-and-scully-meet-the-were-monster-is-a-treat-to-be -treasured-28380/.

34. Chuck Bowen, "*The X-Files* Recap: Season 10, Episode 3, 'Mulder and Scully Meet the Were-Monster,'" Slant Magazine, February 2, 2016, https://www .slantmagazine.com/tv/the-x-files-recap-season-10-episode-3-mulder-and-scully -meet-the-were-monster/.

35. Bowen, "*The X-Files* Recap."

36. Hills, "Cult TV Revival," 310.

TRULY, TRULY, TRULY OUTRAGED: ANTI-FANDOM AND THE LIMITS OF NOSTALGIA

1. For reference, the narratively similar *Pitch Perfect 2* (Elizabeth Banks, 2015) reached $69 million on its opening weekend and returned $1,891 per screen.

2. "*Jem and the Holograms*," Box Office Mojo, https://www.boxofficemojo.com /title/tt3614530/ (accessed July 27, 2021).

3. Jason Guerassio, "This Movie Did So Terribly that Universal Has Pulled It from Over 2,000 Theaters," *Business Insider*, November 15, 2018, https://www .businessinsider.com/box-office-jem-and-the-holograms-did-universal-yanked-it -after-two-weeks-2015-11.

4. This term is attributed to Kenner Toys executive Bernard Loomis, who successfully campaigned to acquire the license to Star Wars action figures in 1976.

5. Toyetic programming dominated children's media production in the 1980s, resulting in the Children's Television Act of 1990, which banned direct advertising of tie-in toy lines and food products.

6. Rick Altman, *The American Film Musical* (Bloomington: Indiana University Press, 1987).

7. In an interview, Christy Marx discusses her childhood love of superhero comics: "I was a fanatic about comic books, an absolute fanatic. I don't know

why, since as a little girl that was considered kind of odd. . . . As a teenager, I was drawing my own comics, and I was creating a lot of strong kick-ass girl characters" (email interview with author, June 26, 2020). Indeed, *Jem and the Holograms* functions as a kind of fan fic for Marx, who was always creating her own female superheroes to supplement the void of women's representation in the genre.

8. Jerrica Benton, "Exclusive!! *Jem and the Holograms* Movie Announcement," YouTube, March 20, 2014, https://www.youtube.com/watch?v=yzVnNVrunAE.

9. Benton, "Exclusive!!"

10. Benton, "Exclusive!!"

11. Hillary Crosley Coker, "Here's the New *Jem and the Holograms* Trailer. I Think I Hate It," Jezebel, May 13, 2015, https://jezebel.com/heres-the-new-jem -and-the-holograms-trailer-i-think-i-1704160551.

12. Jonathan Gray, "Antifandom and the Moral Text: Television without Pity and Textual Dislike," *American Behavioral Scientist* 48, no. 7 (2005): 840–58.

13. Gray, "Antifandom and the Moral Text," 845.

14. Vivi Theodoropoulou, "The Anti-Fan within the Fan: Awe and Envy in Sport Fandom," in *Fandom*, ed. Jonathan Gray, Cornel Sandvoss, and C. Lee Harrington (New York: New York University Press, 2007), 325.

15. Emma A. Jane, "'Your a Ugly, Whorish Slut': Understanding E-bile," *Feminist Media Studies* 14, no. 4 (2014): 531–46.

16. Suzanne Scott, *Fake Geek Girls: Fandom, Gender, and the Convergence Culture Industry* (New York: New York University Press, 2019).

17. Charges that Marvel fans (or even Marvel Studios) were doing the same to "review bomb" DC movies led to changes in how RottenTomatoes handles its audience reviews.

18. Jonathan Gray, "How Do I Dislike Thee? Let Me Count the Ways," in *Anti-Fandom: Dislike and Hate in the Digital Age*, ed. Melissa A. Click (New York: New York University Press, 2019), 25–41.

19. Anne Gilbert, "Hatewatch with Me: Anti-Fandom as Social Performance," in *Anti-Fandom: Dislike and Hate in the Digital Age*, ed. Melissa A. Click (New York: New York University Press, 2019), 63.

20. Darryn King, "Here's What Happens When Men Try and Make 'Jem and the Holograms,'" Cartoon Brew, May 13, 2015, https://www.cartoonbrew .com/feature-film/heres-what-happens-when-men-try-to-make-jem-and-the -holograms-113080.html.

21. For her part, Marx had this to say: "The Jem animation series had: independent young women taking charge of a music company and music careers, Jerrica's secret identity as Jem and the consequences of it, the struggle to maintain a loving home for foster girls, the Jem/Jerrica/Rio love triangle, Synergy was a very cool holographic computer with a personality, [and] female friendships. The live-action film did have the female friendships, but other than that they had: teenage girls not in control of their lives, no foster girls, no

secret identity for Jem, no love triangle, they gave the music company to Rio instead of Jerrica, a silly toy robot that wasn't remotely like Synergy" (personal communication, June 26, 2020).

22. The close friendship between secondary characters Kimber and Stormer has been an active site of queer engagement, as fans have drawn out the subtextual cues to generate fan fiction that centralizes a romantic relationship.

23. Sara Gwenllian Jones, "The Sex Lives of Cult Television Characters," *Screen* 43, no. 1 (2002): 88.

24. Kate Erbland, "How the 'Jem and the Holograms' Movie Manipulates Its Biggest Fans," IndieWire, October 22, 2015, https://www.indiewire.com/2015/10/how-the-jem-and-the-holograms-movie-manipulates-its-biggest-fans-56325/.

25. Derek Johnson, *Transgenerational Media Industries* (Ann Arbor: University of Michigan Press, 2019), 9.

26. Marx echoes these sentiments, stating: "[*Jem*] epitomized the 80s in look, sound, and feel, so if you wanted to reinvigorate the original 80s feel, it would • need to be done in retro fashion. BUT it would still be entirely possible to update it as long as the fundamental elements remained true, as long as the heart of the show was carried forward. The big mistake of the live-action movie is that it did neither. It didn't maintain the heart of the show while updating it, and it didn't take advantage of the 80s nostalgia because they updated it. Fans instinctively know when something is done wrong or done for the wrong reasons, whether they can articulate it or not. They know that a couple of guys dressed like frat boys casually waving Jem dolls around doesn't represent the original creative vision. That was a huge misstep" (personal communication, June 26, 2020).

27. Geoff Berkshire, "Film Review: 'Jem and the Holograms,'" *Variety*, October 22, 2015, https://variety.com/2015/film/reviews/jem-and-the-holograms-film-review-1201623589/.

28. Rebecca Williams, "'Anyone Who Calls Muse a *Twilight* Band Will Be Shot on Sight': Music, Distinction, and the 'Interloping Fan' in the *Twilight* Franchise," *Popular Music and Society* 36, no. 3 (2013): 327–42.

29. Chickbait, "Jem Reacts—to the New *Jem and the Holograms* Trailer," YouTube, June 9, 2015, https://www.youtube.com/watch?v=TVQ9r3Smooo&t=183s.

30. Chickbait, "Truly Outrageous: A Jem Fan Film," YouTube, May 30, 2018, https://www.youtube.com/watch?v=oS_zRhaX1Wk&t=2s.

LIKE FATHER, LIKE DAUGHTER: THE INTERGENERATIONAL PASSING OF DOCTOR WHO AND STAR WARS FANDOM IN THE FAMILIAL CONTEXT

1. Andy Bennett, "Punk's Not Dead: The Continuing Significance of Punk Rock for an Older Generation of Fans," *Sociology* 40, no. 2 (2006): 227–30; C. Lee Harrington and Denise Bielby, "Autobiographical Reasoning in Long-Term Fandom," *Transformative Works and Cultures* 5 (2010), https://doi.org/10.3983

/twc.2010.0209; Susan Napier, "The World of Anime Fandom in America," *Mechademia* 1, no. 1 (2006): 56; Nicola Smith, "Parenthood and the Transfer of Capital in the Northern Soul Scene," in *Aging and Youth Cultures*, ed. Andy Bennett and Paul Hodkinson (London: Bloomsbury Academic, 2013), 160; Julie Tinson, Gary Sinclair, and Dimitrios Kolyperas, "Sport Fandom and Parenthood," *European Sport Management Quarterly* 17, no. 3 (2017): 382–83; Laura Vroomen, "Kate Bush: Teen Pop and Older Female Fans," in *Music Scenes*, ed. Andy Bennett and Richard A Petersen (Nashville, TN: Vanderbilt University Press, 2004), 244–45; Rachel Wood, Benjamin Litherland, and Elizabeth Reed, "Girls Being Rey: Ethical Cultural Consumption, Families, and Popular Feminism," *Cultural Studies* 34, no. 4 (2020), https://doi.org/10.1080/09502386.2019.1656759.

2. Tinson, Sinclair, and Kolyperas, "Sport Fandom and Parenthood," 372.

3. Matt Hills, *Fan Cultures* (London: Routledge, 2002), 126.

4. Harrington and Bielby, "Autobiographical Reasoning."

5. Harrington and Bielby, "Autobiographical Reasoning"; Line Nybro Petersen, "*Gilmore Girls* Generations: Disrupting Generational Belonging in Long-term Fandom," *Celebrity Studies* 9, no. 2 (2018): 226–28; Nick Stevenson, "Talking to Bowie Fans: Masculinity, Ambivalence and Cultural Citizenship," *European Journal of Cultural Studies* 12, no. 1 (2009): 84–85; Neta Yodovich, "'A Little Costumed Girl at a Sci-Fi Convention': Boundary Work as a Main Destigmatization Strategy among Women Fans," *Women's Studies in Communication* 39, no. 3 (2016): 301–2.

6. Matt Hills, "Introduction: Fandom from Cradle to Grave?," *Journal of Fandom Studies* 7, no. 2 (2019): 90.

7. Line Nybro Petersen, "'The Florals': Female Fans over 50 in the *Sherlock* Fandom," *Transformative Works and Cultures* 23 (2017), http://dx.doi.org/10.3983/twc.2017.0956; Christine Scodari, "'No Politics Here': Age and Gender in Soap Opera 'Cyberfandom,'" *Women's Studies in Communication* 21, no. 2 (1998): 180; Christine Scodari, "Breaking Dusk: Fandom, Gender/Age Intersectionality, and the '*Twilight* Moms,'" in *Aging, Media and Culture*, ed. C. Lee Harrington, Denise Bielby, and Anthony R. Bardo (Lanham, MD: Lexington Books, 2014), 144–45.

8. Paul Booth and Peter Kelly, "The Changing Faces of *Doctor Who* Fandom: New Fans, New Technologies, Old Practices," *Participations* 10, no. 1 (2013): 61; Matt Hills, "'The One You Watched When You Were Twelve': Regenerations of *Doctor Who* and Enduring Fandom's 'Life-Transitional Objects,'" *Journal of British Cinema and Television* 14, no. 2 (2017): 216.

9. Tonya Anderson, "Still Kissing Their Posters Goodnight: Female Fandom and the Politics of Popular Music," *Journal of Audience and Reception Studies* 9, no. 2 (2012): 240; C. Lee Harrington and Denise D. Bielby, "A Life Course Perspective on Fandom," *International Journal of Cultural Studies* 13, no. 5 (2010): 429; Harrington and Bielby, "Autobiographical Reasoning"; C. Lee Harrington, Denise D. Bielby, and Anthony R. Bardo, "Life Course Transitions and the Future of Fandom," *International Journal of Cultural Studies* 14, no. 6 (2011): 568; Hills,

"Introduction"; Petersen, "'The Florals.'"

10. Henry Jenkins, "Afterword: The Future of Fandom," in *Fandom: Identities and Communities in a Mediated World*, ed. Cornel Sandvoss, C. Lee Harrington, and Jonathan Gray (New York: New York University Press, 2007), 359; Melanie Kohnen, "'The Power of Geek': Fandom as a Gendered Commodity at Comic-Con," *Creative Industries Journal* 7, no. 1 (2014): 75; Lynn Zubernis and Katherine Larsen, *Fandom at the Crossroads* (Newcastle upon Tyne: Cambridge Scholars, 2012), 59.

11. Camille Bacon-Smith, *Enterprising Women: Television Fandom and the Creation of Popular Myth* (Philadelphia: University of Pennsylvania Press, 1992), 17; Garry Crawford and Victoria K. Gosling, "The Myth of the 'Puck Bunny': Female Fans and Men's Ice Hockey," *Sociology* 38, no. 3 (2004): 486.

12. Scodari, "Breaking Dusk," 144–45; CarrieLynn D. Reinhard, *Fractured Fandoms: Contentious Communication in Fan Communities* (Lanham, MD: Lexington Books, 2018), 7.

13. Daniel Cavicchi, *Tramps Like Us: Music and Meaning among Springsteen Fans* (Oxford: Oxford University Press, 1998), 62; Hills, *Fan Cultures*, 5.

14. Derek Johnson, "'May the Force Be with Katie': Pink Media Franchising and the Postfeminist Politics of HerUniverse," *Feminist Media Studies* 14, no. 6 (2014): 897.

15. Petersen, "The Florals."

16. Johnson, "'May the Force Be with Katie,'" 899–904.

17. Sarah Banet-Weiser, *Kids Rule! Nickelodeon and Consumer Citizenship* (Durham, NC: Duke University Press, 2007), 70; Angela McRobbie, *The Aftermath of Feminism: Gender, Culture and Social Change* (London: Sage, 2009), 40–41.

18. Jeffrey A. Brown, "#WheresRey: Feminism, Protest, and Merchandising Sexism in Star Wars: The Force Awakens," *Feminist Media Studies* 18, no. 3 (2018): 338; Suzanne Scott, "#Wheresrey?: Toys, Spoilers, and the Gender Politics of Franchise Paratexts," *Critical Studies in Media Communication* 34, no. 2 (2017): 138.

19. Johnson, "'May the Force Be with Katie,'" 40–41; Banet-Weiser, *Kids Rule!*, 70; Wood, Litherland, and Reed, "Girls Being Rey."

20. Brown, "#WheresRey," 338.

EXAMINING POP MUSIC FANDOM THROUGH A GENERATIONAL LENS

1. Angela McRobbie, "Rock and Sexuality," in *On Record*, ed. Simon Frith and Andrew Goodwin (London: Routledge, 1990), 317–32.

2. Matt Hills, "When the Pet Shop Boys Were 'Imperial': Fans' Self-Aging and the Neoliberal Life Course of 'Successful' Text-Aging," *Journal of Fandom Studies* 7, no. 2 (2019): 151–67; Lauren Istvandy, *The Lifetime Soundtrack:*

Music and Autobiographical Memory (Sheffield: Equinox, 2019); Nancy Baym, Daniel Cavicchi, and Norma Coates, "Music Fandom in the Digital Age: A Conversation," in *The Routledge Companion to Media Fandom*, ed. Melissa A. Click and Suzanne Scott (New York: Routledge, 2018), 141–52; C. Lee Harrington and Denise D. Bielby, "Aging, Fans, and Fandom," in *The Routledge Companion to Media Fandom*, eds. Melissa A. Click and Suzanne Scott (New York: Routledge, 2018), 406–15.

3. Ryan Lizardi, *Mediated Nostalgia: Individual Memory and Contemporary Mass Media* (Lanham, MD: Lexington Books, 2015).

4. John Seabrook, *The Song Machine: Inside the Hit Factory* (New York: Norton, 201); Hannah Ewens, *Fangirls: Scenes from Modern Music Culture* (Austin: University of Texas Press, 2020).

5. C. Lee Harrington and Denise D. Bielby, "A Life Course Perspective on Fandom," *International Journal of Cultural Studies* 13, no. 5 (2010): 429–50.

6. Mark Duffett, "Introduction: Directions in Music Fan Research: Undiscovered Territories and Hard Problems," *Popular Music and Society* 36, no. 3 (2013): 299–304.

7. Mark Duffett, *Understanding Fandom: An Introduction to the Study of Media Fan Culture* (New York: Bloomsbury Academic, 2015), 154.

8. C. Lee Harrington and Denise D. Bielby, "Autobiographical Reasoning in Long-Term Fandom," *Transformative Works and Cultures* 5 (2010), https://doi.org/10.3983/twc.2010.0209.

9. Harrington and Bielby, "Life Course Perspective."

10. Matt Hills, "Patterns of Surprise," *American Behavioral Scientist* 48, no. 7 (2005): 801–21.

11. Hills, "Patterns of Surprise."

12. Matt Hills, "Returning to Becoming a Fan Stories: Theorising Transformational Objects and the Emergence/Extension of Fandom," in *The Ashgate Research Companion to Fan Cultures*, ed. Linda Duits, Koos Zwaan, and Stijn Reijnders (London: Routledge, 2018), 9–21.

13. Simone Driessen, "'I'll Never Break Your Heart': The Perpetual Fandom of the Backstreet Boys," in *Everybody Hurts: Transitions, Endings, and Resurrections in Fan Cultures*, ed. Rebecca Williams (Iowa City: University of Iowa Press, 2018), 41.

14. Andy Bennett and Paul Hodkinson, *Aging and Youth Culture: Music, Style, and Identity* (London: Bloomsbury, 2013).

15. Istvandy, *Lifetime Soundtrack*, 18.

16. Nick Stevenson, "Talking to Bowie Fans: Masculinity, Ambivalence and Cultural Citizenship," *European Journal of Cultural Studies* 12, no. 1 (2009): 79–98.

17. Maud Lavin, "Patti Smith: Aging, Fandom, and Libido," *Transformative Works and Cultures* 20 (2015), https://doi.org/10.3983/twc.2015.0658.

18. Lavin, "Patti Smith."

19. Tonya Anderson, "Still Kissing Their Posters Goodnight: Female Fandom

and the Politics of Popular Music," *Journal of Audience and Reception Studies*, 9, no. 9 (2012): 239–64.

20. Anderson, "Still Kissing Their Posters Goodnight."

21. Bennett and Hodkinson, *Aging and Youth Culture.*

22. Istvandy, *Lifetime Soundtrack*, 15.

23. Bennett and Hodkinson, *Aging and Youth Culture.*

24. Rukmini Pande, *Squee from the Margins: Fandom and Race* (Iowa City: University of Iowa Press, 2018).

25. The Backstreet Boys had their first performance together as a group (after auditioning for Lou Pearlman) in 1993. They released the following albums: *Backstreet Boys* (1996), *Backstreet's Back* (1997), *Millenium* (1998), *Black & Blue* (2000), *The Hits—Chapter One* (2001), *Never Gone* (2005), *Unbreakable* (2007), *This Is Us* (2009), *In a World Like This* (2013), and *DNA* (2019). Between 2002 and 2004 the band was on hiatus, and from 2004 to 2011 Kevin Richardson temporarily left the band. These moments were highlighted in a documentary on the band, *Show 'Em What You're Made Of* (Stephen Kijak, 2015).

26. Victoria Clarke and Virginia Braun, "Thematic Analysis," in *Encyclopedia of Critical Psychology*, ed. Thomas Teo (New York: Springer Reference, 2014), 1947–52.

27. Duffett, *Understanding Fandom.*

28. Ewens, *Fangirls.*

29. Anderson, "Still Kissing Their Posters Goodnight."

30. Simone Driessen, "Larger than Life: Exploring the Transcultural Fan Practices of the Dutch Backstreet Boys Fandom," *Participations: Journal of Audience and Reception Studies* 12, no. 2 (2015): 180–96.

31. Harrington and Bielby, "Life Course Perspective."

32. Bennett and Hodkinson, *Aging and Youth Cultures.*

33. Anderson, "Still Kissing Their Posters Goodnight."

34. Ewens, *Fangirls.*

35. Istvandy, *Lifetime Soundtrack.*

36. Stevenson, "Talking to Bowie Fans."

LOOKING BACK, LOOKING BI: QUEERING A LIFELONG FANDOM OF THE BABY-SITTERS CLUB

1. Will Thorne, "Netflix Orders 'Baby-Sitters Club' Reboot," *Variety*, February 28, 2019, https://variety.com/2019/tv/news/netflix-orders-baby-sitters-club-reboot-1203152072/.

2. Scholars have discussed fan identification with characters/groups in a fandom in terms of cosplay, merchandising, and even activism. See, Nicolle Lamerichs, "Stranger than Fiction: Fan Identity in Cosplay," *Transformative Works and Cultures* 7 (2011), https://doi.org/10.3983/twc.2011.0246; Victoria Godwin, "Hogwarts House Merchandise, Liminal Play, and Fan Identities," *Film and*

Merchandise 42, no. 2 (2018), https://doi.org/10.3998/fc.13761232.0042.206; Henry Jenkins, "'Cultural Acupuncture': Fan Activism and the Harry Potter Alliance," *Transformative Works and Cultures* 10 (2012), https://doi.org/10.3983/twc.2012.0305.

3. Jackie Stacey, *Star Gazing: Hollywood Cinema and Female Spectatorship* (London: Routledge, 1994), 159.

4. Stacey, *Star Gazing*, 171.

5. Deborah A. Macey breaks down this patterned representation of four-person female friend groups on TV series that reuse iterations of four "ancient archetypes" of femininity developed by Julia T. Wood in *Gendered Lives* (iron maiden, sex object, mother, child). See Deborah A. Macey, "Ancient Archetypes in Modern Media," in *Media Depictions of Brides, Wives, and Mothers*, ed. Alena Amato Ruggerio (Lanham, MD: Lexington Books, 2012), 49–62.

6. Rachel Shukert and Lucia Aniello, interview, Geena Davis Institute on Gender in Media, June 30, 2020, https://seejane.org/video-members-only/influencer-screening-babysitters-club-video/.

7. C. Lee Harrington and Denise D. Bielby, "A Life Course Perspective on Fandom," *International Journal of Cultural Studies* 13, no. 5 (2010): 446.

8. Tony E. Adams and Andrew F. Herrmann, "Expanding Our Autoethnographic Future," *Journal of Autoethnography* 1, no. 1 (2020): 2.

9. Adrienne Evans and Mafalda Stasi, "Desperately Seeking Methods: New Directions in Fan Studies Research," *Participations* 11, no. 2 (2014): 15; in addition, it includes a detailed accounting of fan scholars using autoethnography.

10. William Strauss and Neil Howe, *Millennials and the Pop Culture* (Great Falls, VA: LifeCourse Associates, 2006), 20.

11. The title for this section comes from Glen Roven, "Say Hello to Your Friends," track 10 on *The Baby-Sitters Club: Songs for My Best Friends*, Warner Bros. Records, 1992, CD.

12. For example, see Joli Jensen, "Fandom as Pathology: The Consequences of Characterization," in *The Adoring Audience*, ed. Lisa A. Lewis (New York: Routledge, 1992), 9–29.

13. This is discussed in any work on feminized media texts. See Janice Radway, *Reading the Romance: Women, Patriarchy, and Popular Literature* (Chapel Hill: University of North Carolina Press, 1984); Elana Levine, ed., *Cupcake, Pinterest, and Ladyporn: Feminized Popular Culture in the Early Twenty-First Century* (Chicago: University of Illinois Press, 2015).

14. Harrington and Bielby, "A Life Course Perspective," 444.

15. The title for this section comes from The Linda Lindas, "Claudia Kishi," written by Bela Salazar, Eloise Wong, Lucia de la Garza, and Mila de la Garza, 2020, https://open.spotify.com/track/5gpNwS8UaDW3lSfx1LayPs.

16. Prolific between 2007 and 2010, the blog, created by Kim Hutt Mayhew, is still available at http://whatclaudiawore.blogspot.com/. Mayhew has moved over to chronicling the book covers and fashion from the Netflix adaptation of the BSC

on Instagram at @covercritiques.

17. Early work on girls' bedroom culture includes Angela McRobbie, *Feminism and Youth Culture* (London: Palgrave, 1991), 1–15.

18. Mary Celeste Kearney, "Productive Spaces: Girls' Bedrooms as Sites of Cultural Production," *Journal of Children and Media* 1, no. 2 (2007): 135–36.

19. For a discussion of model minority stereotypes in children's literature, see Rachel Endo, "Complicating Culture and Difference: Situating Asian American Youth Identities in Lisa Yee's *Millicent Min, Girl Genius* and *Stanford Wong Flunks Big-Time*," *Children's Literature in Education* 40, no. 3 (2009): 235–49.

20. *The Claudia Kishi Club* (Sue Ding, 2020, Netflix). In addition, Claudia's legacy connects to the continuing "taste work" and gendered labor performed by Asian women in fashion today. See Minh-Ha T. Pham, *Asians Wear Clothes on the Internet: Race, Gender, and the Work of Personal Style Blogging* (Durham, NC: Duke University Press, 2015).

21. It should be noted that another member of the BSC, Jessi Ramsey, a junior officer of the club introduced in BSC no. 14, is Black. Jessi's characterization as a Black ballerina who struggles to fit in after moving to town deserves more nuanced analysis beyond the scope of this chapter.

22. Phil Yu, "Claudia and *The Baby-Sitters Club* Books We Really Needed," *Angry Asian Man*, November 29, 2017, http://blog.angryasianman.com/2017/11 /claudia-and-baby-sitters-club-books-we.html.

23. Sarah Kuhn, *Heroine Complex* (New York: DAW Books, 2016); and C. B. Lee, *Not Your Sidekick* (New York: Interlude Press, 2016) are the respective first books in each series.

24. Yumi Sakugawa, "A Few Important Facts about Claudia Lynn Kishi, Age 13," YumiSakugawa, January 16, 2013, https://www.yumisakugawa.com /post/40712345711/claudia-kishi-my-asian-american-female-role.

25. The title for this section comes from Roven, "Say Hello to Your Friends."

26. Lauren Savit, "Examining the Labor of Episodic TV Podcast Hosts," *Transformative Works and Cultures* 34 (2020), https://doi.org/10.3983/twc .2020.1721.

27. Savit, "Examining the Labor."

28. Savit, "Examining the Labor."

29. Suzanne Scott, email correspondence, October 26, 2020.

30. "Baby Nation," private Facebook group, https://www.facebook.com /groups/314613195686489//.

31. Eleanor Patterson, "*The Golden Girls Live*: Residual Television Texts, Participatory Culture, and Queering TV Heritage through Drag," *Feminist Media Studies* 16, no. 5 (2016): 839–40.

32. Patterson, "*The Golden Girls Live*," 841.

33. Emily Weiss, "The Baby-Sitters Club: Where Are They Now?," The Hairpin, January 18, 2011, https://www.thehairpin.com/2011/01/the-baby-sitters -club-where-are-they-now/.

34. Alexis Swerdloff, "Ann M. Martin on the Enduring Appeal of *The Baby-Sitters Club* and Rebooting Another Children's Series," *Vulture*, September 5, 2016, https://www.vulture.com/2016/09/ann-m-martin-missy-piggle-wiggle.html.

35. Heather Hogan, "Baby-Sitters Club Creator Ann M. Martin Is Queer, How Did I Not Know This," *Autostraddle*, September 6, 2016, https://www.autostraddle.com/baby-sitters-club-creator-ann-m-martin-is-queer-how-did-i-not-know-this-350912/.

36. Eve Kosofsky Sedgwick, *Between Men: English Literature and Male Homosocial Desire* (New York: Columbia University Press, 1985).

37. See Lauren B. McInroy and Shelley L. Craig, "Online Fandom, Identity Milestones, and Self-Identification of Sexual/Gender Minority Youth," *Journal of LGBT Youth* 15, no. 3 (2018): 179–96.

38. The title for this section comes from Roven, "Say Hello to Your Friends."

39. Shukert and Aniello, interview, Geena Davis Institute.

40. Shukert and Aniello, interview, Geena Davis Institute.

THE MAN FROM U.N.C.L.E. FANDOM: A COMMUNITY OF COUSINS

1. "The Golden Anniversary Affair: Celebrating 50 Years of *The Man from U.N.C.L.E*," https://thegoldenanniversaryaffair.weebly.com/headquarters.html (accessed November 13, 2020).

2. Francesca Coppa, "A Brief History of Media Fandom," in *Fan Fiction and Fan Communities in the Age of the Internet*, ed. Karen Hellekson and Kristina Busse (Jefferson, NC: McFarland, 2006), 41–59.

3. Cynthia W. Walker, "Spy Programs," in *The Encyclopedia of Television*, 2nd ed., ed. Horace Newcomb (Chicago: Fitzroy Dearborn, 2004), 2181–85. Norman Felton and Sam Rolfe knew Gene Roddenberry professionally and personally. Felton's Arena Productions produced Roddenberry's first series, *The Lieutenant* (1963–64) and was even approached to do the same for *Star Trek*. Felton turned down the request, guessing that all the required make-up, costumes, and sets would be too expensive. See Cynthia W. Walker, *Work/Text: Investigating The Man from U.N.C.L.E.* (New York: Hampton Press, 2013), 70–74.

4. Cynthia W. Walker, "The Future Just Beyond the Coat Hook: Technology, Politics and the Postmodern Sensibility in the Man From U.N.C.L.E.," in *Channeling the Future*, ed. Lincoln Geraghty (Plymouth, UK: Scarecrow Press, 2009), 41–58.

5. Walker, *Work/Text*, 207–11.

6. Leslie Raddatz, "The Mystic Cult of Millions: The People from U.N.C.L.E.," *TV Guide*, March 19, 1966, 15–18.

7. Walker, *Work/Text*, 297; Jon Heitland, *The Man from U.N.C.L.E. Book* (New York: St. Martin's Press, 1987), 201.

8. The Spy Commander, "The Man From U.N.C.L.E. Curse," The Spy Command, November 9, 2011, https://hmssweblog.wordpress.com/2011/11/09/the-man-from-u-n-c-l-e-curse; "Man from U.N.C.L.E. 'Curse' Strikes Again: Tom Cruise Backs Out of Project," Cinema Retro, May 24, 2013, https://cinemaretro.com/index.php?/archives/7476-MAN-FROM-U.N.C.L.E.-CURSE-STRIKES-AGAIN-TOM-CRUISE-BACKS-OUT-OF-PROJECT.html.

9. *The Man from U.N.C.L.E.* was "cool" not only in the popular but also in the McLuhanesque sense of the word. See Marshall McLuhan, *Understanding Media* (New York: McGraw-Hill, 1964).

10. Heitland, *The Man from U.N.C.L.E. Book*, 54.

11. Joel Cymrot, "The Cat with the Gat from U.N.C.L.E.," *Gun World*, May 1965, 24, 26–27; "What a Weapon for a One Man Army!," *TV Guide*, February 6, 1965, 12–14.

12. "Great TV Spy Scramble," *Life*, October 1, 1965, 118–20; Cynthia W. Walker, "Mr. Bond's Neighborhood: Domesticating the Superspy for American Television," in *James Bond and Popular Culture*, ed. Michele Brittany (Jefferson, NC: McFarland, 2014), 86.

13. "Our Man with UNcle," *Secretariat*, February 16, 1966, 13.

14. Anthony Enns, "The Fans from UNCLE: The Marketing and Reception of the Swinging '60s Spy Phenomenon," *Journal of Popular Film and Television* 28, no. 4 (2000): 124–32; Brian Paquette and Paul Howley, *The Toys from U.N.C.L.E.: Memorabilia and Collectors Guide* (Worchester: Entertainment Publishing, 1990).

15. Many of these letters are archived in the Norman Felton Collection, Special Collections Department, University of Iowa, Iowa City, Iowa.

16. Barry Sonnenfeld, Ed Solomon, Walter F. Parkes, and Laurie MacDonald, *Men in Black* (New York: Newmarket Press, 1997), 19; Frank Lovece, "'The Man from U.N.C.L.E.' TV Series Was Big!," *Newsday*, August 9, 2015, https://www.theledger.com/news/20150809/the-man-from-uncle-tv-series-was-big/1.

17. Heitland, *The Man from U.N.C.L.E. Book*, 194.

18. Paula Smith, "The U.N.C.L.E. Diaspora and the Great Ingatherings," *Z.I.N.E.S.* 9 (1995): 20–21.

19. Sue Cole, "The History of U.N.C.L.E. HQ: A Brief Look at How This Newsletter Has Evolved and Progressed over the Years," *U.N.C.L.E. HQ Newsletter* 193/194 (1995): 5–7.

20. Cynthia W. Walker, "Coming in from the Cold: Gender, the Internet and *Man from U.N.C.L.E.* Fandom" (presentation, Console-ing Passions, Madison, Wisconsin, April 25–28, 1996).

21. The results of the 2014 survey are reported in Cynthia W. Walker, "Fifty Years of *The Man From U.N.C.L.E.*: How the Ever-Changing Media Sustained and Shaped One of the Oldest Fan Communities," in *Television, Social Media, and Fan Culture*, ed. Alison F. Slade, Amber J. Narro, and Dedria Givens-Carroll (Lanham, MD: Lexington Press, 2015), 353–74.

22. Vaughn compared his character in British crime drama *Hustle* (2004–

12), an experienced con man named Albert Stroller, to a retired Napoleon Solo. On the long-running American series *NCIS* (2003–present), in which McCallum played Dr. Donald "Ducky" Mallard, there were occasional callbacks to McCallum's previous role. For example, in a second season episode, "Meat Puzzle," when Mark Harmon's Jethro Gibbs was asked what Ducky looked like when he was young, Gibbs replied, "Illya Kuryakin." Nevertheless, except for a reunion in the extras on the 2007 DVD set, Vaughn and McCallum never shared the screen again.

23. The most recent survey of U.N.C.L.E. fandom was conducted on Survey Monkey in July 2020 with 322 responses.

24. Cynthia W. Walker and Amy H. Sturgis, "Sexy Nerds: Illya Kuryakin, Mr. Spock, and the Image of the Cerebral Hero in TV Drama," in *Common Sense: Intelligence as Presented on Popular Television*, ed. Lisa Holderman (New York: Lexington Books, 2008), 201–16.

25. Stephanie Schorow, "Second Fiddle, First in Our Hearts," *Boston Herald*, March 12, 1997, section 3, 47.

26. "The Greatest Thing since Peanut Butter and Jelly," *TV Guide*, April 17, 1965, 6–9.

27. Henry Jenkins, *Textual Poachers: Television Fans and Participatory Culture* (New York: Routledge, 1992).

28. Survey results, July 2020.

29. Adam Chitwood, "A 'Man from U.N.C.L.E.' Sequel Is Being Written," *Collider*, April 17, 2017, https://collider.com/man-from-uncle-2-armie-hammer/.

30. David Edelstein, "*The Man From U.N.C.L.E.* Is Sexy, Breezy, Bond-like Fun," *Vulture*, August 14, 2015, https://www.vulture.com/2015/08/movie-review -the-man-from-uncle-shines.html.

31. TheBlokeFromUNCLE, "The Man From UNCLE—The Not So Different Affair," YouTube, October 28, 2015, https://www.youtube.com/watch?v =UfLN5ErVFyY.

32. Chitwood, reporting on a possible sequel, quotes Hammer as saying, "I actually recently talked to Lionel Wigram, the producer and co-writer with Guy, about a *Man from U.N.C.L.E.* sequel, and I was like, 'Dude if you don't start writing this script I'm gonna show up at your house and cut all of the tires of all of your cars, I swear to God.'" See Chitwood, "A 'Man from U.N.C.L.E.' Sequel Is Being Written."

33. Elizabeth Wagmeister, "Armie Hammer Dropped from Another Film, 'Billion Dollar Spy,' in Wake of Sexual Assault Allegations," *Variety*, March 29, 2021, https://variety.com/2021/film/news/armie-hammer-fired-movie-billion- dollar-spy-sex-allegations-1234902364/; Julie Miller, "The Fall of Armie Hammer: A Family Saga of Sex, Money, Drugs, and Betrayal," *Vanity Fair*, March 11, 2021, https://www.vanityfair.com/hollywood/2021/03/the-fall-of-armie-hammer-a -family-saga-of-sex-money-drugs-and-betrayal.

34. The Spy Commander, "The Man from U.N.C.L.E. Curse Strikes Again."

FANS OF FEMALE FILM STARS IN TURKEY:
THE CASE OF TÜRKAN ŞORAY

1. Engin Ayça, "Türk Sineması Seyirci İlişkileri," *Kurgu* 11 (1992): 117.

2. Serpil Kırel, *Yeşilçam Öykü Sineması* (Istanbul: Babil, 2005), 114.

3. Özge Özyılmaz Yıldızcan, *Erken Cumhuriyet Dönemi'nde Hollywood'un Alımlanması: Kadınlar, Gençler ve Modernlik* (PhD dissertation, İstanbul University, 2013), 55.

4. Dilek Kaya-Mutlu, "Bringing Stars Home: Yesilcam Cinema from the Perspective of Audience Letters" (presentation, The Glow in Their Eyes: Global Perspectives on Film Cultures, Film Exhibition and Cinemagoing conference, Brussels, Belgium, December 14–16, 2007).

5. This may indicate an avenue for further study analyzing audience letters in film magazines.

6. Kaya-Mutlu, "Bringing Stars Home."

7. Dilek Kaya-Mutlu, "Between Tradition and Modernity: Yeşilçam Melodrama, Its Stars, and Their Audiences," *Middle Eastern Studies* 46, no. 3 (2010): 418.

8. Donald Horton and R. Richard Wohl, "Mass Communication and Para-Social Interaction: Observations on Intimacy at a Distance," *Psychiatry* 19, no. 3 (1956): 215.

9. Even today, when asked about Turkish cinema's female stars, most people reference Yeşilçam-era actors like Şoray, Fatma Girk, Hülya Koçyiğit, and Filiz Akın.

10. Agah Özgüç, *Türk Sinemasında Cinselligin Tarihi* (Istanbul: Parantez Yayınları, 2000), 41.

11. Kırel, *Yeşilçam Öykü Sineması*, 87.

12. Seçil Büker, "Film Ateşli Bir Öpüşmeyle Bitmiyor," in *Kültür Fragmanları*, ed. Deniz Kandiyoti and Ayşe Saktanber (Istanbul: Metis, 2003), 160.

13. *Alaturca* means in the Ottoman/Turkish style. It pairs with the term *alafranga*, which indicates a European style. Nilüfer Göle, "Sosyolog Gözüyle Dört Kadın," in *Dört Yapraklı Yonca: Onların Sihri Neydi?*, ed. Bircan Usallı Silan (Istanbul: Epsilon, 2004), 435.

14. Türkan Şoray, *Sinemam ve Ben* (Istanbul: Turkiye Isbankası, 2012), 327, 328.

15. Markus Wohlfeil and Susan Whelan, "'Saved!' by Jena Malone: An Introspective Study of a Consumer's Fan Relationship with a Film Actress," *Journal of Business Research* 65, no. 4 (2012): 511.

16. Lucy Bennett, "Tracing Textual Poachers: Reflections on the Development of Fan Studies and Digital Fandom," *Journal of Fandom Studies* 2, no. 1 (2014): 7.

17. Bennett, "Tracing Textual Poachers."

18. Stephen J. Gould, "An Introspective Genealogy of My Introspective Genealogy," *Marketing Theory* 8, no. 4 (2008): 407–24, https://doi.org/10.1177/1470593108096543.

19. Wohlfeil and Whelan, "'Saved!,'" 517.

20. Sibel (last name withheld), interview by the author, October 26, 2018.

21. Yağız Yılmaz, interview by the author, January 25, 2019.

22. Hasan (last name withheld) and Burak (last name withheld), interview by the author, October 25, 2018.

23. Female fan (name withheld), interview by the author, September 28, 2018.

"I NAMED MY DAUGHTER RIPLEY": FAN GIFTING AND INTERNAL HIERARCHIES IN THE ALIEN FANDOM

1. Pamela Church Gibson, "'You've Been in My Life So Long I Can't Remember Anything Else': Into the Labyrinth with Ripley and the Alien," in *Keyframes*, ed. Matthew Tinkcom and Amy Villarejo (London: Routledge, 2001), 43.

2. Christine A. Wooley, "Visible Fandom: Reading *The X-Files* through X-Philes," *Journal of Film and Video* 53, no. 4 (2001): 29.

3. Kevin Dixon, "Learning the Game: Football Fandom Culture and the Origins of Practice," *International Review for the Sociology of Sport* 48, no. 3 (2012): 339.

4. Martin Barker, Kate Egan, Tom Phillips, and Sarah Ralph, *Alien Audiences: Remembering and Evaluating a Classic Movie* (London: Palgrave Macmillan, 2016); Janelle Vermaak, "Fans of the *Alien* Film Franchise: Creating a Fan-Specific Checklist," in *Gender and Contemporary Horror in Comics, Games, and Transmedia*, ed. Robert Shail, Samantha Holland, and Steven Gerrard (West Yorkshire: Emerald Press, 2019), 135–50.

5. Barker et al., *Alien Audiences*, 45.

6. Mark Jancovich and Nathan Hunt, "The Mainstream, Distinction, and Cult TV," in *Cult Television*, ed. Sarah Gwenllian-Jones and Roberta E. Pearson (Minneapolis: University of Minnesota Press, 2004), 27–43; Leora Hadas, "The Web Planet: How the Changing Internet Divided *Doctor Who* Fan Fiction Writers," *Transformative Works and Cultures* 3 (2009), http://journal .transformativeworks.org/index.php/twc/article/view/129/101; Rebecca Williams, "Desiring the Doctor: Identity, Gender, and Genre in Online Science Fiction Fandom," in *British Science Fiction Film and Television*, ed. James Leggott and Tobias Hochscherf (Jefferson, NC: McFarland, 2011), 167–77.

7. Andrea MacDonald, "Uncertain Utopia: Science Fiction Media Fandom and Computer Mediated Communication," in *Theorizing Fandom*, ed. Cheryl Harris and Alison Alexander (New York: Hampton Press, 1998), 131–52.

8. Camille Bacon-Smith, *Enterprising Women: Television Fandom and the Creation of Popular Myth* (Philadelphia: University of Pennsylvania Press, 1992).

9. Karen Hellekson, "A Fannish Field of Value: Online Fan Gift Culture," *Cinema Journal* 48, no. 4 (2009): 114.

10. Barker et al., *Alien Audiences*, 73.

11. Barker et al., *Alien Audiences*, 44.

12. Dixon, "Learning the Game," 339.

13. Barker et al., *Alien Audiences*, 60.

14. Joanne Garde-Hansen, *Media and Memory* (Edinburgh: Edinburgh University Press, 2011), 31.

15. Roger Aden, *Popular Stories and Promised Lands: Fan Cultures and Symbolic Pilgrimages* (Tuscaloosa: University of Alabama Press, 1999), 79.

16. Cornel Sandvoss, *Fans: The Mirror of Consumption* (Cambridge: Polity Press, 2005).

17. Henry Jenkins, "'Do You Enjoy Making the Rest of Us Feel Stupid?': alt. tv.twinpeaks, The Trickster Author, and Viewer Mastery," in *Full of Secrets*, ed. David Lavery (Detroit: Wayne State University Press, 1995), 51–69.

18. Matt Hills, *Fan Cultures* (London: Routledge, 2002), xxxii.

19. Elizabeth Wilson, *Cultural Passions: Fans, Aesthetes and Tarot Readers* (London: I. B. Tauris, 2013).

20. Henry Jenkins, *The Wow Climax: Tracing the Emotional Impact of Popular Culture* (New York: New York University Press, 2007).

21. Vermaak, "Fans of the *Alien* Film Franchise."

22. Barker et al., *Alien Audiences*, 111.

23. Pierre Bourdieu, *Distinction: A Social Critique of the Judgement of Taste* (Cambridge, MA: Harvard University Press, 1984).

24. Lawrence Grossberg, "Is There a Fan in the House?: The Affective Sensibility of Fandom," in *The Adoring Audience: Fan Culture and Popular Media*, ed. Lisa A. Lewis (London: Routledge, 1992), 50–65; Sue Brower, "Fans as Tastemakers: Viewers for Quality Television," in *The Adoring Audience: Fan Culture and Popular Media*, ed. Lisa A. Lewis (London: Routledge, 1992), 163–84.

25. Hills, *Fan Cultures*; Michel de Certeau, *The Practice of Everyday Life* (Berkeley: University of California Press, 1984).

26. Grossberg, "Is There a Fan in the House?"; Hills, *Fan Cultures*.

27. Grossberg, "Is There a Fan in the House?"; Hills, *Fan Cultures*.

28. Jackie Byars, Jeff Gould, Peter Fitting, Judith Newton, Tony Safford, Clayton Lee, and Charles Elkins, "Symposium on *Alien*," *Science Fiction Studies* 7, no. 3 (1980): 278–304.

29. Kristina Busse, "Geek Hierarchies, Boundary Policing, and the Gendering of the Good Fan," *Participations* 10, no. 1 (2013): 75.

30. Busse, "Geek Hierarchies," 74.

31. Brigid Cherry, "Refusing to Refuse to Look: Female Viewers of the Horror Film," in *Horror, the Film Reader*, ed. Mark Jancovich (London: Routledge, 2002), 169–78; Brigid Cherry, *Horror* (London: Routledge, 2009).

32. Barker et al., *Alien Audiences*.

33. Busse, "Geek Hierarchies," 74.

34. Matt Hills, "'Twilight Fans' Represented in Commercial Paratexts and Inter-Fandoms: Resisting and Repurposing Negative Fan Stereotypes," in *Genre*,

Notes to Pages 114–120 207

Reception, and Adaptation in the Twilight Series, ed. Anne Morey (Burlington: Ashgate Publishing, 2012), 113–29.

35. Busse, "Geek Hierarchies," 74.

36. Stephen Hinerman, "'I'll Be Here with You': Fans, Fantasy and the Figure of Elvis," in *The Adoring Audience: Fan Culture and Popular Media*, ed. Lisa A. Lewis (London: Routledge, 1992), 107–34.

37. Andrew Slack, "Cultural Acupuncture and a Future for Social Change," Huffington Post, May 25, 2011, https://www.huffpost.com/entry/cultural-acupuncture-and_b_633824; Henry Jenkins, "'Cultural Acupuncture': Fan Activism and the Harry Potter Alliance," *Transformative Works and Cultures* 10 (2012), doi:10.3983/twc.2012.0305.

38. Devin Maloney, "The Most Feminist Moments in Sci-fi History," *The Cut*, July 2014, http://nymag.com/thecut/2014/07/most-feminist-moments-in-sci-fi-history.html.

39. Hills, "'Twilight' Fans Represented."

"THE POWER OF THE JANE AUSTEN FANDOM": BRIDGING GENERATIONAL GAPS WITH *THE LIZZIE BENNET DIARIES*

1. Claudia L. Johnson, "Austen Cults and Cultures," in *The Cambridge Companion to Jane Austen*, 2nd ed., ed. Edward Copeland and Juliet McMaster (Cambridge: Cambridge University Press, 2006), 232.

2. Gabrielle Malcolm, ed., *Fan Phenomena: Jane Austen* (Bristol: Intellect, 2015); Steven Morris, "Jane Austen Banknote Unveiled—With Strange Choice of Quotation," *The Guardian*, July 18, 2017, https://www.theguardian.com/business/2017/jul/18/jane-austen-banknote-unveiled-with-strange-choice-of-quotation.

3. Johnson, "Austen Cults and Cultures," 232.

4. Devoney Looser, "The Cult of *Pride and Prejudice* and Its Author," in *The Cambridge Companion to Pride and Prejudice*, ed. Janet Todd (Cambridge: Cambridge University Press, 2013), 174–85.

5. Looser, "The Cult of *Pride and Prejudice*," 180.

6. Thomas Leitch, *Film Adaptation and Its Discontents: From* Gone with the Wind *to* The Passion of the Christ (Baltimore: Johns Hopkins University Press, 2007), 9.

7. Looser, "The Cult of *Pride and Prejudice*," 180–82.

8. Of course, Firth and Macfadyen are not the only options. A Janeite could easily answer Laurence Olivier (*Pride and Prejudice*, 1940), Matthew Rhys (*Death Comes to Pemberley*, 2013), Martin Henderson (*Bride and Prejudice*, 2004), or Daniel Vincent Gordh (*The Lizzie Bennet Diaries*, 2012–2013).

9. Holly Luetkenhaus and Zoe Weinstein, *Austentatious: The Evolving World of Jane Austen Fans* (Iowa City: University of Iowa Press, 2019), 2.

10. Juliet McMaster, *Jane Austen the Novelist: Essays Past and Present* (London:

Palgrave Macmillan, 1996), 5; Claire Harman, *Jane's Fame: How Jane Austen Conquered the World* (Edinburgh: Canongate Books, 2009), 229.

11. C. Lee Harrington and Denise Bielby, "A Life Course Perspective on Fandom," *International Journal of Cultural Studies* 13, no. 5 (2010): 431.

12. Göran Bolin, "Media Generations: Objective and Subjective Media Landscapes and Nostalgia among Generations of Media Users," *Participations* 11, no. 2 (2014): 109.

13. Line Nybro Petersen, "*Gilmore Girls* Generations: Disrupting Generational Belonging in Long-Term Fandom," *Celebrity Studies* 9, no. 2 (2018): 220.

14. Bolin, "Media Generations," 109.

15. Bolin, "Media Generations," 113.

16. Luetkenhaus and Weinstein, *Austentatious*, 9, 13.

17. Leitch, *Film Adaptation*, 9.

18. The Lizzie Bennet Diaries, "Vidcon Interruption—Ep: 25," YouTube, July 2, 2012, https://youtu.be/hU6nVwRPcp8.

19. Meredith Dabek, "Replies, Retweets, and Reblogs: Modes of Participation in *The Lizzie Bennet Diaries*," *Paradoxa* 29 (2017): 263–86.

20. Susan C. Greenfield, "*Pride and Prejudice* at 200: Stop Looking for Mr. Darcy!," *Ms. Magazine*, January 28, 2013, http://msmagazine.com/blog/2013/01/28/pride-and-prejudice-at-200-stop-looking-for-mr-darcy/; Kaite Welsh, "*Pride and Prejudice* at 200: The Best Jane Austen Small-Screen Adaptations," *The Guardian*, January 28, 2013, https://www.theguardian.com/tv-and-radio/tvandradioblog/2013/jan/28/youtube-austen-pride-and-prejudice.

21. Linda Hutcheon, *A Theory of Adaptation*, 2nd ed. (London: Routledge, 2013), 3–4.

22. The Lizzie Bennet Diaries, "A Wedding," Pemberley Digital, April 21, 2012, http://www.pemberleydigital.com/a-wedding/.

23. The Lizzie Bennet Diaries, "The Most Awkward Dance Ever—Ep: 7," YouTube, April 30, 2012, https://youtu.be/-SPDXorOuds.

24. Hutcheon, *A Theory*, 18–20, 176.

25. Leitch, *Film Adaptation*, 82.

26. Bernie Su, "Lizzie Bennet Diaries BTS: Why Is He 'Bing Lee'?", Tumblr, April 21, 2012, https://berniesu.tumblr.com/post/21510376101/lizzie-bennet-diaries-bts-why-is-he-bing-lee.

27. Bernie Su, "Lizzie Bennet BTS: Hunsford Arc Part 1 AKA Collins and Collins," Tumblr, October 27, 2012, https://berniesu.tumblr.com/post/34433495877/lizzie-bennet-bts-hunsford-arc-part-1-aka-collins.

28. It is difficult to determine the gender breakdown of the worldwide Austen fandom. However, the demographics of my survey respondents are closely aligned with the results from a 2008 survey of Austen fans conducted by the Jane Austen Society of North America. See Jeanne Kiefer, "Anatomy of a Janeite: Results from *The Jane Austen Survey 2008*," *Persuasions On-Line* 29, no. 1 (2008), http://www.jasna.org/persuasions/on-line/vol29no1/kiefer.html.

29. Among those I reached out to were transmedia producer Jay Bushman, transmedia editor Alexandra Edwards, executive producer Jenni Powell, and writers Kate Noble, Margaret Dunlap, and Rachel Kiley.

30. This may also be the result of recruiting survey respondents via social media. It is likely that the respondents (regardless of age) had a preexisting familiarity with digital media platforms and therefore less of a knowledge gap with regard to LBD's YouTube videos and tweets.

31. The Lizzie Bennet Diaries, "The Green Bean Gelatin Plan—Ep: 19," YouTube, June 11, 2012, https://youtu.be/ce_URjhJ3Xs.

32. Greenfield, "Pride and Prejudice at 200"; Allegra Tepper, "Lizzie in Real Life: Social and Narrative Immersion through Transmedia in *The Lizzie Bennet Diaries*," *Film Matters* 6, no. 1 (2015): 46.

33. Lori H. Zerne, "Ideology in *The Lizzie Bennet Diaries*," *Persuasions On-Line* 34, no. 1 (2013), http://www.jasna.org/persuasions/on-line/vol34no1/zerne.html.

34. Jane Austen, *The Annotated Pride and Prejudice*, 2nd ed., ed. David Shapard (New York: Random House, 2012), Kindle loc. 4319.

35. Hank Green, "I Am Hank Green, Co-Creator, Executive Producer, and Occasional Writer for *The Lizzie Bennet Diaries*," Reddit, August 14, 2012, https://www.reddit.com/r/LizzieBennet/comments/13rx7y/i_am_hank_green_cocreator_executive_producer_and/.

36. Luetkenhaus and Weinstein, *Austentatious*, 14–15.

37. Louisa Stein, *Millennial Fandom: Television Audiences in the Transmedia Age* (Iowa City: University of Iowa Press, 2015), 162.

38. Leitch, *Film Adaptation*, 70.

39. Leitch, *Film Adaptation*, 70.

40. Noelle M. Kozak, "New Media Adaptations of Classic Literature: From *Pride and Prejudice* to *The Lizzie Bennet Diaries*," *Inquiries Journal* 8, no. 10 (2016), http://www.inquiriesjournal.com/articles/1468/new-media-adaptations-of-classic-literature-from-pride-and-prejudice-to-the-lizzie-bennet-diaries.

41. Looser, "The Cult of *Pride and Prejudice*," 185.

42. Lauren Berlant, *The Female Complaint: The Unfinished Business of Sentimentality in Amerian Culture* (Durham, NC: Duke University Press, 2008), viii, 5.

STAR WARS FANS, GENERATIONS, AND IDENTITY

1. Fredric Jameson, "Nostalgia for the Present," *South Atlantic Quarterly* 88, no. 2 (1989): 517–37; Dale Pollock, *Skywalking: The Life and Films of George Lucas* (New York: Da Capo, 1999), 186.

2. Dan Golding, *Star Wars after Lucas* (Minnesota: University of Minnesota Press, 2019).

3. Golding, *Star Wars after Lucas*; Matthew Freeman, "Rebuilding Transmedia *Star Wars*: Strategies of Branding and Unbranding a Galaxy Far, Far Away," in

Disney's Star Wars: *Forces of Production, Promotion, and Reception*, ed. William Proctor and Richard McCulloch (Iowa City: University of Iowa Press, 2019), 23–38; Matt Hills, "Transmedia Spectacle and Transownership Storytelling as Seen on TV: *Star Wars* from the *Holiday Special* to *Rebels*," in *Disney's* Star Wars: *Forces of Production, Promotion, and Reception*, ed. William Proctor and Richard McCulloch (Iowa City: University of Iowa Press, 2019), 39–52; Michelle Kent, "'You Die! You Know That, Right? You Don't Come Back!': Fans Negotiating Disney's (De)Stabilized *Star Wars* Canon," in *Disney's* Star Wars: *Forces of Production, Promotion, and Reception*, ed. William Proctor and Richard McCulloch (Iowa City: University of Iowa Press, 2019), 221–36; William Proctor and Matthew Freeman, "The First Step into a Smaller World: The Transmedia Economy of *Star Wars*," in *Revisiting Imaginary Worlds*, ed. Mark J. P. Wolf (London: Routledge, 2016), 223–45.

4. Adam Rogers, "The Force Will Be with Us, Always," *Wired*, November 2015, https://www.wired.com/2015/11/building-the-star-wars-universe/.

5. Heather Urbanski, *The Science Fiction Reboot: Canon, Innovation and Fandom in Refashioned* (Jefferson, NC: McFarland, 2013), 7.

6. Jennifer Pearson, "'I Wanted a Movie Mothers Could Take Their Daughters to': J.J. Abrams on Why He Cast a Strong Female Lead in Star Wars: The Force Awakens," *Daily Mail*, December 1, 2015, http:// www.dailymail.co.uk/tvshowbiz /article-3339834/J-J-Abrams-cast-strong-female-lead-Star-Wars-Force-Awakens. html.

7. See Neta Yodovich's chapter in this volume for more on the phenomenon of fathers passing their love of Star Wars on to their children.

8. Carrie Fisher, *The Princess Diarist* (New York: Blue Rider, 2016), 230.

9. This viewing idea, which proposes an order of episodes IV, V, II, III, and finally VI, skipping I entirely, was proposed and popularized by blogger Rod Hilton in 2011 as a way of making the viewing experience more rewarding, more protective of plot twists, and more shielded from appearances of Jar Jar Binks. Alex Fitzpatrick, "This Is the Best Way to Watch *Star Wars* This Weekend," *Time*, April 10, 2015, https://time.com/3817072/star-wars-download-machete-order/.

10. Pim van den Berg, "Execute Order 66: How *Star Wars* Memes Became Indebted to Fascist Dictatorship," Institute of Network Cultures, November 23, 2018, https://networkcultures.org/longform/2018/11/23/execute-order-66-how -star-wars-memes-became-indebted-to-fascist-dictatorship/.

11. BBC Staff, "*Star Wars*: Jar Jar Binks Actor Ahmed Best Considered Suicide," BBC News, July 4, 2018, https://www.bbc.com/news/entertainment -arts-44708983; Kirsten Chuba, "*Star Wars* Actress Kelly Marie Tran Leaves Social Media after Months of Harassment," *Variety*, June 5, 2018, https://variety .com/2018/biz/news/star-wars-kelly-marie-tran-leaves-social-media -harassment-1202830892/.

12. Bryan Young, "Once Shunned, Jar Jar Actor Ahmed Best Gets a Standing Ovation," SyFy Wire, April 15, 2019, https://www.syfy.com/syfywire/star-wars

-daily-once-shunned-jar-jar-actor-ahmed-best-gets-a-standing-ovation; Kimberly Yam, "Kelly Marie Tran Gets Emotional as Fans Chant Her Name at Star Wars Celebration," Huffington Post, March 13, 2019, https://www.huffingtonpost.com .au/entry/kelly-marie-tran-fans-star-wars-celebration_n_5cb0c45ae4b098b9a2d 35127?rii8n.

13. Göran Bolin, *Media Generations: Experience, Identity, and Mediatised Social Change* (New York: Routledge, 2017).

14. Bolin, *Media Generations*, 115.

15. Thomas Elsaesser, "Cinephilia or the Uses of Disenchantment," in *Cinephilia: Movies, Love, and Memory*, ed. Marijke de Valck and Malte Hagener (Amsterdam: Amsterdam University Press, 2005), 35.

16. William Proctor and Richard McCulloch, "From the House that George Built to the House of Mouse," in *Disney's* Star Wars: *Forces of Production, Promotion, and Reception*, ed. William Proctor and Richard McCulloch (Iowa City: Iowa University Press, 2019), 4.

17. Golding, *Star Wars after Lucas*, 41–64.

18. A fuller discussion of the politics of Star Wars can be found in Golding, *Star Wars after Lucas*, 20–40.

19. Matt Miller, "The Year *Star Wars* Fans Finally Ruined *Star Wars*," *Esquire*, December 13, 2018, http://www.esquire.com/entertainment/movies/a25560063 /how-fans-ruined-star-wars-the-last-jedi-2018/.

20. Robin Wood, *Hollywood from Vietnam to Reagan* (New York: Columbia University Press, 1986), 147; emphasis in original.

21. For example, following the sale to Disney in 2013, Lucas remarked, "But now, with the internet, it's gotten very vicious and very personal. You just say, 'Why do I need to do this?'" Quoted in Golding, *Star Wars after Lucas*, 38.

22. Suzanne Scott, *Fake Geek Girls: Fandom, Gender, and the Convergence Culture Industry* (New York: New York University Press, 2019).

23. Stuart Hall, "Notes on Deconstructing 'The Popular,'" in *People's History and Socialist Theory*, ed. Raphael Samuel (London: Routledge, 1981), 239.

ROADS GO EVER ON AND ON: FAN FICTION AND ARCHIVAL INFRASTRUCTURES AS MARKERS OF THE AFFIRMATIONAL-TRANSFORMATIONAL CONTINUUM IN TOLKIEN FANDOM

1. Andrea MacDonald, "Uncertain Utopia: Science Fiction Media Fandom and Computer Media Communication," in *Theorizing Fandom*, ed. Cheryl Harris and Alison Alexander (New York: Hampton Press, 1998), 131–52.

2. Kristina Busse, *Framing Fan Fiction: Literary and Social Practices in Fan Fiction Communities* (Iowa City: University of Iowa Press, 2017), 101.

3. Kristin Thompson, "Gollum Talks to Himself: Problems and Solutions in Peter Jackson's *The Lord of the Rings*," in *Picturing Tolkien: Essays on Peter Jackson's*

The Lord of the Rings Film Trilogy, ed. Janice M. Bogstad and Philip E. Kaveny (Jefferson, NC: McFarland, 2011), 42–43.

4. As a brief sample, Cheryl Harris describes fandoms as fans' chosen and self-constructed "social and cultural environment," while Nancy Reagin and Anne Rubenstein think of fandoms as the "communities" that congregate around a popular text. See Cheryl Harris, "Introduction: Theorizing Fandom: Fans, Subculture, and Identity," in *Theorizing Fandom: Fans, Subculture, and Identity*, ed. Cheryl Harris and Alison Alexander (New York: Hampton Press, 1998), 4; Nancy Reagin and Anne Rubenstein, "'I'm Buffy, and You're History': Putting Fan Studies into History," *Transformative Works and Cultures* 6 (2011), https://doi.org/10.3983/twc.2011.0272.

5. Dawn Walls-Thumma, "Diving into the Lacuna: Fan Studies, Methodologies, and Mending the Gaps," *Transformative Works and Cultures* 33 (2020), https://doi.org/10.3983/twc.2020.1871.

6. Elana Shefrin, "*Lord of the Rings, Star Wars*, and Participatory Fandom: Mapping New Congruencies between the Internet and Media Entertainment Culture," *Critical Studies in Media Communication* 21, no. 3 (2004): 261–81; Simone Murray, "'Celebrating the Story the Way It Is': Cultural Studies, Corporate Media and the Contested Utility of Fandom," *Continuum* 18, no. 1 (2004): 7–25; Kirsten Pullen, "*The Lord of the Rings* Online Blockbuster Fandom: Pleasure and Commerce," in *The Lord of the Rings: Popular Culture in Global Context*, ed. Ernest Mathjis (London: Wallflower Press, 2006), 172–88; Matt Hills, "Realising the Cult Blockbuster: *The Lord of the Rings* Fandom and Residual/ Emergent Cult Status in 'the Mainstream,'" in *The Lord of the Rings: Popular Culture in Global Context*, ed. Ernest Mathjis (London: Wallflower Press, 2006), 160–71; Bertha Chin and Jonathan Gray, "'One Ring to Rule Them All': Pre-Viewers and Pre-Texts of the *Lord of the Rings* Films," *Intensities* 2 (2001), https://intensitiescultmedia.files.wordpress.com/2012/12/chin-and-gray-one-ring-to-rule-them-all.pdf; Maggie Parke, "LOTR: One Digital Fandom to Initiate Them All," in *Fan Phenomena: The Lord of the Rings*, ed. Lorna Piatti-Farnell (Bristol: Intellect, 2016), 18–25; Robin Reid, "Breaking of the Fellowship: Competing Discourses of Archives and Canons in *The Lord of the Rings* Internet Fandom," in *How We Became Middle-Earth: A Collection of Essays on* The Lord of the Rings, ed. Adam Lam and N. Oryschuk (Zollikofen, Switzerland: Walking Tree, 2007); Lars Konzack, "The Subcreation of J.R.R. Tolkien's Middle-earth and How It Became Transmedial Culture," in *Revisiting Imaginary Worlds: A Subcreation Studies Anthology*, ed. Mark J. P. Wolf (Abingdon, UK: Routledge, 2016), 69–82.

7. Robin Reid, "Thrusts in the Dark: Slashers' Queer Practices," *Extrapolation* 50, no. 3 (2009): 463–83; Megan B. Abrahamson, "J.R.R. Tolkien, Fanfiction, and 'the Freedom of the Reader,'" *Mythlore* 32, no. 1 (2016): 55–74; Amy Sturgis, "Make Mine 'Movieverse': How the Tolkien Fan Fiction Community Learned to Stop Worrying and Love Peter Jackson," in *Tolkien on Film: Essays on Peter Jackson's* The Lord of the Rings, ed. Janet Brennan Croft (Altadena, CA: Mythopoeic

Press, 2005); Amy Sturgis, "Reimagining Rose: Portrayals of Tolkien's Rosie Cotton in Twenty-First Century Fan Fiction," *Mythlore* 24, no. 3 (2006), https:// dc.swosu.edu/mythlore/vol24/iss3/10; Dawn Walls-Thumma, "Affirmational and Transformational Values and Practices in the Tolkien Fanfiction Community," *Journal of Tolkien Research* 8, no. 1 (2019), https://scholar.valpo.edu /journaloftolkienresearch/vol8/iss1/6; Maria K. Alberto, "'The Effort to Translate': Fan Film Culture and the Works of J.R.R. Tolkien," *Journal of Tolkien Research* 3, no. 3 (2016), https://scholar.valpo.edu/journaloftolkienresearch/vol3/iss3/2/.

8. There are notable exceptions, though. Sheenagh Pugh discusses the affirmational tendencies of literary fandoms, which value a highly circumscribed definition of canon to include the interpretive, moral, and even stylistic dispositions of the original creator. See Sheenagh Pugh, *The Democratic Genre: Fan Fiction in a Literary Context* (Bridgend, Wales: Seren, 2005).

9. The rise and development of these Tolkien fandom generations also corresponds with understandings of fan migration, which Brianna Dym and Casey Fiesler have characterized as fandom being "an ever-evolving community of nomads, migrating across platforms and constantly attracting new members across generations." See Brianna Dym and Casey Fiesler, "Generations, Migrations, and the Future of Fandom's Private Space," *Transformative Works and Cultures* 28 (2018), https://journal.transformativeworks.org/index.php/twc /article/view/1583. For Tolkien fandom, we note that different generations are also demarcated by factors occurring in tandem with fan migrations. For instance, Martin Barker and Ernest Mathijs's 2003–2004 Lord of the Rings Project, a fifteen-month research study of audience reactions to Jackson's films that drew over 24,000 participants from twenty countries, and the initial 2014–2015 Tolkien Fanfiction Survey reveal a massive upsurge of interest spurred by Jackson's films, which facilitated many new fans' entry into the fan fiction writing side of Tolkien fandom.

10. This survey was approved by the Institutional Review Board (IRB) of American Public University. The second iteration was approved by the IRB of the University of Utah.

11. The full methodology of this study is available in Dawn Walls-Thumma, "Data on Tolkien Fanfiction Culture and Practices, 1st Edition," DawnFelagund.com, 2019, http://dawnfelagund.com/file/DataOnTolkien FanfictionCultureAndPractices1.pdf.

12. Henry Jenkins, *Textual Poachers: Television Fans and Participatory Culture* (New York: Routledge, 1992); Camille Bacon-Smith, *Enterprising Women: Television Fandom and the Creation of Popular Myth* (Philadelphia: University of Pennsylvania Press, 1992).

13. The lack of sexual content can be seen in a 1955 *Observer* review, in which Scottish poet Edwin Muir maintains that "all the characters [in *LOTR*] are boys masquerading as adult heroes . . . hardly one of them knows anything about women, except by hearsay." See also Brenda Partridge, "No Sex Please—We're

Hobbits: The Construction of Female Sexuality in *The Lord of the Rings*," in *J.R.R. Tolkien: This Far Land*, ed. Robert Giddings (London: Vision, 1983), 179–97.

14. Marion Zimmer Bradley, "How Dragged Were My Heels: Sex in Science Fiction," Tolkien Fanzines (Marquette University collection) 5 (1961): 7–8, https://cdm16280.contentdm.oclc.org/digital/collection/p16280coll10/id/714.

15. For a sample of this discussion, see https://groups.google.com/g/rec.arts.books.tolkien/c/LHNpwDNimNo/m/3G_JVudoJZEJ.

16. For more, see https://groups.google.com/d/topic/rec.arts.books.tolkien/I7Z30UyOU_s/discussion; J. R. R. Tolkien, *The Letters of J.R.R. Tolkien*, ed. Humphrey Carpenter and Christopher Tolkien (Boston: Houghton Mifflin, 1981), 371.

17. A 1996 plea to "tone down the level of sex" on the RABT newsgroup provides one such example. See https://groups.google.com/g/rec.arts.books.tolkien/c/TiZXQQvyb1E/m/3XD0WsH20W8J.

18. Prembone, "The NEW TildeFAQ," July 10, 1999, https://groups.google.com/g/rec.arts.books.tolkien/c/Rxgn3V41IwM/m/STwaU7thfaAJ.

19. In 1998, RABT member Johan Winge conducted an informal poll of newsgroup members. Of the respondents who indicated their sex, just 26 percent identified as women.

20. Most fans did pick up the books, and the Tolkien fan fiction side at least seems to remain primarily book based. For example, despite being administered in the midst of *The Hobbit* film trilogy's release, the 2014–2015 Tolkien Fanfiction Survey recorded that less than 0.5 percent of responding authors wrote fan fiction using only the films as their basis.

21. Sturgis, "Make Mine 'Movieverse,'" 286.

22. Susan Booker estimates that in 2004 nearly 10 percent of fan fiction websites were Tolkien-related. Susan Booker, "Tales Around the Internet Campfire: Fan Fiction in Tolkien's Universe," in *Tolkien on Film: Essays on Peter Jackson's The Lord of the Rings*, ed. Janet Brennan Croft (Altadena, CA: Mythopoeic Press, 2005), 259.

23. This has changed even more in just the past few years, as Tumblr's controversial "porn ban" or "nipplepocalypse" of December 2018 limited explicit sexual content in ways that included much fan art, and users began migrating to less censorious platforms, including "closed" platforms like Discord.

24. Fanlore, "Kink Meme," https://fanlore.org/wiki/Kink_Meme (accessed July 27, 2020).

25. For example, Femslash February and Legendarium Ladies April address the all-too-common absence of women in the canon and Tolkien-based fan fiction by encouraging new stories about women characters.

26. The Textual Ghosts Project by fan fiction writer Elleth provides an apt illustration of the ease with which Tolkien fan fiction writers use both types of fannish expression along the affirmational-transformational continuum. Elleth's list includes all the unnamed women who must have existed in Tolkien's book

canon as wives and mothers of named male characters. The list has been used as a resource and an imperative encouraging fellow fan fiction authors to write about the women of Middle-earth. This artifact draws from both affirmational and transformational values: it is an exhaustive and impressive collection of the canon, representing intensive labor and expertise with the full range of Tolkien's work, yet it functions to make room for fan creators' own interests, experiences, and beliefs. Elleth, "The Textual Ghosts Project," https://web.archive.org /web/20200120090450/http://elleth.x10host.com/textualghosts.htm (accessed July 27, 2020).

27. Fanlore, "Least Expected," https://fanlore.org/wiki/Least_Expected (accessed July 27, 2020).

28. Ty Rosenthal, "Warm Beds Are Good: Sex and Libido in Tolkien's Writing," *Mallorn* 42 (2004), 11, emphasis added.

29. Rosenthal, "Warm Beds," 11.

30. For example, Stories of Arda disallowed explicit sexual content and all slash, Library of Moria included only slash, the Open Scrolls Archive archived only het, and the Henneth-Annûn Story Archive ostensibly allowed any type or degree of sexual content but also used a review panel, which, some argued, functioned as a de facto barrier to certain fan works, particularly slash. See Kristi Lee Brobeck, "Under the Waterfall: A Fan Fiction Community's Analysis of Their Self-Representation and Peer Review," *Refractory: A Journal of Entertainment Media* 5 (2004), http://refractory.unimelb.edu.au/2004/02/03/under-the -waterfall-a-fanfiction-communitys-analysis-of-their-self-representation-and-peer -review-kristi-lee/.

31. Reid, "Breaking of the Fellowship"; Brobeck, "Under the Waterfall."

32. Rosenthal, "Warm Beds," 11.

33. Access to early Tolkien zines through the Marquette University collection and similar endeavors is extremely limited, but the small sample of fan fiction available through these venues is authored predominantly by men—a significant difference from many other fandoms extant at this point, in which women wrote most of the fan fiction.

34. Elsewhere Walls-Thumma has documented how vicious and ubiquitous the denunciations of Mary Sues became in early second-generation Tolkien fandom. See Walls-Thumma, "Affirmational and Transformational Values and Practices," 25–26.

35. Walls-Thumma, "Affirmational and Transformational Values and Practices," 25–26.

36. Ika Willis, "Keeping Promises to Queer Children: Making Space (for Mary Sue) at Hogwarts," in *Fan Fiction and Fan Communities in the Age of the Internet*, ed. Karen Hellekson and Kristina Busse (Jefferson, NC: McFarland), 163.

37. Emil Johansson, "Population by Race and Sex," LOTRProject, 2014, http:// lotrproject.com/statistics/.

38. Pugh, *The Democratic Genre*, 19. Pugh's distinction between fans who

want "more of" versus "more from" the canon could be seen as an earlier representation of the affirmational-transformational continuum.

39. These sites were chosen because they allow authors to input characters from a prepopulated list and a story summary. We used the former to find female characters' names and the latter to determine whether they had leading roles. Because the SWG archive opened in 2007, it does not have data for 2003. We must also note that Walls-Thumma is the founder of the SWG, and both authors are active participants there.

40. Elyanna (@itariilles), "My Statement on Tolkien 2019," Tumblr, June 21, 2020; Andrew Rearick, "Why Is the Only Good Orc a Dead Orc?: The Dark Face of Racism Examined in Tolkien's World," *Modern Fiction Studies* 50, no. 4 (2004): 861–74. Robin Reid has also published an excellent bibliographic essay covering work on race in Tolkien studies more generally. Robin Reid, "Race in Tolkien Studies: A Bibliographic Essay," in *Tolkien and Alterity*, ed. Christopher Vaccaro and Yvette Kisor (Cham, Switzerland: Palgrave Macmillan, 2017), 33–74.

"FANNISH SENSIBILITIES": FISSURES IN THE SHERLOCK HOLMES FANDOM

1. Al Shaw, "The Adventure of the Windy City Giants," in *About Being a Sherlockian: 60 Essays Celebrating the Sherlock Holmes Community*, ed. Christopher Redmond (Rockville, MD: Wildside Press, 2017), 75.

2. Christopher Redmond, "Introduction," in *About Being a Sherlockian: 60 Essays Celebrating the Sherlock Holmes Community*, ed. Christopher Redmond (Rockville, MD: Wildside Press, 2017), 7–8.

3. Angela Fowler, "The Adventure of the Inexperienced Academic," in *About Being a Sherlockian: 60 Essays Celebrating the Sherlock Holmes Community*, ed. Christopher Redmond (Rockville, MD: Wildside Press, 2017), 194.

4. Fowler, "The Adventure of the Inexperienced Academic," 194.

5. Andrew J. Peck, "A Case of Irregularity," in *About Being a Sherlockian: 60 Essays Celebrating the Sherlock Holmes Community*, ed. Christopher Redmond (Rockville, MD: Wildside Press, 2017), 73.

6. Wendy C. Fries, "The Adventure of the Scarlet Thread," in *About Being a Sherlockian: 60 Essays Celebrating the Sherlock Holmes Community*, ed. Christopher Redmond (Rockville, MD: Wildside Press, 2017), 148.

7. Ashley D. Polasek, "Traditional Transformations and Transmedial Affirmations: Blurring the Boundaries of Sherlockian Fan Practices," *Transformative Works and Cultures* 23 (2017), https://doi.org/10.3983/twc.2017.0911.

8. Polasek, "Traditional Transformations."

9. Mattias Boström, *From Holmes to Sherlock: The Story of the Men and Women Who Created an Icon*, trans. Michael Gallagher (New York: Mysterious Press, 2018), 123.

10. Ann K. McClellan, "*Tit-Bits*, New Journalism, and Early Sherlock Holmes

Notes to Pages 158–163 217

Fandom," *Transformative Works and Cultures* 23 (2017), https://doi.org/10.3983/twc.2017.0816.

11. McClellan, "*Tit-Bits.*"

12. Boström, *From Holmes to Sherlock*, 141.

13. Boström, *From Holmes to Sherlock*, 201.

14. Boström, *From Holmes to Sherlock*, 201–3.

15. Boström, *From Holmes to Sherlock*, 206.

16. Boström, *From Holmes to Sherlock*, 255.

17. "Subscribe / Renew the BSJ," Baker Street Irregulars, December 6, 2019, https://bakerstreetirregulars.com/2001/05/01/subscribe-bsj/.

18. Boström, *From Holmes to Sherlock*, 408.

19. Boström, *From Holmes to Sherlock*, 207.

20. Harrison Hunt, "The Adventure of the Irregular Historian," in *About Being a Sherlockian: 60 Essays Celebrating the Sherlock Holmes Community*, ed. Christopher Redmond (Rockville, MD: Wildside Press, 2017), 70.

21. Andrew L. Solberg and Robert S. Katz, "Fandom, Publishing, and Playing the Grand Game," *Transformative Works and Cultures* 23 (2017), https://doi.org/10.3983/twc.2017.0825.

22. Boström, *From Holmes to Sherlock*, 480.

23. Boström, *From Holmes to Sherlock*, 480.

24. Boström, *From Holmes to Sherlock*, 480.

25. Louisa Ellen Stein and Kristina Busse, eds., *Sherlock and Transmedia Fandom: Essays on the BBC Series* (Jefferson, NC: McFarland, 2012); Jennifer Wojton and Lynnette R. Porter, *Sherlock and Digital Fandom: The Meeting of Creativity, Community and Advocacy* (Jefferson, NC: McFarland, 2018); Ann K. McClellan, *Sherlock's World: Fan Fiction and the Reimagining of BBC's Sherlock* (Iowa City: University of Iowa Press, 2018).

26. Roberta Pearson, "'Good Old Index': Or, the Mystery of the Infinite Archive," in *Sherlock and Transmedia Fandom: Essays on the BBC Series*, ed. Louisa Ellen Stein and Kristina Busse (Jefferson, NC: McFarland, 2012), 155.

27. Quoted in Pearson, "'Good Old Index,'" 155.

28. Line Nybro Petersen, "'The Florals': Female Fans over 50 in the *Sherlock* Fandom," *Transformative Works and Cultures* 23 (2017), https://doi.org/10.3983/twc.2017.0956.

29. As quoted in Wojton and Porter, *Sherlock and Digital Fandom*, 76.

30. Boström, *From Holmes to Sherlock*, 50.

31. Boström, *From Holmes to Sherlock*, 372.

32. Quoted in Boström, *From Holmes to Sherlock*, 118.

33. Lyndsay Faye, "A Study in Semblance," in *About Being a Sherlockian: 60 Essays Celebrating the Sherlock Holmes Community*, ed. Christopher Redmond (Rockville, MD: Wildside Press, 2017), 154.

34. Quoted in McClellan, *Sherlock's World*, 123.

35. Polasek, "Traditional Transformations."

36. Boström, *From Holmes to Sherlock*, 367.

37. Sanna Nyqvist, "Authorship and Authenticity in Sherlock Holmes Pastiches," *Transformative Works and Cultures* 23 (2017), https://doi.org/10.3983/twc.2017.0834.

38. Faye, "A Study in Semblance," 153.

39. Lyndsay Faye, "Upon the Clear Distinction between Fandom and the Baker Street Irregulars," Criminal Element, May 9, 2018, http://www.criminalelement.com/upon-the-clear-distinction-between-fandom-and-the-baker-street-irregulars-lyndsay-faye-sherlock-holmes-arthur-conan-doyle-elementary.

40. Boström, *From Holmes to Sherlock*, 340.

41. Julia Carlson Rosenblatt, "From Outside to Inside," *Transformative Works and Cultures* 23 (2017), https://doi.org/10.3983/twc.2017.0920.

42. Rosenblatt, "From Outside to Inside."

43. Rosenblatt, "From Outside to Inside."

44. Rosenblatt, "From Outside to Inside."

45. Lydnsay Faye, "Inside the Baker Street Irregulars," Tor.com, March 22, 2012, https://www.tor.com/2012/03/22/inside-the-baker-street-irregulars/.

46. Thomas J. Francis, "The Adventure of the Most Interesting People," in *About Being a Sherlockian: 60 Essays Celebrating the Sherlock Holmes Community*, ed. Christopher Redmond (Rockville, MD: Wildside Press, 2017), 61–62.

47. "About," Baker Street Babes, http://bakerstreetbabes.com/about/ (accessed July 30, 2020).

48. Peck, "A Case of Irregularity," 73.

49. Kristina Manente, "Preface," in *The One Fixed Point in a Changing Age: A New Generation on Sherlock Holmes*, ed. Kristina Manente, Maria Fleischhack, Sarah Roy, and Taylor Blumenberg (Indianapolis: Gasogene Books, 2014), v.

50. Polasek, "Traditional Transformations."

THE FANDOM IS A WELCOMING PLACE UNLESS I KNOW MORE THAN YOU: GENERATIONS, MENTORSHIP, AND SUPER-FANS

1. Agnès Pécolo and Myriam Bahuaud, "Générations," in *Abécédaire*, ed. Gino Gramaccia (Bordeaux: Presses Universitaires de Bordeaux, 2013), 89–93; translation by author.

2. Agnès Pécolo, "Identité Générationnelle," *Publictionnaire*, October 16, 2017, http://publictionnaire.huma-num.fr/notice/identite-generationnelle/.

3. Henry Jenkins, *Textual Poachers: Television Fans and Participatory Culture* (New York: New York University Press, 1992).

4. Nick Abercrombie and Brian Longhurst, *Audiences: A Sociological Theory of Performance and Imagination* (London: Sage, 1998).

5. Henry Jenkins, "La 'Filk' et la Construction Sociale de la Communauté

des Fans de Science-Fiction," in *Cultural Studies: Anthologie*, ed. Hervé Glévarec, Eric Macé, and Eric Maigret (Paris: Armand Colin, 2008), 212–22; translation by author.

6. Sarah M. Corse and Jaime Hartless, "Sci-fi and Skimpy Outfits: Making Boundaries and Staking Claims to *Star Trek: Into Darkness*," in *Fan Girls and the Media: Creating Characters, Consuming Culture*, ed. Adrienne Trier-Bienick (London: Rowman and Littlefield, 2015), 1–20.

7. Paul Booth, *Digital Fandom: New Media Studies* (New York: Peter Lang, 2010), 20.

8. Booth, *Digital Fandom*, 22.

9. Mélanie Bourdaa, "Taking a Break from All Your Worries: *Battlestar Galactica* et les Nouvelles Pratiques Télévisuelles des Fans," *Questions de Communication* 22 (2012): 235–50.

10. See Neta Yodovich's chapter in this volume for specific analysis of fandom passed from parent to child.

11. Henry Jenkins, Mimi Ito, and danah boyd, *Participatory Culture in a Networked Era* (New York: Polity Press, 2016), 4.

12. Rebecca W. Black, *Adolescence and Online Fan Fiction* (New York: Peter Lang, 2008).

13. Jenkins, Ito, and boyd, *Participatory Culture*, 19.

14. The original letter is not available anymore on Dirk Benedict's website, but you can find a copy here: https://qcurtius.com/2017/02/09/dirk-benedicts-lost-in-castration/ (accessed November 3, 2020).

15. "Fandom Forward's Camp GLA 2021," Protego Foundation, July 16, 2021, https://www.protegofoundation.org/blog/fandom-forwards-camp-gla-2021.

16. Mélanie Bourdaa, "May We Meet Again: Social Bonds, Activities and Identities in the #Clexa Fandom," in *A Companion to Media Fandoms and Fan Studies*, ed. Paul Booth (Hoboken, NJ: Wiley-Blackwell, 2018), 385–400.

Bibliography

Abercrombie, Nick, and Brian Longhurst. *Audiences: A Sociological Theory of Performance and Imagination.* London: Sage, 1998.

Abrahamson, Megan B. "J.R.R. Tolkien, Fanfiction, and 'The Freedom of the Reader.'" *Mythlore* 32, no. 1 (2013). https://dc.swosu.edu/mythlore/vol32/iss1/5.

Adams, Tony E., and Andrew F. Herrmann. "Expanding Our Autoethnographic Future." *Journal of Autoethnography* 1, no. 1 (2020): 1–8.

Aden, Roger. *Popular Stories and Promised Lands: Fan Cultures and Symbolic Pilgrimages.* Tuscaloosa: University of Alabama Press, 1999.

Alberto, Maria. "'The Effort to Translate': Fan Film Culture and the Works of J.R.R. Tolkien." *Journal of Tolkien Research* 3, no. 3 (2016). http://scholar.valpo.edu/journaloftolkienresearch/vol3/iss3/2.

Altman, Rick. *The American Film Musical.* Bloomington: Indiana University Press, 1987.

Anderson, Tonya. "Still Kissing Their Posters Goodnight: Female Fandom and the Politics of Popular Music." *Journal of Audience and Reception Studies* 9, no. 2 (2012): 239–64.

Austen, Jane. *The Annotated Pride and Prejudice,* 2nd ed. Edited by David Shapard. New York: Random House, 2012.

Austin, Thomas. *Hollywood Hype and Audiences: Selling and Watching Popular Film in the 1990s.* Manchester: Manchester University Press, 2002.

Ayça, Engin. "Türk Sineması Seyirci İlişkileri." *Kurgu* 11 (1992): 117–33.

Bacon-Smith Camille. *Enterprising Women: Television Fandom and the Creation of Popular Myth.* Philadelphia: University of Pennsylvania Press, 1992.

Banet-Weiser, Sarah. *Empowered: Popular Feminism and Popular Misogyny.* Durham, NC: Duke University Press, 2018.

———. *Kids Rule!: Nickelodeon and Consumer Citizenship.* Durham, NC: Duke University Press, 2007.

Barker, Martin, Kate Egan, Tom Phillips, and Sarah Ralph. *Alien Audiences: Remembering and Evaluating a Classic Movie.* London: Palgrave Macmillan, 2016.

Baym, Nancy, Daniel Cavicchi, and Norma Coates. "Music Fandom in the Digital Age: A Conversation." In *The Routledge Companion to Media Fandom,* edited by Melissa A. Click and Suzanne Scott, 141–52. New York: Routledge, 2018.

Bennett, Andy. "Punk's Not Dead: The Continuing Significance of Punk Rock for an Older Generation of Fans." *Sociology* 40, no. 2 (2006): 219–35.

Bennett, Andy, and Paul Hodkinson. *Aging and Youth Culture: Music, Style, and Identity.* London: Bloomsbury, 2013.

Bennett, Lucy. "Tracing Textual Poachers: Reflections on the Development of Fan Studies and Digital Fandom." *Journal of Fandom Studies* 2, no. 1 (2014): 5–20.

Berlant, Lauren. *The Female Complaint: The Unfinished Business of Sentimentality in American Culture.* Durham, NC: Duke University Press, 2008.

Black, Rebecca W. *Adolescence and Online Fan Fiction.* New York: Peter Lang, 2008.

Bogdan, Robert, and Sari Knopp Biklen. *Qualitative Research for Education.* Boston: Allyn and Bacon, 1992.

Bolin, Göran. *Media Generations: Experience, Identity, and Mediatised Social Change.* New York: Routledge, 2017.

———. "Media Generations: Objective and Subjective Media Landscapes and Nostalgia Among Generations of Media Users." *Participations* 11, no. 2 (2014): 103–31.

Booker, Susan. "Tales around the Internet Campfire: Fan Fiction in Tolkien's Universe." In *Tolkien on Film: Essays on Peter Jackson's The Lord of the Rings,* edited by Janet Brennan Croft, 259–82. Altadena, CA: Mythopoeic Press, 2005.

Booth, Paul. *Digital Fandom: New Media Studies.* New York: Peter Lang, 2010.

Booth, Paul, and Peter Kelly. "The Changing Faces of *Doctor Who* Fandom: New Fans, New Technologies, Old Practices." *Participations* 10, no. 1 (2013): 56–72.

Boström, Mattias. *From Holmes to Sherlock: The Story of the Men and Women Who Created an Icon.* Translated by Michael Gallagher. New York: Mysterious Press, 2018.

Bourdaa, Mélanie. "'May We Meet Again': Social Bonds, Activities, and Identities in the #Clexa Fandom." In *A Companion to Media Fandom and Fan Studies,* edited by Paul Booth, 385–400. Hoboken, NJ: Wiley-Blackwell, 2018.

———. "Taking a Break from All Your Worries: *Battlestar Galactica* et les Nouvelles Pratiques Télévisuelles des Fans." *Questions de Communication* 22 (2012): 235–50.

Bourdieu, Pierre. *Distinction: A Social Critique of the Judgement of Taste.* Cambridge, MA: Harvard University Press, 1984.

Bridgeman, Teresa. "Time and Space." In *The Cambridge Companion to Narrative,* edited by David Herman, 52–65. Cambridge: Cambridge University Press, 2007.

Brobeck, Kristi Lee. "Under the Waterfall: A Fan Fiction Community's Analysis of Their Self-Representation and Peer Review." *Refractory: A Journal of Entertainment Media* 5 (2004). http://refractory.unimelb.edu.au/2004/02/03/under-the-waterfall-a-fanfiction-communitys-analysis-of-their-self-representation-and-peer-review-kristi-lee/.

Brower, Sue. "Fans as Tastemakers: Viewers for Quality Television." In *The Adoring Audience: Fan Culture and Popular Media,* edited by Lisa A. Lewis, 163–84. London: Routledge, 1992.

Brown, Jeffrey A. "#WheresRey: Feminism, Protest, and Merchandising Sexism in *Star Wars: The Force Awakens.*" *Feminist Media Studies* 18, no. 3 (2018): 335–348.

Büker, Seçil. "Film Ateşli Bir Öpüşmeyle Bitmiyor." In *Kültür Fragmanları*, edited by Deniz Kandiyoti and Ayşe Saktanber, 159–82. Istanbul: Metis, 2003.

Bury, Rhiannon. *Cyberspaces of Their Own: Female Fandoms Online.* New York: Peter Lang, 2005.

Busse, Kristina. *Framing Fan Fiction: Literary and Social Practices in Fan Fiction Communities.* Iowa City: University of Iowa Press, 2017.

———. "Geek Hierarchies, Boundary Policing, and the Gendering of the Good Fan." *Participations* 10, no. 1 (2013): 73–91.

Byars, Jackie, Jeff Gould, Peter Fitting, Judith Newton, Tony Safford, Clayton Lee, and Charles Elkins. "Symposium on *Alien.*" *Science Fiction Studies* 7, no. 3 (1980): 278–304.

Cavicchi, Daniel. *Tramps Like Us: Music and Meaning among Springsteen Fans.* Oxford: Oxford University Press, 1998.

Cherry, Brigid. *Horror.* London: Routledge, 2009.

———. "Refusing to Refuse to Look: Female Viewers of the Horror Film." In *Horror: The Film Reader*, edited by Mark Jancovich, 169–78. London: Routledge, 2002.

Chin, Bertha, and Jonathan Gray. "'One Ring to Rule Them All': Pre-Viewers and Pre-Texts of the *Lord of the Rings* Films." *Intensities: The Journal of Cult Media* 2 (2001). https://intensitiescultmedia.files.wordpress.com/2012/12/chin-and-gray-one-ring-to-rule-them-all.pdf.

Clarke, Victoria, and Virginia Braun. "Thematic Analysis." In *Encyclopedia of Critical Psychology*, edited by Thomas Teo, 1947–1952. New York: Springer Reference, 2014.

Coppa, Francesca. "A Brief History of Media Fandom." In *Fan Fiction and Fan Communities in the Age of the Internet*, edited by Karen Hellekson and Kristina Busse, 41–59. Jefferson, NC: McFarland, 2006.

Corse, Sarah M., and Jaime Hartless. "Sci-fi and Skimpy Outfits: Making Boundaries and Staking Claims to *Star Trek: Into Darkness.*" In *Fan Girls and the Media: Creating Characters, Consuming Culture*, edited by Adrienne Trier-Bienick, 1–20. London: Rowman and Littlefield, 2015.

Crawford, Garry, and Victoria K. Gosling. "The Myth of the 'Puck Bunny': Female Fans and Men's Ice Hockey." *Sociology* 38, no. 3 (2004): 477–93.

Dabek, Meredith. "Replies, Retweets, and Reblogs: Modes of Participation in *The Lizzie Bennet Diaries.*" *Paradoxa* 29 (2017): 263–86.

de Certeau, Michel. *The Practice of Everyday Life.* Berkeley: University of California Press, 1984.

Dixon, Kevin. "Learning the Game: Football Fandom Culture and the Origins of Practice." *International Review for the Sociology of Sport* 48, no. 3 (2012): 334–48.

Driessen, Simone. "'I'll Never Break Your Heart': The Perpetual Fandom of the

Backstreet Boys." In *Everybody Hurts: Transitions, Endings, and Resurrections in Fan Cultures*, edited by Rebecca Williams, 31–42. Iowa City: University of Iowa Press, 2018.

———. "Larger than Life: Exploring the Transcultural Fan Practices of the Dutch Backstreet Boys Fandom." *Participations: Journal of Audience and Reception Studies* 12, no. 2 (2015): 180–96.

Duffett, Mark. "Introduction: Directions in Music Fan Research: Undiscovered Territories and Hard Problems." *Popular Music and Society* 36, no. 3 (2013): 299–304.

———. *Understanding Fandom: An Introduction to the Study of Media Fan Culture.* New York: Bloomsbury, 2013.

Dym, Brianna, and Casey Fiesler. "Generations, Migrations, and the Future of Fandom's Private Spaces." *Transformative Works and Cultures* 28 (2018). http://dx.doi.org/10.3983/twc.2018.1583.

Elsaesser, Thomas. "Cinephilia or the Uses of Disenchantment." In *Cinephilia: Movies, Love, and Memory*, edited by Marijke de Valck and Malte Hagener, 27–43. Amsterdam: Amsterdam University Press, 2005.

Endo, Rachel. "Complicating Culture and Difference: Situating Asian American Youth Identities in Lisa Yee's *Millicent Min, Girl Genius* and *Stanford Wong Flunks Big-Time*." *Children's Literature in Education* 40, no. 3 (2009): 235–49.

Enns, Anthony. "The Fans from UNCLE: The Marketing and Reception of the Swinging '60s Spy Phenomenon." *Journal of Popular Film and Television* 28, no. 4 (2000): 124–32.

Evans, A., and M. Stasi. "Desperately Seeking Methods: New Directions in Fan Studies Research." *Participations* 11, no. 2 (2014): 4–23.

Ewens, Hannah. *Fangirls: Scenes from Modern Music Culture.* Austin: University of Texas Press, 2020.

Fairclough-Isaacs, Kirsty. "Celebrity Culture and Aging." In *Routledge Handbook of Cultural Gerontology*, edited by Julia Twigg and Wendy Martin, 361–68. New York: Routledge, 2015.

Faye, Lyndsay. "A Study in Semblance." In *About Being a Sherlockian: 60 Essays Celebrating the Sherlock Holmes Community*, edited by Christopher Redmond, 153–56. Rockville, MD: Wildside Press, 2017.

Fisher, Carrie. *The Princess Diarist.* New York: Blue Rider, 2016.

Fowler, Angela. "The Adventure of the Inexperienced Academic." In *About Being a Sherlockian: 60 Essays Celebrating the Sherlock Holmes Community*, edited by Christopher Redmond, 192–95. Rockville, MD: Wildside Press, 2017.

Francis, Thomas J. "The Adventure of the Most Interesting People." In *About Being a Sherlockian: 60 Essays Celebrating the Sherlock Holmes Community*, edited by Christopher Redmond, 59–63. Rockville, MD: Wildside Press, 2017.

Freeman, Matthew. "Rebuilding Transmedia *Star Wars*: Strategies of Branding and Unbranding a Galaxy Far, Far Away." In *Disney's Star Wars: Forces of Production, Promotion, and Reception*, edited by William Proctor and Richard

McCulloch, 23–38. Iowa City: University of Iowa Press, 2019.

Fries, Wendy C. "The Adventure of the Scarlet Thread." In *About Being a Sherlockian: 60 Essays Celebrating the Sherlock Holmes Community*, edited by Christopher Redmond, 147–49. Rockville, MD: Wildside Press, 2017.

Garde-Hansen, Joanne. *Media and Memory*. Edinburgh: Edinburgh University Press, 2011.

Garner, Ross. "The Mandalorian Variation: Gender, Institutionality, and Discursive Constraints in Star Wars Rebels." In *Disney's* Star Wars: *Forces of Production, Promotion, and Reception*, edited by William Proctor and Richard McCulloch, 109–22. Iowa City: University of Iowa Press, 2019.

Geraghty, Christine. *Now a Major Motion Picture: Film Adaptations of Literature and Drama*. Plymouth: Rowman and Littlefield, 2008.

Gibson, Pamela Church. "'You've Been in My Life So Long I Can't Remember Anything Else': Into the Labyrinth with Ripley and the Alien." In *Keyframes: Popular Cinema and Cultural Studies*, edited by Matthew Tinkcom and Amy Villarejo, 35–51. London: Routledge, 2001.

Gilbert, Anne. "Hatewatch with Me: Anti-Fandom as Social Performance." In *Anti-Fandom: Dislike and Hate in the Digital Age*, edited by Melissa A. Click, 62–80. New York: New York University Press, 2019.

Godwin, Victoria. "Hogwarts House Merchandise, Liminal Play, and Fan Identities." *Film and Merchandise* 42, no. 2 (2018). https://doi.org/10.3998/fc.13761232.0042.206.

Golding, Dan. *Star Wars after Lucas*. Minneapolis: University of Minnesota Press, 2019.

Göle, Nilüfer. "Sosyolog Gözüyle Dört Kadın." In *Dört Yapraklı Yonca: Onların Sihri Neydi?*, edited by Bircan Usallı Silan, 433–50. Istanbul: Epsilon, 2004.

Gould, Stephen J. "An Introspective Genealogy of My Introspective Genealogy." *Marketing Theory* 8, no. 4 (2008): 407–24. https://doi.org/10.1177/1470593108096543.

Gray, Jonathan. "Antifandom and the Moral Text: Television without Pity and Textual Dislike." *American Behavioral Scientist* 48, no. 7 (2005): 840–58.

Gray, Jonathan. "How Do I Dislike Thee? Let Me Count the Ways." In *Anti-Fandom: Dislike and Hate in the Digital Age*, edited by Melissa A. Click, 25–41. New York: New York University Press, 2019.

Grossberg, Lawrence. "Is There a Fan in the House?: The Affective Sensibility of Fandom." In *The Adoring Audience: Fan Culture and Popular Media*, edited by Lisa A. Lewis, 50–65. London: Routledge, 1992.

Hadas, Leora. "The Web Planet: How the Changing Internet Divided *Doctor Who* Fan Fiction Writers." *Transformative Works and Cultures* 3 (2009). https://doi.org/10.3983/twc.2009.0129.

Hall, Stuart. "Notes on Deconstructing 'The Popular.'" In *People's History and Socialist Theory*, edited by Raphael Samuel, 227–39. London: Routledge, 1981.

Harman, Claire. *Jane's Fame: How Jane Austen Conquered the World*. Edinburgh:

Bibliography 225

Canongate Books, 2009.

Harrington, C. Lee, and Denise D. Bielby. "Aging, Fans, and Fandom." In *The Routledge Companion to Media Fandom*, edited by Melissa A. Click and Suzanne Scott, 406–15. New York: Routledge, 2018.

———. "Autobiographical Reasoning in Long-Term Fandom." *Transformative Works and Cultures* 5 (2010). https://doi.org/10.3983/twc.2010.0209.

———. "A Life Course Perspective on Fandom." *International Journal of Cultural Studies* 13, no. 5 (2010): 429–50.

Harrington, C. Lee, Denise D. Bielby, and Anthony R. Bardo. "Life Course Transitions and the Future of Fandom." *International Journal of Cultural Studies* 14, no. 6 (2011): 567–90.

Harris, Cheryl. "Introduction: Theorizing Fandom: Fans, Subculture and Identity." In *Theorizing Fandom: Fans, Subculture, and Identity*, edited by Cheryl Harris and Alison Alexander, 3–8. New York: Hampton Press, 1998.

Heitland, Jon. *The Man from U.N.C.L.E. Book*. New York: St. Martin's Press, 1987.

Hellekson, Karen. "A Fannish Field of Value: Online Fan Gift Culture." *Cinema Journal* 48, no. 4 (2009): 113–18.

Hills, Matt. "Cult TV Revival: Generational Seriality, Recap Culture, and the 'Brand Gap' of *Twin Peaks: The Return*." *Television and New Media* 19, no. 4 (2018): 310–27.

———. *Fan Cultures*. London: Routledge, 2002.

———. "Introduction: Fandom from Cradle to Grave?" *Journal of Fandom Studies* 7, no. 2 (2019): 87–92.

———. "'The One You Watched When You Were Twelve': Regenerations of *Doctor Who* and Enduring Fandom's 'Life-Transitional Objects.'" *Journal of British Cinema and Television* 14, no. 2 (2017): 213–30.

———. "Patterns of Surprise." *American Behavioral Scientist* 48, no. 7 (2005): 801–21.

———. "Psychoanalysis and Digital Fandom: Theorizing Spoilers and Fans' Self-Narratives." In *Producing Theory in a Digital World*, edited by Rebecca Ann Lind, 105–22. New York: Peter Lang, 2012.

———. "Realising the Cult Blockbuster: *The Lord of the Rings* Fandom and Residual/Emergent Cult Status in 'the Mainstream.'" In *The Lord of the Rings: Popular Culture in Global Context*, edited by Ernest Mathjis, 160–71. London: Wallflower Press, 2006.

———. "Returning to Becoming a Fan Stories: Theorising Transformational Objects and the Emergence/Extension of Fandom." In *The Ashgate Research Companion to Fan Cultures*, edited by Linda Duits, Koos Zwaan, and Stijn Reijnders, 9–21. London: Routledge, 2018.

———. "Transmedia Spectacle and Transownership Storytelling as Seen on TV: *Star Wars* from the *Holiday Special* to *Rebels*." In *Disney's Star Wars: Forces of Production, Promotion, and Reception*, edited by William Proctor and Richard McCulloch, 39–52. Iowa City: University of Iowa Press, 2019.

———. "'Twilight' Fans Represented in Commercial Paratexts and Inter-Fandoms: Resisting and Repurposing Negative Fan Stereotypes." In *Genre, Reception, and Adaptation in the Twilight Series*, edited by Anne Morey, 113–29. Burlington: Ashgate, 2012.

———. "When the Pet Shop Boys Were 'Imperial': Fans' Self-Aging and the Neoliberal Life Course of 'Successful' Text-Aging." *Journal of Fandom Studies* 7, no. 2 (2019): 151–67.

Hinerman, Stephen. "'I'll Be Here With You': Fans, Fantasy and the Figure of Elvis." In *The Adoring Audience: Fan Culture and Popular Media*, edited by Lisa A. Lewis, 107–34. London: Routledge, 1992.

Horton, Donald, and R. Richard Wohl. "Mass Communication and Para-Social Interaction: Observations on Intimacy at a Distance." *Psychiatry* 19, no. 3 (1956): 215–29.

Hunt, Harrison. "The Adventure of the Irregular Historian." In *About Being a Sherlockian: 60 Essays Celebrating the Sherlock Holmes Community*, edited by Christopher Redmond, 68–70. Rockville, MD: Wildside Press, 2017.

Hutcheon, Linda. *A Theory of Adaptation*, 2nd ed. London: Routledge, 2013.

Istvandy, Lauren. *The Lifetime Soundtrack: Music and Autobiographical Memory*. Sheffield: Equinox Publishing, 2019.

Jameson, Fredric. "Nostalgia for the Present." *South Atlantic Quarterly* 88, no. 2 (1989): 517–37.

Jancovich, Mark, and Nathan Hunt. "The Mainstream, Distinction, and Cult TV." In *Cult Television*, edited by Sarah Gwenllian-Jones and Roberta E. Pearson, 27–43. Minneapolis: University of Minnesota Press, 2004.

Jane, Emma A. "'Your a Ugly, Whorish Slut': Understanding E-bile." *Feminist Media Studies* 14, no. 4 (2014): 531–46.

Jenkins, Henry. "Afterword: The Future of Fandom." In *Fandom: Identities and Communities in a Mediated World*, edited by Jonathan Grey, Cornel Sandvoss, and C. Lee Harrington, 357–64. New York: New York University Press, 2007.

———. "'Cultural Acupuncture': Fan Activism and the Harry Potter Alliance." *Transformative Works and Cultures* 10 (2012). https://doi.org/10.3983/twc.2012.0305.

———. 'Do You Enjoy Making the Rest of Us Feel Stupid?': alt.tv.twinpeaks, The Trickster Author, and Viewer Mastery." In *Full of Secrets: Critical Approaches to Twin Peaks*, edited by David Lavery, 51–69. Detroit: Wayne State University Press, 1995.

———. "La 'filk' et la Construction Sociale de la Communauté des Fans de Science-Fiction." In *Cultural Studies: Anthologie*, edited by Glévarec Hervé, Eric Macé, and Eric Maigret, 212–22. Paris: Armand Colin, 2008.

———. *Textual Poachers: Television Fans and Participatory Culture*. London: Routledge, 1992.

———. *The Wow Climax: Tracing the Emotional Impact of Popular Culture*. New York: New York University Press, 2007.

Jenkins, Henry, Mimi Ito, and danah boyd. *Participatory Culture in a Networked Era*. New York: Polity Press, 2016.

Jenkins, Richard. *Social Identity*. New York: Routledge, 2004.

Jensen, Joli. "Fandom as Pathology: The Consequences of Characterisation." In *The Adoring Audience: Fan Culture and Popular Media*, edited by Lisa A. Lewis, 9-29. London: Routledge, 1992.

Jerslev, Anne, and Line Nybro Petersen. "Introduction: Aging Celebrities, Aging Fans, and Aging Narratives in Popular Media Culture." *Celebrity Studies* 9, no. 2 (2018): 157–65.

Johnson, Claudia L. "Austen Cults and Cultures." In *The Cambridge Companion to Jane Austen*, 2nd ed., edited by Edward Copeland and Juliet McMaster, 232–47. Cambridge: Cambridge University Press, 2006.

Johnson, Derek. "'May the Force Be with Katie': Pink Media Franchising and the Postfeminist Politics of HerUniverse." *Feminist Media Studies* 14, no. 6 (2014): 895–911.

———. *Transgenerational Media Industries*. Ann Arbor: University of Michigan Press, 2019.

Jones, Bethan. "The Fandom Is Out There: Social Media and *The X-Files* Online." In *Fan CULTure: Essays on Participatory Fandom in the 21st Century*, edited by Kristin M. Barton and Jonathan Malcolm Lampley, 92–105. Jefferson, NC: McFarland, 2012.

Jones, Gwenllian Sara. "The Sex Lives of Cult Television Characters." *Screen* 43, no. 1 (2002): 79–90.

Kaya-Mutlu, Dilek. "Between Tradition and Modernity: Yeşilçam Melodrama, Its Stars, and Their Audiences." *Middle Eastern Studies* 46, no. 3 (2010): 417–31.

———. "Bringing Stars Home: Yeşilçam Cinema from the Perspective of Audience Letters." Paper presented at The Glow in Their Eyes: Global Perspectives on Film Cultures, Film Exhibition and Cinemagoing conference, Brussels, Belgium, December 14–16, 2007.

Kearney, Mary Celeste. "Productive Spaces: Girls' Bedrooms as Sites of Cultural Production." *Journal of Children and Media* 1, no. 2 (2007): 126–41.

Keegan, Cael. "In Praise of the Bad Transgender Object: *Rocky Horror*." *Flow*, November 28, 2019. https://www.flowjournal.org/2019/11/in-praise-of-the -bad/.

Kent, Michelle. "'You Die! You Know That, Right? You Don't Come Back!': Fans Negotiating Disney's (De)Stabilized *Star Wars* Canon." In *Disney's* Star Wars: *Forces of Production, Promotion, and Reception*, edited by William Proctor and Richard McCulloch, 221–36. Iowa City: University of Iowa Press, 2019.

Kiefer, Jeanne. "Anatomy of a Janeite: Results from *The Jane Austen Survey 2008*." *Persuasions On-Line* 29, no. 1 (2008). http://www.jasna.org/persuasions /on-line/vol29no1/kiefer.html.

Kırel, Serpil. *Yeşilçam Öykü Sineması*. Istanbul: Babil, 2005.

Kohnen, Melanie. "'The Power of Geek': Fandom as Gendered Commodity at

Comic-Con." *Creative Industries Journal* 7, no. 1 (2014): 75–78.

Konzack, Lars. "The Subcreation of J.R.R. Tolkien's Middle-Earth and How It Became Transmedial Culture." In *Revisiting Imaginary Worlds: A Subcreation Studies Anthology*, edited by Mark J. P. Wolf, 69–82. Abingdon: Routledge, 2016.

Kozak, Noelle M. "New Media Adaptations of Classic Literature: From *Pride and Prejudice* to *The Lizzie Bennet Diaries*." *Inquiries Journal* 8, no. 10 (2016). http://www.inquiriesjournal.com/articles/1468/new-media-adaptations-of -classic-literature-from-pride-and-prejudice-to-the-lizzie-bennet-diaries.

Lamerichs, Nicolle. "Stranger than Fiction: Fan Identity in Cosplay." *Transformative Works and Cultures* 7 (2011). https://doi.org/10.3983 /twc.2011.0246.

Lavery, David, Angela Hague, and Marla Cartwright. "Introduction: Generation X—*The X-Files* and the Cultural Moment." In *Deny All Knowledge: Reading the X-Files*, edited by David Lavery, Angela Hague, and Marla Cartwright, 1–21. London: Faber and Faber, 1996.

Lavin, Maud. "Patti Smith: Aging, Fandom, and Libido." *Transformative Works and Cultures* 20 (2015). https://doi.org/10.3983/twc.2015.0658.

Leitch, Thomas. *Film Adaptation and Its Discontents: From* Gone with the Wind *to* The Passion of the Christ. Baltimore: Johns Hopkins University Press, 2007.

Levine, Elana, ed. *Cupcakes, Pinterest, and Ladyporn: Feminized Popular Culture in the Early Twenty-First Century*. Chicago: University of Illinois Press, 2015.

Lizardi, Ryan. *Mediated Nostalgia: Individual Memory and Contemporary Mass Media*. Lanham, MD: Lexington Books, 2015.

Looser, Devoney. "The Cult of *Pride and Prejudice* and Its Author." In *The Cambridge Companion to Pride and Prejudice*, edited by Janet Todd, 174–85. Cambridge: Cambridge University Press, 2013.

Lowry, Brian. *The Truth Is Out There: The Official Guide to The X-Files*. New York: Harper-Collins, 1995.

Luetkenhaus, Holly, and Zoe Weinstein. *Austentatious: The Evolving World of Jane Austen Fans*. Iowa City: University of Iowa Press, 2019.

Lyons, Siobhan. "From the Elephant Man to Barbie Girl: Dissecting the Freak from the Margins to the Mainstream." *M/C Journal* 23, no. 5 (2020). https://doi.org/10.5204/mcj.1687.

MacDonald, Andrea. "Uncertain Utopia: Science Fiction Media Fandom and Computer Media Communication." In *Theorizing Fandom: Fans, Subculture and Identity*, edited by Cheryl Harris and Alison Alexander, 131–52. New York: Hampton Press, 1998.

Macey, Deborah A. "Ancient Archetypes in Modern Media." In *Media Depictions of Brides, Wives, and Mothers*, edited by Alena Amato Ruggerio, 49–62. Lanham, MD: Lexington Books, 2012.

Malcolm, Gabrielle, ed. *Fan Phenomena: Jane Austen*. Bristol: Intellect, 2015.

Manente, Kristina. "Preface." In *The One Fixed Point in a Changing Age: A New*

Generation on Sherlock Holmes, edited by Kristina Manente, Maria Fleischhack, Sarah Roy, and Taylor Blumenberg, v–vi. Indianapolis: Gasogene Books, 2014.

Massanari, Adrienne. "#Gamergate and the Fappening: How Reddit's Algorithm, Governance, and Culture Support Toxic Technocultures." *New Media and Society* 19, no. 3 (2015): 329–46.

McClellan, Ann K. *Sherlock's World: Fan Fiction and the Reimagining of BBC's Sherlock*. Iowa City: University of Iowa Press, 2018.

———. "'Tit-Bits,' New Journalism, and Early Sherlock Holmes Fandom." *Transformative Works and Cultures* 23 (2017). https://doi.org/10.3983/twc.2017.0816.

McInroy, Lauren B., and Shelley L. Craig. "Online Fandom, Identity Milestones, and Self-Identification of Sexual/Gender Minority Youth." *Journal of LGBT Youth* 15, no. 3 (2018): 179–96.

McLuhan, Marshall. *Understanding Media*. New York: McGraw-Hill, 1964.

McMaster, Juliet. *Jane Austen the Novelist: Essays Past and Present*. London: Macmillan, 1996.

McRobbie, Angela. *The Aftermath of Feminism: Gender, Culture and Social Change*. London: Sage, 2009.

———. *Feminism and Youth Culture*. London: Palgrave, 1991.

———. "Rock and Sexuality." In *On Record: Rock, Pop, and the Written Word*, edited by Simon Frith and Andrew Goodwin, 317–32. London: Routledge, 1990.

Milner, Ryan. "FCJ-156 Hacking the Social: Internet Memes, Identity Antagonism, and the Logic of Lulz." *Fibreculture Journal* 22 (2013): 62–92. http://twentytwo.fibreculturejournal.org/fcj-156-hacking-the-social-internet-memes-identity-antagonism-and-the-logic-of-lulz/.

Murray, Simone. "'Celebrating the Story the Way It Is': Cultural Studies, Corporate Media and the Contested Utility of Fandom." *Continuum* 18, no. 1 (2004): 7–25.

Napier, Susan. "The World of Anime Fandom in America." *Mechademia* 1, no. 1 (2006): 47–63.

Napoli, Philip M. *Audience Economics: Media Institutions and the Audience Marketplace*. New York: Columbia University Press, 2003.

Nyqvist, Sanna. "Authorship and Authenticity in Sherlock Holmes Pastiches." *Transformative Works and Cultures* 23 (2017). https://doi.org/10.3983/twc.2017.0834.

Özgüç, Agah. *Türk Sinemasında Cinselligin Tarihi*. Istanbul: Parantez Yayınları, 2000.

Pande, Rukmini. *Squee from the Margins: Fandom and Race*. Iowa City: Iowa University Press, 2018.

Paquette, Brian, and Paul Howley. *The Toys from U.N.C.L.E.: Memorabilia and Collectors Guide*. Worchester: Entertainment Publishing, 1990.

Parke, Maggie. "LOTR: One Digital Fandom to Initiate Them All." In *Fan*

Phenomena: The Lord of the Rings, edited by Lorna Piatti-Farnell, 18–25. Bristol: Intellect, 2016.

Parks, Lisa. "Special Agent or Monstrosity: Finding the Feminine in *The X-Files*." In *Deny All Knowledge: Reading The X-Files*, edited by David Lavery, Angela Hague, and Marla Cartwright, 121–34. London: Faber and Faber, 1996.

Partridge, Brenda. "No Sex Please—We're Hobbits: The Construction of Female Sexuality in *The Lord of the Rings*." In *J.R.R. Tolkien: This Far Land*, edited by Robert Giddings, 179–97. London: Vision, 1983.

Patterson, Eleanor. "*The Golden Girls Live*: Residual Television Texts, Participatory Culture, and Queering TV Heritage through Drag." *Feminist Media Studies* 16, no. 5 (2016): 838–851.

Pearson, Roberta. "'Good Old Index': Or, the Mystery of the Infinite Archive." In *Sherlock and Transmedia Fandom: Essays on the BBC Series*, edited by Louisa Ellen Stein and Kristina Busse, 150–64. Jefferson, NC: McFarland, 2012.

Peck, Andrew J. "A Case of Irregularity." In *About Being a Sherlockian: 60 Essays Celebrating the Sherlock Holmes Community*, edited by Christopher Redmond, 71–73. Rockville, MD: Wildside Press, 2017.

Pécolo, Agnès. "Identité Générationnelle." In Publictionnaire: Dictionnaire Encyclopédique et Critique des Publics, October 16, 2017. http://publictionnaire.huma-num.fr/notice/identite-generationnelle/.

Pécolo, Agnès, and Myriam Bahuaud. "Générations." In *Abécédaire: Vingt Ans de Recherches et de Publications en Communication des Organisations*, edited by Gino Gramaccia, 89–93. Bordeaux: Presses Universitaires de Bordeaux, 2013.

Petersen, Line Nybro. "'The Florals': Female Fans over 50 in the *Sherlock* Fandom." *Transformative Works and Cultures* 23 (2017). http://dx.doi .org/10.3983/twc.2017.0956.

———. "*Gilmore Girls* Generations: Disrupting Generational Belonging in Long-Term Fandom." *Celebrity Studies* 9, no. 2 (2018): 213–30.

Pham, Minh-Ha T. *Asians Wear Clothes on the Internet: Race, Gender, and the Work of Personal Style Blogging*. Durham, NC: Duke University Press, 2015.

Polasek, Ashley D. "Traditional Transformations and Transmedial Affirmations: Blurring the Boundaries of Sherlockian Fan Practices." *Transformative Works and Cultures* 23 (2017). https://doi.org/10.3983/twc.2017.0911.

Pollock, Dale. *Skywalking: The Life and Films of George Lucas*. New York: Da Capo Press, 1999.

Proctor, William. "'Bitches Ain't Gonna Hunt No Ghosts': Totemic Nostalgia, Toxic Fandom and the *Ghostbusters* Platonic." *Palabra Clave* 20, no. 4 (2017): 1105–41.

Proctor, William, and Matthew Freeman. "The First Step into a Smaller World: The Transmedia Economy of *Star Wars*." In *Revisiting Imaginary Worlds*, edited by Mark J. P. Wolf, 223–45. London: Routledge, 2016.

Proctor, William, and Richard McCulloch. "From the House that George Built to the House of Mouse." In *Disney's* Star Wars: *Forces of Production, Promotion, and Reception*, edited by William Proctor and Richard McCulloch, 1–19. Iowa City: Iowa University Press, 2019.

Pugh, Sheenagh. *The Democratic Genre: Fan Fiction in a Literary Context*. Bridgend, Wales: Seren, 2005.

Pullen, Kirsten. "*The Lord of the Rings* Online Blockbuster Fandom: Pleasure and Commerce." In *The Lord of the Rings: Popular Culture in Global Context*, edited by Ernest Mathjis, 172–88. London: Wallflower Press, 2006.

Radway, Janice. *Reading the Romance: Women, Patriarchy, and Popular Literature*. Chapel Hill: University of North Carolina Press, 1984.

Reagin, Nancy, and Anne Rubenstein. "'I'm Buffy, and You're History': Putting Fan Studies into History." *Transformative Works and Cultures* 6 (2011). https://doi.org/10.3983/twc.2011.0272.

Rearick, Anderson. "Why Is the Only Good Orc a Dead Orc? The Dark Face of Racism Examined in Tolkien's World." *Modern Fiction Studies* 50, no. 4 (2004): 861–74.

Redmond, Christopher. "Introduction." In *About Being a Sherlockian: 60 Essays Celebrating the Sherlock Holmes Community*, edited by Christopher Redmond, 7–10. Rockville, MD: Wildside Press, 2017.

Reid, Robin. "Breaking of the Fellowship: Competing Discourses of Archives and Canons in *The Lord of the Rings* Internet Fandom." In *How We Became Middle-Earth: A Collection of Essays on* The Lord of the Rings, edited by Adam Lam and N. Oryschuk, 347–70. Zollikofen, Switzerland: Walking Tree, 2007.

———. "Race in Tolkien Studies: A Bibliographic Essay." In *Tolkien and Alterity*, edited by Christopher Vaccaro and Yvette Kisor, 33–74. Cham, Switzerland: Palgrave Macmillan, 2017.

———. "Thrusts in the Dark: Slashers' Queer Practices." *Extrapolation* 50, no. 3 (2009): 463–83.

Reinhard, Carrie Lynn D. *Fractured Fandoms: Contentious Communication in Fan Communities*. Lanham, MD: Lexington Books, 2018.

Rosenblatt, Julia Carlson. "From Outside to Inside." *Transformative Works and Cultures* 23 (2017). https://doi.org/10.3983/twc.2017.0920.

Rosenthal, Ty. "Warm Beds Are Good: Sex and Libido in Tolkien's Writing." *Mallorn* 42 (2004). https://ansereg.com/WarmBedsareGood.pdf.

Sandvoss, Cornel. *Fans: The Mirror of Consumption*. Cambridge: Polity Press, 2005.

Savit, Lauren. "Examining the Labor of Episodic TV Podcast Hosts." *Transformative Works and Cultures* 34 (2020). https://doi.org/10.3983/twc.2020.1721.

Scodari, Christine. "Breaking Dusk: Fandom, Gender/Age Intersectionality, and the '*Twilight* Moms.'" In *Aging, Media and Culture*, edited by C. Lee Harrington, Denise Bielby, and Anthony R. Bardo, 143–54. Lanham, MD: Lexington Books, 2014.

———. "No Politics Here: Age and Gender in Soap Opera 'Cyberfandom.'"

Women's Studies in Communication 21, no. 2 (1998): 168–87.

Scott, Suzanne. *Fake Geek Girls: Fandom, Gender, and the Convergence Culture Industry.* New York: New York University Press, 2019.

———. "#Wheresrey?: Toys, Spoilers, and the Gender Politics of Franchise Paratexts." *Critical Studies in Media Communication* 34, no. 2 (2017): 138–47.

Seabrook, John. *The Song Machine: Inside the Hit Factory.* New York: Norton, 2015.

Sedgwick, Eve Kosofsky. *Between Men: English Literature and Male Homosocial Desire.* New York: Columbia University Press, 1985.

Shaw, Al. "The Adventure of the Windy City Giants." In *About Being a Sherlockian: 60 Essays Celebrating the Sherlock Holmes Community,* edited by Christopher Redmond, 74–77. Rockville, MD: Wildside Press, 2017.

Shefrin, Elana. "*Lord of the Rings, Star Wars,* and Participatory Fandom: Mapping New Congruencies between the Internet and Media Entertainment Culture." *Critical Studies in Media Communication* 21, no. 3 (2004): 261–81.

Smith, Nicola. "Parenthood and the Transfer of Capital in the Northern Soul Scene." In *Aging and Youth Cultures,* edited by Andy Bennett and Paul Hodkinson, 159–72. London: Bloomsbury Academic, 2013.

Solberg, Andrew L., and Robert S. Katz. "Fandom, Publishing, and Playing the Grand Game." *Transformative Works and Cultures* 23 (2017). https://doi .org/10.3983/twc.2017.0825.

Sonnenfeld, Barry, Ed Solomon, Walter F. Parkes, and Laurie MacDonald. *Men in Black: The Script and the Story Behind the Film.* New York: Newmarket Press, 1997.

Şoray, Türkan. *Sinemam ve Ben.* Istanbul: Turkiye Isbankası, 2012.

Stacey, Jackie. *Star Gazing: Hollywood Cinema and Female Spectatorship.* London: Routledge, 2013.

Stein, Louisa. *Millennial Fandom: Television Audiences in the Transmedia Age.* Iowa City: University of Iowa Press, 2015.

Stein, Louisa Ellen, and Kristina Busse, eds. *Sherlock and Transmedia Fandom: Essays on the BBC Series.* Jefferson, NC: McFarland, 2012.

Stevenson, Nick. "Talking to Bowie Fans: Masculinity, Ambivalence and Cultural Citizenship." *European Journal of Cultural Studies* 12, no. 1 (2009): 79–98.

Strauss, William, and Neil Howe. *Millennials and the Pop Culture.* Great Falls, VA: LifeCourse Associates, 2006.

Sturgis, Amy. "Make Mine 'Movieverse': How the Tolkien Fan Fiction Community Learned to Stop Worrying and Love Peter Jackson." In *Tolkien on Film: Essays on Peter Jackson's The Lord of the Rings,* edited by Janet Brennan Croft, 283–305. Altadena, CA: Mythopoeic Press, 2005.

———. "Reimagining Rose: Portrayals of Tolkien's Rosie Cotton in Twenty-First Century Fan Fiction." *Mythlore* 24, no. 3 (2006). https://dc.swosu.edu /mythlore/vol24/iss3/10.

Tepper, Allegra. "Lizzie in Real Life: Social and Narrative Immersion through

Transmedia in *The Lizzie Bennet Diaries*." *Film Matters* 6, no. 1 (2015): 45–51.

Theodoropoulou, Vivi. "The Anti-Fan within the Fan: Awe and Envy in Sport Fandom." In *Fandom: Identity and Communities in a Mediated World*, edited by Jonathan Gray, Cornel Sandvoss, and C. Lee Harrington, 316–27. New York: New York University Press, 2007.

Thompson, Kristin. "Gollum Talks to Himself: Problems and Solutions in Peter Jackson's *The Lord of the Rings*." In *Picturing Tolkien: Essays on Peter Jackson's The Lord of the Rings Film Trilogy*, edited by Janice M. Bogstad and Philip E. Kaveny, 25–45. Jefferson, NC: McFarland, 2011.

Tinson, Julie, Gary Sinclair, and Dimitrios Kolyperas. "Sport Fandom and Parenthood." *European Sport Management Quarterly* 17, no. 3 (2017): 370–91.

Tolkien, J. R. R. *The Letters of J.R.R. Tolkien*. Edited by Humphrey Carpenter and Christopher Tolkien. Boston: Houghton Mifflin, 1981.

Urbanski, Heather. *The Science Fiction Reboot: Canon, Innovation and Fandom in Refashioned Franchises*. Jefferson, NC: McFarland, 2013.

Vermaak, Janelle. "Fans of the *Alien* Film Franchise: Creating a Fan-Specific Checklist." In *Gender and Contemporary Horror in Comics, Games and Transmedia*, edited by Robert Shail, Samantha Holland, and Steven Gerrard, 135–50. West Yorkshire: Emerald Press, 2019.

Vroomen, Laura. "Kate Bush: Teen Pop and Older Female Fans." In *Music Scenes: Local, Translocal and Virtual*, edited by Andy Bennett and Richard A. Petersen, 328–53. Nashville, TN: Vanderbilt University Press, 2004.

Walker, Cynthia W. "Fifty Years of *The Man from U.N.C.L.E.*: How the Ever-Changing Media Sustained and Shaped One of the Oldest Fan Communities." In *Television, Social Media, and Fan Culture*, edited by Alison F. Slade, Amber J. Narro, and Dedria Givens-Carroll, 353–74. Lanham, MD: Lexington Books, 2015.

———. "The Future Just beyond the Coat Hook: Technology, Politics, and the Postmodern Sensibility in *The Man From U.N.C.L.E.*" In *Channeling the Future: Essays in Science Fiction and Fantasy Television*, edited by Lincoln Geraghty, 41–58. Plymouth, UK: Scarecrow Press, 2009.

———. "Mr. Bond's Neighborhood: Domesticating the Superspy for American Television." In *James Bond and Popular Culture: Essays on the Influence of the Fictional Superspy*, edited by Michele Brittany, 80–102. Jefferson, NC: McFarland, 2014.

———. "Spy Programs." In *The Encyclopedia of Television*, 2nd ed., edited by Horace Newcomb, 2181–85. Chicago: Fitzroy Dearborn, 2004.

———. *Work/Text: Investigating The Man from U.N.C.L.E.* New York: Hampton Press, 2013.

Walker, Cynthia W., and Amy H. Sturgis. "Sexy Nerds: Illya Kuryakin, Mr. Spock, and the Image of the Cerebral Hero in TV Drama." In *Common Sense: Intelligence as Presented on Popular Television*, edited by Lisa Holderman, 201–16. New York: Lexington Books, 2008.

Walls-Thumma, Dawn. "Affirmational and Transformational Values and

Practices in the Tolkien Fanfiction Community." *Journal of Tolkien Research* 8, no. 1 (2019). https://scholar.valpo.edu/journaloftolkienresearch/vol8/iss1/6.

———. "Diving into the Lacuna: Fan Studies, Methodologies, and Mending the Gaps." *Transformative Works and Cultures* 33 (2020). https://doi.org/10.3983/twc.2020.1871.

Williams, Rebecca. "'Anyone Who Calls Muse a *Twilight* Band Will Be Shot on Sight': Music, Distinction, and the 'Interloping Fan' in the *Twilight* Franchise." *Popular Music and Society* 36, no. 3 (2013): 327–42.

———. "Desiring the Doctor: Identity, Gender, and Genre in Online Science Fiction Fandom." In *British Science Fiction Film and Television*, edited by James Leggott and Tobias Hochscherf, 167–77. Jefferson, NC: McFarland, 2011.

Willis, Ika. "Keeping Promises to Queer Children: Making Space (for Mary Sue) at Hogwarts." In *Fan Fiction and Fan Communities in the Age of the Internet*, edited by Karen Hellekson and Kristina Busse, 153–70. Jefferson, NC: McFarland, 2006.

Wills, Emily Regan. "The Political Possibilities of Fandom: Transformational Discourses on Gender and Power in *The X-Files* Fandom." Paper presented at the Midwest Political Science Association conference, Chicago, IL, April 2–5, 2009.

Wilson, Elizabeth. *Cultural Passions: Fans, Aesthetes and Tarot Readers*. London: I. B. Tauris, 2013.

Wohlfeil, Markus, and Susan Whelan. "'Saved!' by Jena Malone: An Introspective Study of a Consumer's Fan Relationship with a Film Actress." *Journal of Business Research* 65, no. 4 (2012): 511–19.

Wojton, Jennifer, and Lynnette R. Porter. *Sherlock and Digital Fandom: The Meeting of Creativity, Community and Advocacy*. Jefferson, NC: McFarland, 2018.

Wood, Rachel, Benjamin Litherland, and Elizabeth Reed. "Girls Being Rey: Ethical Cultural Consumption, Families and Popular Feminism." *Cultural Studies* 34, no. 4 (2020). https://doi.org/10.1080/09502386.2019.1656759.

Wood, Robin. *Hollywood from Vietnam to Reagan*. New York: Columbia University Press, 1986.

Wooley, Christine A. "Visible Fandom: Reading *The X-Files* through X-Philes." *Journal of Film and Video* 53, no. 4 (2001): 29–53.

Yıldızcan, Özge Özyılmaz. *Erken Cumhuriyet Dönemi'nde Hollywood'un Alımlanması: Kadınlar, Gençler ve Modernlik*. PhD dissertation, Istanbul University, 2013.

Yodovich, Neta. "'A Little Costumed Girl at a Sci-Fi Convention': Boundary Work as a Main Destigmatization Strategy among Women Fans." *Women's Studies in Communication* 39, no. 3 (2016): 289–307.

Yu, Sabrina Qiong. "Introduction: Performing Stardom: Star Studies in Transformation and Expansion." In *Revisiting Star Studies*, edited by Sabrina Qiong Yu and Guy Austin, 1–24. Edinburgh: Edinburgh University Press, 2017.

Zerne, Lori H. "Ideology in *The Lizzie Bennet Diaries.*" *Persuasions On-Line* 34, no. 1 (2013). http://www.jasna.org/persuasions/on-line/vol34no1/zerne.html.

Zubernis, Lynn, and Katherine Larsen. *Fandom at the Crossroads: Celebration, Shame and Fan/Producer Relationships.* Newcastle upon Tyne: Cambridge Scholars, 2012.

Index

The A Team, 95
Abrams, J. J., 138
aca-fan, 80
Adams, Tony E., 79–80
adaptation, 123–32, 161
adulthood, 74–77
The Adventures of Sherlock Holmes, 163
Adventuresses of Sherlock Holmes, 170
affirmational fandom, 149–60
ageism, 63
aging, 33–42
Alien: fandom, 112–22; film franchise, 112–22
Amick, Mädchen, 34, 37, 40
Anakin Skywalker, 135
Anderson, Gillian, 23, 26–32, 37–42
Anderson, Tonya, 70
Angry Asian Man (podcast), 84
anti-fandom, 47–50
Archive of Our Own (AO3), 154
Ashbrook, Dana, 36
Asian identity, 79, 82–84, 127
Aşk Rüzgarı, 101
"Astronomy" (short story), 167–68
Austin, Thomas, 22
authenticity, 172–80

Baby Boomers, 3, 33–35, 39
Baby-Sitters Club (franchise), 78–89
The Baby-Sitters Club Club (podcast), 85–86
Backstreet Boys fandom, 68–77
Baker Street Babes, 170
Baker Street Irregulars, 162, 163, 167, 169–70
Baker Street Journal, 164, 171
Banet-Weiser, Sarah, 19
Bardo, Anthony R., 24
Barker, Martin, 114, 117
Battlestar Galactica: original series, 178; 2004 reboot, 175, 178–79
becoming-a-fan, 72–74
#BelieveInSherlock, 165
Bennett, Andy, 69
Bennett, Lucy, 107
Best, Ahmed, 140, 145
Bielby, Denise, 4, 10, 24, 69, 79, 81, 88, 124
bisexuality, 79
Black, Rebecca W., 177
Boba Fett, 147
Bolin, Göran, 124–25, 140
Booth, Paul, 174
Boström, Matthias, 163
Botox, 38
Bourdieu, Pierre, 117
boyd, danah, 176, 178
Bridgeman, Teresa, 23
Brower, Sue, 117
Büker, Seçil, 104
Busse, Kristina, 26, 118–20, 166

camp, 50–51, 52–53
Carter, Chris, 21, 26–32
Cavill, Henry, 90, 98–99
Cherry, Brigid, 120
cine-magazines, 102–03, 104
cinephilia, 140
The Claudia Kishi Club, 83

The Clone Wars, 143
collecting, 106, 110–11
comic book fandom, 62
coming out, 88
competition, 110
Coppa, Francesca, 90–91
Corse, Sarah M., 174
cross-generational, 33–37
cultural acupuncture, 180
Cumberbatch, Benedict, 162, 165, 171

Darceymania, 124
dark side of fandom, 9
Darth Vader, 143
David Bowie fandom, 70, 76
de Certeau, Michel, 117
diversity, 4, 6
Doctor Who: fandom, 57–67;
    franchise, 91–92
Doyle, Sir Arthur Conan, 161, 163
Duchovny, David, 36, 37–42
Duffett, Mark, 69
Duran Duran fandom, 70
Dust and Shadow, 167

Earper fandom, 179–80
Eick, David, 178
Elementary, 161, 165, 166
Elizabeth/Lizzie Bennet, 125–26,
    128–29, 131
Elsaesser, Thomas, 140
Erbland, Kate, 49–50
Evans, Adrienne, 80

Fairclough-Isaacs, Kristy, 38
family, 175–76
fan: age, 24, 33–42, 102, 110, 127–28;
    definition, 173–74; etymology, 173;
    good vs. bad, 179;
    identification, 78–79

fan fiction, 94–98, 139, 149–60, 162,
    166–68, 174, 177
fanatic, 173
fangirl, 1; stereotypes of, 75–76, 161, 171
fanzine, 151
fat Monica, 1
fathers and sons, 138
Faye, Lyndsay, 167
Felton, Norman, 90
femininity, 119–20
Fenn, Sherilyn, 34, 38, 40
Firth, Colin, 123
Fisher, Carrie, 138
The Force Awakens, 11, 64, 138, 142,
    143, 146
formative years, 72–77
Fowler, Angela, 162
Freeman, Martin, 166
Friends, 1–2
Friends of Irene Adler, 170
Fries, Wendy, 162

Garner, Ross, 11
Gary (Carrie Fisher's dog), 140–42
gatekeeping, 176–77
Geena Davis Institute on Gender in
    Media, 13, 14, 89
Gen X, 3, 21, 33–34, 43
Gen Z, 3, 15, 21, 43
gender, 96–98, 109–10
generation, 122, 140; defined
    sociologically, 3, 10; gap, 132; as life
    course, 4; by medium, 4
Ghostbusters: 1984 film, 11–13; 2016
    film, 9, 13–14, 48
gifting, 112–13, 114
The Girl from U.N.C.L.E., 92
girls' bedrooms, 83
Golden Anniversary Affair, 90
The Golden Girls: fandom, 86, 79: *The*

238   *Index*

Golden Girls LIVE, 86
Göle, Nilüfer, 104
Grand Game, 162, 164
Grant, Hugh, 90
Gray, Jonathan, 47
Green, Hank, 130
Greenring, Tanner, 85–86
Grossberg, Lawrence, 117–18

Hadas, Leora, 26, 114
Hall, Stuart, 146
Hammer, Armie, 90, 98–99;
    allegations against, 99
Hannah Montana, 51
Harman, Claire, 124
Harrington, C. Lee, 4, 10, 24, 69, 79,
    81, 88, 124
Hartless, Jaime, 174
hate-watching, 48–49
Hellekson, Karen, 114
Heroine Complex, 84
Herrmann, Andrew F., 79–80
hierarchy, 113, 177–78
Hills, Matt, 12, 26, 39, 41, 57, 69,
    117–18, 120–21
Hinerman, Stephen, 120
The Hobbit, 149–60
Hodkinson, Paul, 69
homophobia, 1
homosexuality, 110
Horton, Donald, 103
Howe, Neil, 80
Hunt, Nathan, 114
Hutcheon, Linda, 126

Inner Circle, 90, 91–92, 94
inter-fandom, 121; antagonism, 26;
    stereotyping, 120
inter-generational, 5–6, 57, 66, 136–38,
    175

Iraq War, 145
Istvandy, Lauren, 71
Ito, Mizuko, 176, 178

Jameson, Frederic, 135
Jancovich, Mark, 114
Jane Austen fandom, 123–32
Janeites, 123–32
Janeitism, 123
Jar Jar Binks, 140, 142
Jem and the Holograms, 43–53
Jenkins, Henry, 97, 117, 173, 176, 178
Jenkins, Richard, 12
Johnlock, 166
Johnson, Claudia L., 123
Johnson, Derek, 3, 6, 63–64, 86
Jones, Leslie, 9
Jones, Sara Gwenllian, 49

Katz, Richard, 165
Kaya-Mutlu, Dilek, 103, 104
Kearney, Mary Celeste, 83
Keegan, Cael, 19
kink meme, 154
kinship, 58
KIrel, Serpil, 104
Kishi, Claudia, 79, 82–84
Kuhn, Sarah, 83
Kuryakin, Illya, 90, 93, 96, 98, 99

The L Word: original series, 15–16;
    Generation Q, 9, 15–16
Ladd Jr., Alan, 135
The Last Jedi, 142, 143
Latinx representation, 89
Lavin, Maud, 70
Least Expected, 155
Lee, C. B., 83
Lee, Sheryl, 34
legacy film, 136–37

Index   239

Leitch, Thomas, 123, 127
lesbian, 87
letters, 91, 104
LGBTQIA+, 180
Lipton, Peggy, 33, 40
The Lizzie Bennet Diaries, 125–32
Looser, Devoney, 123
Lord of the Rings: book, 149–60; fandom, 149–60; film franchise, 149–60
love, 106, 108, 109–10
Lowry, Brian, 22
Lucas, Charlotte, 129
Lucas, George, 135, 145
Lucasfilm, 135–48
Luetkenhaus, Holly, 124
Luke Skywalker, 135
Lydia Bennet, 129–30

Macfadyen, Matthew, 124
MacLachlan, Kyle, 33, 37–42
Man from U.N.C.L.E.: 2015 film, 90, 98–99; fandom, 90–100; television series, 90–100
The Mandalorian, 147
Manente, Kristina, 170–71
Martin, Ann M., 88
Marx, Christy, 43–50
Mary Sue, 157
Massanari, Adrienne, 13
McCallum, David, 90, 91–92, 96, 98
McClellan, Ann K., 166, 167
McCulloch, Richard, 142
McMaster, Juliet, 124
media conglomeration, 6
MediaWest Con, 95
A Memoir of Jane Austen, 123
memorabilia, 73, 105
mentorship, 110, 172–80
merchandise, 44, 63, 93–94

#MeToo, 20–32
Meyer, Nicholas, 167
Middle-earth, 149–60
Millennials, 3, 21, 33–34, 43, 80
Miller, Matt, 145, 146
misogyny, 19, 20
model minority stereotype, 83
Moore, Ronald D., 178–79
Morley, Christopher, 163
motherhood, 64–65, 76
mothers and daughters, 138
Mr. Collins, 129
musical, 45

Netherlands, 68–77
newbie, 177
nonbinary, 12, 18
nostalgia, 2, 11–14, 20, 43, 135–36
Nyqvist, Sanna, 168

obsession_inc, 150, 155
One Day at a Time: 2017 reboot, 9, 16–18; original series, 16–17
Özgüç, Agah, 104

Padmé Amidala, 147
Parachute_Silks, 167–68
parasocial relationship, 103, 109
parent-child relationships, 57
Partridge, Brenda, 151
pastiche, 168
Patterson, Eleanor, 86
Patti Smith fandom, 70
Pearson, Rebecca, 166
Peck, Andrew J., 162
Pécolo, Agnès, 172
Pegg, Simon, 142
Petersen, Line Nybro, 63, 166
The Phantom Menace, 135, 138, 140
podcast, 85–86

240 *Index*

Polasek, Ashley, 162
Ponda Baba, 139
Porter, Lynette, 166
post-youth, 69–77
Professor Moriarty, 164, 165
Pride and Prejudice, 123–32
Prigge, Matt, 39
The Princess Diarist, 138
Proctor, William, 12–13, 142

queer: identification, 86; queerness, 160; reading, 86–87

Reagan/Reaganite politics, 145
reboot, 4–5, 9, 50; culture, 2, 4, 9–19, 78–79, 86
Redmond, Christopher, 161–62
Regan-Wills, Emily, 29
remake, 4–5, 9
representation, 89, 145
Return of the Jedi, 140
reunion tour, 77
Revenge of the Sith, 139, 143, 147
revival, 4–5, 9
Rey, 11, 32, 63, 64–65, 147
Ripley, 118–21
The Rise of Skywalker, 135, 143
Ritchie, Guy, 90
Robie, Wendy, 40
Rogue One, 137
Rolfe, Sam, 90
Rosenblatt, Julia Carlson, 170
Rosenthal, Ty, 155
ruined childhood, 11–14

Sackhoff, Katee, 178
same-sex desire, 151
Savit, Lauren, 85–86
Scholastic Book Fair, 81
Scott, Andrew, 165

Scott, Suzanne, 48, 86
Scully effect, 4, 14, 20
Seitz, Matt Zoller, 13
The Seven Per-Cent Solution, 167
Shaw, Al, 161
Shepherd, Jack, 85–86
Sherlock, 161, 165–66
Sherlock Holmes: fandom, 161–71; texts, 161–71
Sherlock Holmes Society, 169–70
Shukert, Rachel, 79, 89
Sidekick Squad, 84
Silmarillion Writers Guild, 158
The Silmarillion, 150
Slack, Andrew, 180
slash, 152, 155, 166
Solberg, Andrew, 165
Solo, Napoleon, 90, 93, 96, 98, 99
Şoray, Türkan, 101–11
Stacey, Jackie, 79
Star Trek, 91–92
Star Wars: fandom, 57–67, 135–48; franchise, 135–48
Starbuck, 178
stars as family, 104
Stasi, Mafalda, 80
Stein, Louisa Ellen, 166
Stevenson, Nick, 70
Stories of Arda, 158
Strauss, William, 80
A Study in Scarlet, 161
Su, Bernie, 127
Sumner Gary Hunnewell fanzine collection, 151
super fan, 178
superhero, 45, 50–51

teen sexuality, 18
textual poaching, 97, 174
Theodoropulou, Vivi, 47–48

Index 241

Thomas, Kristy, 78, 79, 87
Tico, Rose, 139–40
Tit-Bits, 163, 167
Tolkien, J. R. R., 149–60; fandom, 149–60
toyetic, 44, 52
toys, 61
Tran, Kelly Marie, 139–40
trans: character, 15, 89; representation, 12, 15, 19; rights, 16; transphobia, 1, 13, 19, 20
transformational fandom, 149–60
transgenerational, 2–3, 5–6, 43, 101, 102, 106, 110–11, 170, 177
travel, 74–76
Tumblr, 154, 165, 166
Twin Peaks, 33–42

Urbanski, Heather, 23–24, 29, 137

Vaughn, Robert, 90, 95
Vietnam War, 145
Vikander, Alicia, 99

Walrus Man, 139
Watson, Dr. John, 166
Weaver, Sigourney, 120, 121
Weinberg, Scott, 139
Weinstein, Zoe, 124
#WheresRey, 64–65
Whigham, Lionel, 90
William Darcy, 123, 124, 125, 126, 131
Williams, Rebecca, 51, 114
Willis, Ika, 157–58
Wise, Ray, 33–34, 36
Wohl, R. Richard, 103
Wojton, Jennifer, 166
Wood, Robin, 145
Wynonna Earp, 179–80

The X-Files, 20–32, 33–34, 36–42

Yeşilçam, 101–04
youth, 68–77
Yu, Sabrina Qiong, 38

Fandom & Culture

A Fan Studies Primer:
Method, Research, Ethics
edited by Paul Booth and
Rebecca Williams

Queerbaiting and Fandom:
Teasing Fans through
Homoerotic Possibilities
edited by Joseph Brennan

Gaming Masculinity: Trolls,
Fake Geeks, and the Gendered
Battle for Online Culture
by Megan Condis

Emo: How Fans Defined
a Subculture
by Judith May Fathallah

Johnny Cash International: How and
Why Fans Love the Man in Black
by Michael Hinds and
Jonathan Silverman

Fandom as Classroom
Practice: A Teaching Guide
edited by Katherine
Anderson Howell

Star Attractions: Twentieth-
Century Movie Magazines
and Global Fandom
edited by Tamar Jeffers
McDonald and Lies Lanckman

Fandom, the Next Generation
edited by Bridget Kies
and Megan Connor

Straight Korean Female Fans
and Their Gay Fantasies
by Jungmin Kwon

Aussie Fans: Uniquely Placed
in Global Popular Culture
edited by Celia Lam and
Jackie Raphael

Austentatious: The Evolving
World of Jane Austen Fans
by Holly Luetkenhaus
and Zoe Weinstein

Sherlock's World: Fan Fiction and
the Reimagining of BBC's Sherlock
by Ann K. McClellan

Fandom, Now in Color: A
Collection of Voices
edited by Rukmini Pande

Squee from the Margins:
Fandom and Race
by Rukmini Pande

Disney's Star Wars: *Forces of Production, Promotion, and Reception*
edited by William Proctor and Richard McCulloch

Re-living the American Frontier: Western Fandoms, Reenactment, and Historical Hobbyists in Germany and America since 1900
by Nancy Reagin

Fan Sites: Film Tourism and Contemporary Fandom
by Abby S. Waysdorf

Everybody Hurts: Transitions, Endings, and Resurrections in Fan Cultures
edited by Rebecca Williams